THE SONS OF THE CLERGY

Randall Cantuar

President.

THE SONS
OF THE CLERGY

SOME RECORDS OF TWO HUNDRED AND
SEVENTY-FIVE YEARS

BY ERNEST HAROLD PEARCE

Litt.D., D.D., F.S.A.

BISHOP OF WORCESTER
TREASURER OF THE CORPORATION AND OF THE FESTIVAL

QUOD EORUM MINIMIS MIHI

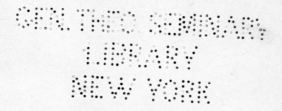
LONDON
JOHN MURRAY, ALBEMARLE STREET, W.

FIRST EDITION . March, 1904
SECOND EDITION 1928

Printed in Great Britain by
Hazell, Watson & Viney, Ld., London and Aylesbury.

TO

THE MOST REVEREND

RANDALL
LORD ARCHBISHOP OF CANTERBURY

THE SIXTEENTH OCCUPANT OF
HIS HIGH OFFICE
WHO HAS ALSO BEEN PRESIDENT OF
THE CORPORATION OF
THE SONS OF THE CLERGY

WITH DUTIFUL REGARD

PREFACE TO THE SECOND EDITION

ON April 24th, 1929, we shall keep, please God, what we call the 275th Festival of the Sons of the Clergy. We call it so, not because we deny that there have been any gaps in a series which is still without rival in the story of the Church of England. There were modifications during the Great War ; there was a gap during the General Strike ; there are some early years which have no memorial. On the other hand, the series may, and, indeed, I believe it does, date back behind 1655, which is the first Festival of which we have any record.

When the Corporation more than five and twenty years ago was looking forward to its 250th Festival, a young City Incumbent, then newly elected to the Court of Assistants, who had attended these Festivals as a schoolboy with a " pink ticket " from his head-master, thought that he might help the Charity by a study of its records. If I were turned loose, he said, among the court-minutes and committee-books and other documents, some light must surely be thrown on the efforts of our oldest Church society to accomplish the thing whereto it had set itself, and something might at the same time be added to the story of the English Church during all those years.

Churchmen, of whom it is the habit to speak lightly either as High Tories or as Latitudinarians or as bloated pluralists, would be somehow better able to speak with their enemies in the gate, when it was realised that their time and their money and their sermons and their good fellowship were unselfishly devoted to the relief of the widow and the fatherless among the households of the clergy of their day.

But history, even what Creighton would call " true history," was only a fraction of the book's purpose. Sir Paget Bowman and the author then—like Mr. A. C. Rowden and the author now—were out for unblushing propaganda. We wanted this ancient society to be known because to know it is to love it, and to love it is to seek to do it good.

The book, as issued in 1904, has long been out of print. The actual writing of it was done during a holiday in a remote Suffolk village, with no apparatus except the note-book which I had compiled in the Court-room at 2 Bloomsbury Place. But, with a few exceptions here and there, it stands in this re-issue as it was then written. Any additions are in the form of footnotes, many of them due to the splendid work accomplished by the Venns, father and son, in their compilation of *Alumni Cantabrigienses* or by T. A. Walker in that of his *Admissions to Peterhouse*. These

help you to trace the personalities and the careers of
the men, often quite unknown to fame, to whom the
work of " the Corporation of Clergymen's Sons " was
a passion. The only real additions are that a brief
chapter has been added to cover some changes which
five and twenty years have inevitably brought, and
that the list of Festival preachers has been amplified
to the present date.

The purpose, then, is not history, but propaganda.
We want the Corporation to be more widely known
and to be more clearly appreciated by those who can
help it.

It breaks the heart of a historian, to whom names
are sacrosanct, to confess that the title of the Charity
is against it ; but in a sense this is true. We have
some splendid partners in another ship, whose sign is
" The Poor Clergy Relief Corporation." Now, there
is a name which tells at once ; it raises no doubts ; so
down it goes in a man's last will and testament for a
legacy ; nor could anything give greater pleasure to
Bloomsbury Place than to read that the gift has been
made to Tavistock Place. But ask such a man to
insert similar mention of " The Sons of the Clergy "
in his will and he is likely to exclaim, " Who are
they ? " or even " What is that ? " This book will
have been written in vain unless it shows him that
under this ancient and mysterious title there is con-

cealed a considerable company of Christian men and women, subject to no conditions of birth or status or education, whose only bond is a desire to remedy the distresses and to ease the struggles of the clergy, their widows, their unmarried daughters, and, perhaps above all, their boys and girls who are starting out to make their way in life.

Or again, there are those who know vaguely what are the purposes of the Festival and of the Corporation, but who have heard that in the course of centuries our society by public generosity and careful management has been able to invest considerable funds. That is quite true. But it is the purpose of our story to show that, when the recipients are so numerous, and when there are so many others whom we ought to be able to help, an income of £36,000 from invested funds and real property is all too small for the need. We are merely palliating poverty when we distribute this sum, and our £5,000 of annual receipts, among 3,224 persons—which was the number in 1927.

But, above all, the heart of the Registrar and the heart of the recorder is towards those who can offer themselves willingly as Stewards of the 275th Festival. To do so is not only to fall into line with the custom which represents the oldest feature in the Corporation's long and honoured life, but to have your part

in that section of the work which is the most hopeful
—the aid given to the young for their advancement in
life.

Perhaps it is fair to warn those who succumb to the
blandishments of the Registrar, and who agree to be
among the 275 Stewards of the 275th Festival, that,
pathologically, this is a condition which is highly
infectious and very difficult to shake off. You can
ask Lord Marshall of Chipstead, who caught it, quite
young, from his father forty-seven years ago, has
looked forward to an annual attack of it ever since,
and has inoculated several members of his family with
the same benevolent virus.

Certainly few things could give greater satisfaction
to the Archbishop of Canterbury, whom we are soon
to lose from Lambeth Palace, than the knowledge that
this ancient Corporation is thus renewing its youth,
with its heart-action quite unimpaired—*Quod eorum
minimis mihi.*

I am again indebted to my brother for revising
the proofs—all the more so, because the erstwhile
" Fellow and Dean " of Tenison's College has become
a much busier man since he last helped me in the
same way.

In the years that have passed since the first issue
in 1904 I have had communications from various
historical students. As far as possible, I have added

notes of the information which they have thus given me and have made mention of their names.

I need hardly add that the Registrar, Mr. A. C. Rowden, has given me every possible assistance, or that Sir John Murray, a firm friend of the Charity, has made the most favourable arrangements for the production of the book.

ERNEST WORCESTER.

HARTLEBURY CASTLE.
  September, 1928.

PREFACE TO THE FIRST EDITION

THESE chronicles of the Sons of the Clergy have been compiled as a holiday task from such records as remain at Corporation House. The minutes of the Court of Assistants are complete and continuous from the time of the granting of the Charter, and there are also one or two Committee books. These and a few original papers are our authorities for the annals of the Corporation. The story of the Festival is not so continuous. Its beginnings have almost no memorial, and the earliest surviving minute-book of the Stewards' work opens in 1775. But it has been possible to fill some of the gaps from other sources, such as the sermons preached at Festivals, the records of the Royal Society of Musicians, which Dr. W. H. Cummings and its Secretary kindly consulted for me, and the information placed at my disposal by the Clerk of the Merchant Taylors' Company.

I cannot adequately acknowledge the assistance I have received from Sir Paget Bowman, the Registrar, and from Mr. John Murray, who as a Governor of the Corporation readily consented to publish the book.

Without going into financial details it may be stated that a satisfactory sale of the book will involve some pecuniary benefit to the funds of the Corporation.

But in any case the writer will be more than gratified, if what is here written interests the benevolent Church-man in the 250th anniversary Festival, which we shall celebrate in May, 1904, and incites him to take a practical part in the work of the oldest Church of England society.

I ought to add that I am alone responsible for any *obiter dicta* which may interrupt the even tenor of the story. It is impossible, for instance, to look into the past history and present equipment of the Sons of the Clergy without feeling that here the Church has her central charitable organisation, to which the hundred minor societies of the same sort should be in some way affiliated. All that requires to be done for the temporary assistance of the clergy, beneficed and unbeneficed, for subventing the higher education of their children, and for making some permanent pro-vision for their widows and maiden daughters, could well be achieved through Corporation House, which might be made a clearing house for all such work, if the necessary funds were entrusted to it. This would save deserving applicants the dreary task of picking up unconsidered trifles from several societies at once.

Whatever may be said in regard to such a sugges-tion, my immediate purpose will have been achieved, if Church-people learn from this story that, old as the

Corporation is, the old is still good, and needs only the old generosity to make it better.

It may even be hoped that the Church historian, when he has to deal with the eighteenth century and the last years of the seventeenth, will learn from this record to give a generally despised period its due, as a time when the problem of clerical distress was seriously and benevolently faced.   He will not fail to notice that the men who took up this cause might be doughty and famous champions of opposite policies or beliefs ; but that round the table of the Sons of the Clergy they " were of one heart and soul : and not one of them said that aught of the things that he possessed was his own."

My thanks are due to my brother, the Rev. E. Courtenay Pearce, Fellow and Dean of Corpus Christi College, Cambridge, for reading the proofs and suggesting various alterations.

E. H. P.

The Vicarage,
    King Edward Street, E.C.
        January, 1904.

CONTENTS

2 xvii

CHAPTER IX

LIST OF ILLUSTRATIONS

THE SONS OF THE CLERGY

CHAPTER I

THE CORPORATION AND ITS CHARTER

THE venerable work, of which the following pages give at any rate a longer record than has hitherto been compiled, springs in reality from three distinct impulses, combined to all intents and purposes into one benevolent force. The three are thus described by a footnote in the Festival sermon of 1811, when the Rev. William Douglas, Prebendary of Westminster and Chancellor of Salisbury, was the appointed preacher. He had been saying that but for "those excellent institutions" the "infant family of a clergyman suddenly bereft of their only support" would be left "to the merciful, but to them degrading, provisions of the poor laws." His note adds that the institutions referred to are :—

> THE SOCIETY FOR THE EDUCATION OF THE ORPHANS OF THE CLERGY—THE FESTIVAL OF THE SONS OF THE CLERGY, the Stewards of which defray the whole expence of this anniversary, and apply all the money collected to the apprenticing the children of distressed Clergymen—and THE CORPORATION OF THE SONS OF THE CLERGY, the funds of which are employed in pensions to the widows, and in apprenticing the orphans, of the Clergy.

1

His list violates chronological order, for he puts first what was founded last, but it is a complete statement of the activities of a society which this year counts two centuries and three-quarters of kindly activity, and is the oldest institution connected with the English Church.

It will hardly be possible, in the course of these pages, to keep the three branches of its work distinct, except at the cost of considerable repetition. The Festival, as a public and very venerable function, is entitled to its own story, but the Corporation, as receiving the tangible benefits of the Festival, will be treated in these pages as the " predominant partner " in a truly philanthropic concern. It will appear presently that the definite beginning of the Corporation is only a later stage in the development of the Charity ; for it is known that a sermon was preached in its behalf in St. Paul's Cathedral on November 8th, 1655, and the title-page of that sermon states that its subject was " improved " and the sermon delivered before " the Sons of Ministers, then solemnly assembled." To the circumstances of that sermon we must return later, only stopping now to notice that already the phrase " Sons of Ministers " suggests the existence of the Charity. This at least may be taken as certain, that a name and a cause do not spring complete into public notice on the day that a well-known divine pleads the cause and makes familiar use of the name in the mother church of the capital.

Therefore, for the *origines* of our Charity we must

look at the records of the Festival. Corporate life begins, when it has established its right to existence, and has obtained for itself a charter, and this did not happen till 1678, in the reign of King Charles II., who had been among the *rois en exil* in 1655. Its phraseology is of the sort that might be expected. His Majesty, it says, has been approached by " divers of our loving subjects who are Sons of Clergymen," and this, I take it, is a reference to the technical title which the promoters had taken to themselves at least three-and-twenty years earlier. For it is presently expanded by a phrase which would include any of its present helpers. " Severall charitable and well-disposed persons the children of clergymen and others have appeared very free and forward " in the good work. They have brought assistance to " such of the widdows and children of Loyall and Orthodox clergiemen as are poore and Indigent." Their work, as described in the Charter, includes " placeing out many of the said poore children apprentices," the " maintenance of the others at the Vniversityes," and " the releife of many of the said poor widdowes." In fact, the Charity had obviously been doing good for years before it applied for royal recognition. The Charter goes on to name the first set of Governors, no doubt men who have earned the honour by their activity in the cause, such as " Our Right trustie and well-beloved Cousin, Francis, Earle of Longford in the Kingdome of Ireland," Humphrey Henchman, almost certainly a son of the former Bishop of London, and certain

members of the Dolben family, to whom the Charity
has owed much from first to last. But the Charter
does not set up the title " Sons of the Clergy " ; that
seems to have been settled already by popular usage ;
the Governors are permitted by the King's document
to be known as " Governours of the Charity for the
Releife of the poore Widdowes and Children of Clergymen." This remains for all purposes of investments
and the like the Society's legal title, and (though
the poor applicants use it frequently) in the early
official records the expression " Sons of the Clergy "
is by no means common, except in reference to the
Festival.

Besides the name, the Charter gave them other necessary privileges. They were to have a common seal ;
they might acquire land of the annual value of £2,000
a year ; they could " plead and bee impleaded " ; they
could make constitutions for themselves and inflict
" mulcts and amerciaments " on offenders ; they were
" to assemble themselves togeather at or in their Hall
or any other convenient place within the Citty of
London or Westminster," or indeed elsewhere. Still
more important and, as it happens, more permanent
were the arrangements made by the Charter for the
administration of the Charity. This was to be committed to a " Court of Assistance "—now generally
called " Court of Assistants "—composed of a President, a Vice-President, three Treasurers, and forty-two
" assistants, members of the said corporacon." The
Charter nominated the first Court, with " John Lord

CHARLES II'S CHARTER.

4]

Bishop of Rochester " (Dolben) as President, and Sir Christopher Wren as Vice-President, and ordered that the second Thursday in each November should be the day of annual election, as it still is. In view of the trust imposed in the Assistants, oaths were required of them on their admission to office " for their true and faithfull execution of their respective trusts and places," and in the first instance these were to be taken " before the Lord High Chancellor or the Lord Keeper of the Great Seale of England." Subsequently, the oath was sworn at the first meeting of the Court which the new Assistant might happen to attend. Its exact words were as follows :—

You shall sweare that you will duely and faithfully performe and execute all trusts and offices which are or shalbe committed unto you by the Governors of the Charity for the Releife of poore Widdows and Children of Clergymen, In vertue of his Majesties Charter granted unto them, according to the best of your skill, Soe help you God.

At the same time the Charter appointed certain *ex officio* Visitors, viz. the Archbishop of Canterbury, the Lord High Chancellor, the Archbishop of York, the Lord Keeper of the Great Seal, the Lord High Treasurer, the Lord Bishop of London, the Lord High Almoner, and the Lord Mayor of the City of London. Their duties were practically those of Visitors of colleges and the like. " They or the major part of

them shall heare and determine all differences and
disputes which shall arise touching the ordering and
governement of the said Corporation." I have not
found any case in which they were called in to give
their arbitrament ; but the want of practical interest
in the work of the Charity shown by the holders of
some of these high offices only serves to emphasise
the services of the Archbishops of Canterbury from
Tenison onwards, of an individual Lord Keeper such
as Sir Nathan Wright, of individual Chancellors such
as Thurlow, and of the Lord Mayors of London for
many years past. We may dismiss the Charter with
a notice of its signature : " Witnesse our selfe at
Westminster the first day of July in the Thirtieth
yeare of our Raigne," that is, A.D. 1678.

The Court lost no time in getting to the work set
them by the Charter. It was easy to begin under
legalised conditions a work which had plainly been
freely carried on without the dignity and recognition
which the Charter conferred. Fourteen days after the
signing of the document the first Court of Assistants
met in Jerusalem Chamber at Westminster Abbey, a
room hallowed to Churchmen by many famous associations, but never put to better use than when it
sheltered the first active members of the Corporation.
No doubt they owed the privilege of assembling there
to John Dolben, who, according to a baneful custom,
of which he was the first of eight instances, combined
the see of Rochester with the deanery of Westminster.
Pluralism is not less baneful because its exponents are

devoutly and charitably disposed ; but it can at least be said for Dolben and Sprat and Atterbury and Zachary Pearce and other occupants of these two posts that the Corporation had no keener workers. We shall return to them later. For the moment we are round the table in Jerusalem Chamber on July 15th, 1678. The first need is an executive, and "Mr. Henry Symonds, a member of the Court of Assistants, was chosen Register of this Corporation Nemine Contradicente," while Richard Williams, citizen and Haberdasher, was appointed Messenger. The Treasurers, to whose hands already there were sums of money to be entrusted, gave bonds for their financial soundness, and it will be seen later that this was by no means an inconsiderable formality. Then the members, being convinced that still further sums would come to them, settled the "preamble" to their appeal for subscriptions, and ordered the "necessary books" for records and accounts. Bishop Dolben, their President, Sir Christopher Wren, Vice-President, the Treasurers, and other members " were sworne before the Right Hono^{ble} Heneage Lord Finch, Baron of Daventry, Lord High Chancellor of England," and with the conclusion of that formality the enterprise was started under conditions which to a large extent prevail to this day. And, as it will be impossible to give the names of all who have helped in the charitable work from that day to this, it may be pardonable to insert here, as they stand in the Court-book, the names of this first Court, some of them famous in other connections.

President.

John [Dolben], Lord Bishop of Rochester.*

Vice-President.

Sir Christopher Wren.*

Treasurers.

William Wren.* [1] | James Paul. | Henry Loads.

Assistants.

Francis, Earl of Longford.[2]

Peter [Gunning], Lord Bishop of Ely.*

John [Pearson], Lord Bishop of Chester.*

William [Lloyd], Lord Bishop of Llandaff.*

John [Fell], Lord Bishop of Oxford.*

Sir Joseph Williamson.*

Sir John Robinson.

Sir Thomas Meres.*

Sir William Dolben.*

Sir Samuel Morland.*

Francis Barrett.

William Gregory.* [3]

Sir Andrew Hacket.* [4]

Sir Samuel Clark.

William Breedon.

Dr. William Lloyd.* [5]

Dr. Thomas Sprat.* [6]

Dr. Zachariah Craddock.* [7]

Dr. Nicholas Stanley, M.D.*

Dr. Walter Needham.[8]

Dr. John Mapletoft.* [9]

Dr. Henry Dove.* [10]

Lee Warner.* [11]

Tobias Rustat.*

Charles Wren.* [12]

Arthur Turner.

James Pearce.

Samuel Skinner.

Edward Thornborow.

Obadiah Sedgwick.

Edward Wake.

Charles Beamount.

Thomas Langham.

Charles Porter.

Longworth Cross.

Robert Chapman.

Henry Whistler.

Nathaniel Loddington.

Henry Symmonds.*

John Buchanan.

John Bowerman.

Francis Knowles.

For Notes, see page 9.

The months that intervened between July and the second Thursday in November, the day fixed by the Charter for the Annual General Court, are without record. But the interval was not wasted. The Corporation and the Festival were distinct entities, but the members of either were interested in the other, and by the time the General Court met in Jerusalem Chamber on November 14th, the Festival of 1678 had been held, and therefore Mr. William Wren was requested by the Governors present to thank Dr. Sprat " for his sermon preached before them and others the Sonns of the Clergy at their Anniversary meeting on Thursday the Seaventh day of November instant in the Church of St. Mary L^e Bow, London, and to desire

---

  * Known to have been sons of clergymen.

  [1] Son of Matthew, Bishop of Ely ; knighted 1685 ; M.P. Cambridge, 1685-7.

  [2] LL.D. Oxford at the installation of James, Duke of Ormond, as Chancellor, Aug. 6, 1677. Wood, *Ath. Oxon*, ii. f. 208.

  [3] Knighted 1679, as Baron of the Exchequer ; Judge of King's Bench, 1689.

  [4] Master in Chancery ; son of John Hacket, author of *Scrinia Reserata*, Bishop of Coventry and Lichfield, 1661.

  [5] Then vicar of St. Martin-in-the-Fields ; afterwards Bishop of Worcester.

  [6] Then Prebendary of Westminster ; afterwards Dean of Westminster and Bishop of Rochester.

  [7] Then Prebendary of Chichester ; Provost of Eton, 1681.

  [8] K.S. at Westminster; M.D. Camb., 1664; Physician to the Charterhouse. Wood, *Ath. Oxon*, ii. f. 109.

  [9] Rector of St. Laurence Jewry ; President of Sion College, 1707.

  [10] Vicar of St. Bride, Fleet St. ; President of Sion College, 1687-8.

  [11] Barrister at law.

  [12] Son of Matthew, Bishop of Ely ; died 1681.

him to print the same." The compliment was not paid to subsequent preachers by the General Court, as falling naturally within the sphere of those who managed the Festival ; but on this occasion it was no doubt thought well that the first annual meeting of the Governors under Charter should emphasise the partnership of the Festival and the Corporation. Something more productive than compliments was also engaging the Court's attention. Tobias Rustat, Sir Christopher Wren, Dr. Sprat, and others are soon formed into a special committee " to consider of the most effectuall way for promoteing subscriptions or contributions from the Governors and others towards the charitable ends of this Corporation and to report what they doe to the Court of Assistants." This naturally developed into a permanent Ways and Means Committee, and in 1679 resolved to meet weekly " at Dʳˢ Commons Thursdaies in the afternoone." Its recommendations were soon providing business for the Courts and advertising the Corporation in the country. To begin with, the terms of the Charter were worth making known, and the first item of ordinary expenditure was for printing " five thousand Abstracts of the patent." The printer's bill was before the Court on November 27th, 1678, and the warrant for payment is of sufficient interest to be given as it stands :—

" We praye you Mʳ Wren [*i.e.* William Wren, one of the first batch of Treasurers] be pleased to

pay Ten pounds to Mr Brome according to this
order.
> Joh. Roffen [Dolben].
> Jo. Cestriens [Pearson].
> Chr. Wren.
> Chas. Wren.
> Tho. Sprat.
> Henry Dove."

Nor were they content with circulating copies of
their Royal letters. The Treasurers were empowered
in December to grant letters of attorney " to their
severall ffriends in the Countrey or elsewhere for
gathering contributions," and Mr. Wake, a member
of the Court, was " desired to inquire out the names
of persons in severall counties fitt to be trusted." It is
possible that this Edward Wake was responsible for
a resolution of two years later " that Mr Wm Wake of
Blandford in Dorsetshire have a deputation sent to
him," that is, a legal power to get in subscriptions. As
William Wake, who became Archbishop of Canterbury
in 1716, and was elected President of the Corporation in
1723, was born at Blandford, being the son of William
Wake, we may assume that a relation of his was one of
the members of the first Court, and that his father was
one of the Corporation's earliest helpers in the provinces.

This, then, was the result of the first few months of
chartered activity, a Court elected, a Register and a
Messenger appointed, and the need of money made
known to the country by the efforts of voluntary
helpers. There has been no essential change of method
ever since.

CHAPTER II

PRESIDENTS, VICE-PRESIDENTS, AND GOVERNORS

HAVING sped the society so far on its way, we stop to examine its organisation a little more in detail, and we begin with the uppermost rank of its constitution. The President, along with the rest of the workers, came up for election or re-election on the second Thursday in each November. We have seen that John Dolben was the first to hold the office. He is also the first of many instances in which the Presidents have been no mere figure-heads, but men with an active interest in the work. Of the services of his family to the Charity we shall speak elsewhere. It will be sufficient here to note that at St. Michael's, Cornhill, he had preached the Festival sermon of 1674, four years before the Charter was granted. He presided, as we have seen, over the first General Court, and as Dean of Westminster lent Jerusalem Chamber for the purpose. When the Corporation was in a position to buy land in 1680, and an estate was suggested as their first purchase, it was not acquired till " the Lord President " had been asked to give his approbation. In 1683, on the death of Richard Sterne, Dolben was promoted to the Archbishopric of York. He was " translated in the Long Vacation time," and therefore, as the minutes explain, the members " had not the Opportunity to waite upon his Grace to pay theire

12

respects to him." So Dr. Francis Turner, his successor
as Bishop of Rochester (but not as Dean of Westminster), was asked to write " to excuse them and to
acknowledge his Graces great kindnesse and bounty
to this Corporation." They would no doubt gladly
have re-elected him, but he was of no mind to be an
ornamental chief. He sent a message that " he
intends constantly to reside " in his diocese, and Peter
Gunning, Bishop of Ely, reigned over the Corporation
in his stead.

Gunning was no less zealous for the cause. He, too,
had been the Festival preacher at Bow Church, in 1676.
His name was in the Charter as one of the first set
of Assistants. In 1679, and for ten years after, " the
Great Dyning-roome at Ely House, Holborne, the
Mansion House of the Right Reverend ffather in God
Peter Lord Bishopp of Ely," is given in the minutes as
the meeting-place of the General Courts. In 1681 he
paid in a legacy of £100 from a friend of his, whose
executor he was, and to whom no doubt he suggested
the Corporation as worthy of its place in the will.
Gunning did not live many months after his election
as President, but no man had more sympathy with
those whom the Corporation helps than the reputed
author of the prayer which bids us remember before
God " all those who are any ways afflicted, and distressed, in mind, body, or estate."

To him succeeded Francis Turner, Bishop of Rochester, both in the see of Ely and the presidentship of the
Corporation. He continued to afford to the General

3

Courts the hospitality of Ely House, and, though he does not appear actively in the records of the business, there is one entry indicative of his practical goodwill to the cause. It is dated November, 1692, after his retirement from the see of Ely as a Nonjuror, and after he had been " excused " from the office of President, and it shows that his trials had made no difference to his sense of the needs of the Charity. " A person," it says, " who at present desired to have his name concealed," has offered the Corporation the sum of £1,250 on certain conditions. The principal was to go to the Corporation at his death, but he was to receive interest at the rate of 5 per cent. per annum during his life, and the Corporation was to pay £20 a year " to two or more Clergymens widdows such as should be by him named in his lifetime to be enjoyed by them during their lives." It was only after they had given the security of some City houses for the due fulfilment of the donor's intentions that the members of the Court discovered his identity. As a matter of financial interest, it is worth adding that the £1,250 " and so much more as will make up £1,700 " was at once " lent to their Majesties upon the security of the Act for granting to their Maties four shillings in the pound upon Lands, etc. for one year," and that the Treasurer was " desired to pay in the same and to take four Tallyes for it in his own name." Years later Turner's brother and married daughter appealed to the Corporation, and " did hope that considering how good a Benefactor the sd Bishop had been to this Corporation, this Court

would accept of the recommendation " of a case
for a pension which they were anxious to help :
and the Court was not slow to own the force of
the appeal.

The fourth President, who took Turner's place on
his ejection in 1690, was William Lloyd, Bishop of
St. Asaph, who two years later appears on the minutes
of the General Court as " Ld Bishopp of Coven and
Lichen," a man whose learning and whose friendship
with Gilbert Burnet did not stand in the way of his
promotion. He too was no merely ornamental President. It was he who smoothed the negotiations with
Bishop Burnet in connection with the fee-farm rent on
the Blewberry estate, which the Corporation held till
a few years since. When it was desired in 1695 to
ask for special privilege in respect of taxation for the
Corporation property, it was to him and to Tenison
that the Court turned. The two were asked to " attend
Sʳ Thomas Clarges,[1] one of the Members of the honourable House of Commons, and to crave his aid and
favour in getting the Lands of this Corporation ex-
empted this next year from taxes." He, like Turner,
had his special cases of distress which he was anxious to
help. At one Court he stated (perhaps on Burnet's
behalf) that " William Douglass an Episcopall Minister
who had formerly a benefice in Scotland but was lately
settled in England dyed very poore," and that his wife

---

[1] I think I once read in a vestry-book of St. Martin-in-the-
Fields that Sir Thomas Clarges was a seat-holder in that church,
of which Tenison succeeded W. Lloyd as vicar.

" was now desirous to returne into Scotland but had
not wherewithal to beare the Charges of her Journey,"
towards which the Court gave her forty shillings.
More interest attaches to another *protégé* of Lloyd's.
A few months before his retirement from office he reported that " one — Bedle a Clergymans sonne of about
thirteen or fourteene years of age, grandchild of Bishop
Bedle [1] that great ornament of our Church and Paterne
of Churchmen, who is supported cheefly by the Charity
of Sr Robert Llangley," was in need of £5 towards his
apprenticeship fees.   Lloyd had already arranged with
Tenison to help the case, and the Court was quick to
support his endeavours.   Thus, as far as an interest
in the objects of the Charity is concerned, Lloyd continued active, though at his own desire he was " excused " in 1697 " for the yeare ensueing." [2]

[1] William Bedell, Bishop of Dromore ; d. 1642.
[2] Lloyd had made earlier attempts to be "excused." Years
ago, when I contemplated an edition of Tenison's correspondence,
I made a copy of a letter to him (Lambeth Palace Library, MSS.
942.55) which, as it shows Lloyd's knowledge of his clergy, his
pride in the presidency of our Corporation, and his care for its
Festival-dinner, is worth its space here :—

93. Nov. 27.
MY GOOD LORD,
    I thank God I was not so ill wth ye gripes as my
friends apprehended me to be & y^t ye illness such as it was
is now over.
    There was a mistake in ye mention I made of Mr Gretton in
my former l^r.   There are 2 clergymen of y^t name in Derbyshire.
One of y^m is a scandall to ye Church tho I have no suffic^t proof
to bring him under Church censures. . . . The other Mr Gretton
. . . is a man free from exception & very well spoken of by all
ye best men I know in his neighbourhood.   I saw many of their

And then came Tenison, the fifth of the seventeenth-century Presidents of the Corporation. It is the custom to sneer at Tenison's Whiggish Latitudinarianism, but in connection with the charitable work of the Sons of the Clergy he can show a worthy record. In 1680, two years after the grant of the Charter, he was elected one of the Court of Assistants, and was constant in his attendance. In the following year he preached the Festival sermon at Bow Church. In 1689 he had a chance that he welcomed of bestowing a practical boon on the Charity. John Love,[1] rector of Wood-

hands to his L^{rs} Testimoniall, wch he thought needfull to take along wth him for fear he should be mistaken for y^t wretched man y^t bears the same name but as he saies is not kin to him y^t he knows. . . .

I cannot but take very kindly ye honour y^t is done me by our brethren of ye Corporation of Clergymens Sons in continuing mee to be their President. But I am so much ye more sorry for the wrong they have done themselves by it : for as it is but little service I can do them upon ye place, so I cannot expect to do any at this distance. I can onely hope to be there time enough to see this kinde error mended at their next election. The mean while I thank yor Lo^p for taking care to get ye Venison for their Feast. If yor Lo^p shall be there (wch may be doubted in a sitting of Parlt) I desire you would be pleased to put 2 Guinies for me into ye Bason : or if you are not there yo^{r}self to get somebody els to do it. . . .

Yo^r Ldps most affectionate Servt
W. Cov. & Lich.

For . . . ye Lord Bp of Lincolne
    at his house in St. Martins.

[1] John Love was a son of Richard Love, Master of Corpus Christi, Cambridge (Tenison's College), and Dean of Ely. He was admitted to Clare in 1662 and graduated 1666-7. He was vicar of Everton, Hunts, a Clare College benefice, 1680-85, and died 1688. Venn, *Al. Cantab.*, iii. 107.

church, had left £1,000 at the discretion of Tenison, William Sherlock, Dean of St. Paul's, and Sharp, Dean of Norwich and afterwards Archbishop of York, to dispose of " for charitable uses." " Wherein," he had added, " I desire Clare Hall in Cambridge, the Library or Schoole at St. Martins in the ffeilds [founded by Tenison] and the Clergymenns Sonnes may be considered as in their Wisdomes they shall thinke fitt." Tenison was able to announce that by consent of the trustees the Corporation would receive one-third of the sum in question. In 1692, when he was Bishop of Lincoln, he was still on the Court, and the fact that he attended meetings in January, March, and November (twice), 1693, and April, 1694, need not imply a neglect of his episcopal duties, except in the minds of those who forget that in those days the vast diocese of Lincoln stretched down to the banks of the Thames.   Indeed, it is possible to conclude that he was jealous of his reputation as a regular attendant, for a note is added to the minutes of the meeting of November 15th, 1692, to the following effect :—" The Rt. Reverend father in God Thomas L^d B^p of Lincoln and Sr Thomas Meers K^{nt} [1] two members of this Court, came immediately upon the riseing of the Court and before the members thereof were departed."   Thus it was naturally " by an unanimous consent " that the Governors chose him President in Lloyd's place, and they were evidently not a little proud to be able to describe him in 1694 in their minutes as " Lord Arch-

---

[1] Whig M.P. for Lincoln ; see p. 25.

bishop of Canterbury, primate of all England and Metropolitan." As if to show that the Assistants were conscious of Tenison's past services, it was " ordered that Ten pounds more bee payd to his Grace the Lord Arch Bishop of Canterbury to be disposed of by him for the Relief of such poore widdows and children of Clergymen as his Grace shall judge to be most necessitous." And the Court made use of him in other ways. He was one of the Corporation's first trustees of Palmer's Charity.[1] Their addresses to William III., Anne, and George I., were presented by Tenison. It was through him, as through his successor of to-day, that the Court endeavoured to get practical support from the bench of bishops. For in February, 1700, several Assistants were chosen to " attend the Archbishop and the Bishop of Worcester [William Lloyd, promoted from ' Coven and Lichen,'] to-morrow att eleaven of the Clock to take their directions about applying to the severall Bishops for promoteing the benefitt of the Corporation and to meete att Webbs Coffee house under Scotland yard gate."[2] It was to him also that they turned when they wanted help from the Universities. The records show that he not infrequently presided at Court meetings, and an order of 1711 " That the Messenger summons his Grace the Lord Arch Bishop of Canterbury to every Court of Assistants " may be taken to imply that he had expressed his wish to attend as frequently as possible. Add to his services to the Court his constant support

---

[1] See pp. 46 f.; 115 f.   [2] Close to Sir Christopher Wren's house.

of the Festival—for he and Francis Atterbury and William Lloyd, who preached both in 1679 and 1680, and Adam Littleton, rector of Chelsea, who was their spokesman for three years in succession (1687–1689), were the only men ever asked to preach a second time in its behalf [1]—and it will be easy to see that the Corporation had reason to regret his death.

But in those days the best vote of condolence was the election of a suitable successor. The Governors turned again to Bishop Lloyd, and with his re-election accomplished we might leave the Presidents for the moment and descend to the next rank in this charitable hierarchy, were it not for an incident which happened within a few years. Lloyd's re-election occurred in 1716, but he died shortly after. Next came Philip Bisse,[2] Bishop of Hereford, who with others of his family had shown zeal for the cause, being at that time a member of the Court. He died in 1721, and then came a contested election. " All the Bishops who are of the Court of Assistants," says the minute-book, " being putt in Nominacon, the Bishops of Winton [C. Trimnell] and Rochester [Atterbury] appeared to

[1] Until William Boyd Carpenter, Bishop of Ripon, who had preached as vicar of St. James, Lower Holloway, in 1876, was rightly chosen to preach at the 250th Festival in 1904. Similarly, the President has invited the Dean of St. Paul's, who preached in 1912, to preach at the 275th Festival,—a fine compliment alike to the cathedral and the preacher.

[2] Philip Bisse preached the Festival sermon in 1708, and his brother Thomas in 1716. As Chancellor of Hereford, Thomas Bisse in 1724 converted the Festival of the Three Choirs into that source of charity to clergy-widows which it still is. D. Lysons, *Meeting of the Three Choirs* (1895), pp. 1–5.

be the 2 Bishops who had the Majority and it being
doubtfull who had the Majority of the two the Members
divided in order to be *told* and the Bishop of Winchester
appeared to have the Majority and was declared by
the Treasurer to be elected." It will be seen elsewhere [1] that there was some possible significance in
this contest, but the Court was no doubt glad that
Trimnell's death in 1723 did not leave them in similar
difficulties. Wake, the then Archbishop, was elected
a Governor and President the same day, and there is
a sign of relief in the statement that he was chosen
nemine contradicente. Over thirty years before, Wake's
father had been a worker in Dorsetshire on the Corporation's behalf. But the occasion was of more
than personal importance. It set the policy of always
looking to Lambeth for the President, and the Corporation has never looked in vain. Even when in
1757 it chose Matthew Hutton (then Archbishop of
York), it did so from a shrewd suspicion that he was to
succeed Herring at Canterbury. And the Archbishops
have served the Charity personally ; the signatures of
Secker and Cornwallis and Manners Sutton frequently
attest the confirmation of the minutes ; while the services of latter-day Primates are too well known to
need description. The present Archbishop had been
for many years a member of the Court, when he became
President in 1903. Indeed, his personal interest in the
Charity goes back to the early days of his chaplaincy
to Dr. Tait.[2]

[1] p. 265.   [2] See Chapter XV.

THE VICE-PRESIDENTS

The choice of Sir Christopher Wren as their first Vice-President was something more than a compliment to a distinguished son of a clergyman. It was a recognition of an unwritten rule that laymen should have an equal share in the work of the Charity, and sprang from a desire that the laymen selected should be men of affairs. But in selecting Sir Christopher they happened upon one who was destined to render them service over a long course of years. He had already been a Steward of the Festival in 1676. His name is in the Charter of 1678. He remained Vice-President till 1683, and during his term of office it was resolved that he " bee desired forthwith to provide a Seale for this Corporation," which he did, presenting it at a Court held in Jerusalem Chamber in October, 1680. He was naturally consulted as to purchases of City and other property ; for instance, when they were negotiating in 1681 for the acquisition of " the House in Pancrasse Lane, London, of the yearely value of 70$^{£}$ p. annum," a special note was made that " Mr Vice-President " should be among those who were invited " to treate about the same." A few days later there is a record of " Sr Ch^r Wrens declaration of trust " in respect of £1,500 lodged with the East India Company. In 1683 " at the earnest desire of Sr Ch^r Wren, Knt., Vice-President, the Court did excuse him." Wren, if anyone, could plead at that time a multitude of public obligations, but he did not desert the Sons of the Clergy. In 1685 the Court asked him to help them present an address to James II. Both in 1703 and in 1720 he was again elected an Assistant, but he did not attend during the year, and was consequently " excused " at the following annual meeting. Yet in 1722 they once more desired to have his name on their list, and elected him Vice-President, in succession to Sir Gilbert Dolben, and " the President [Trimnell of Winchester] was pleased to declare that he would acquaint him therewith and desire him to accept of the office." Early in the following year the Court were anxious about his will. Dr. Strahan, of Doctors' Commons, reported " that he has inspected Sr Christopher Wrens will and finds that the Corporation is not mentioned therein." This was no doubt a grievous disappointment, but the Court were not cast down. If the fine old man had left them no legacy, they could at least make sure of his annual subscriptions, which seem not to have been paid with absolute regularity. I have found among the faded papers at Corporation House a statement in the handwriting of Mr. Robert Chapman, one of the Treasurers, giving a list of the subscriptions and other moneys received by him from Williams the Messenger. Pinned on to it are receipts for Common Sewer and Militia taxes, but in the list of " subscriptions received that were due at Michaelmas 1686 " it appears that on January 11th, 1687, there was " Recēd of Sr Christopher Wren, 1 yr. £05. 00. 00," and his friend Flamsteed is in the same list with a sovereign. But in 1700 a sub-committee was desired to " waite upon Sir Christopher Wren about his

subscriptions " ; and now, upon his death, an order
is given that the Register should let his executor have
" an account of his subscription by way of Debtor
and Creditor." The Chancery judges would probably
make short work of such a demand in the present day,
and it is a pity that we do not know the fate it met
with on this occasion.

In 1683, when Sir Christopher asked to be " excused "
from the office of Vice-President, he was succeeded by
his cousin, William Wren, afterwards a knight and
M.P. for Cambridge. He and Charles Wren were
sons of Matthew Wren, Bishop of Ely. As one who
" had suffered for his Majesty's cause " and been
ejected from the University of Cambridge, he was
created M.A. at the Restoration. He had served as
Steward of the 1675 Festival. He was one of the
first set of Treasurers, and was a very regular attendant at the business meetings. He was followed in
1689 by Sir William Gregory, Judge of King's Bench,
and it is easy to see the advantage that the Corporation
stood to gain by having a distinguished lawyer on
its honorary staff. Disputed wills and purchases of
property and transfers of trust were soon daily occur-
rences. Mr. Palmer's Holloway property,[1] for instance, was passed over with its obligations to our
Charity in 1694, and Sir William Gregory was asked
to assist in the arrangements for the transfer of trust.
But his interest in the work was not merely a legal one.
I have before me a widow's letter addressed in 1688

[1] Cf. pp. 115-18.

" To Sergeant Gregory these in all humility present
at Serients Inn in Chancery Lane in London." Her
appeal was evidently attended to, for the letter is
backed with the name of " Mr Baron Gregory " in
the Register's handwriting. " Honble Sir," she writes,
" my humble request is that you wilbe pleased to
speake and assist me for the getting of the three
pounds which was allotted me for the maintenance of
Minnisters widdows out of Doctors Comons, I have
received two paiments already and I am much distressed for this also, I being in a sad condicon. I
would desire you wilbe pleased to help some of my
sons children to place them, for he hath left seauen
of them, so praying for yor assistance therein I humbly
take leave and rest yor distressed servant Anne ffloyde."

His successor, Sir Thomas Meres, had been Commis-
sioner to the Admiralty and sat in the Whig interest
for Lincoln for half a century. Besides his personal
co-operation in the good work during his life—for he
was twice Vice-President, 1696 to 1704, and in 1706
—he left the Corporation a legacy, which his son was
by no means hasty in handing over. Two men who
followed him in office are worth a passing mention.
Among those who accepted a place on the Court of
Assistants in 1699 was " Sr Nathan Wright, Searjant
att Lawe." [1] In 1700 a committee was appointed to

---

[1] Son of Ezekiel Wright, fellow of Emmanuel, Cambridge, and
rector of Thurcaston, Leics., where Latimer, Bishop of Worcester,
was born, and where Richard Hurd, Bishop of Worcester, was rector.
He was born 1653.   Recorder of Leicester, 1680.   Lord Keeper,
1700–1705. Died 1723.

wait on him as " Lord Keeper of the Great Seale of England," and " congratulate him upon his Maties great honour conferred on him," and the occasion was thought to be sufficiently noteworthy for Archbishop Tenison to be asked to go with them. They soon made use of his legal experience, for in the same year came a question whether the Corporation could allow money to be collected *and distributed* in the arch-deaconry of Chester. Could this be done within the terms of the Charter ? So they resolved " to consult my Lord Keeper and such of this Court as are of the Long Robe," and in due course were satisfied that no breach of trust would be involved. Again in 1701 Wright was associated with Tenison in the presentation of an address to William III. at Hampton Court. Lord Keeper Wright was elected Vice-President in 1705, and at the same Court there was chosen as Assistant another member of the Dolben family, which has served the Corporation so well. Sir Gilbert Dol-ben, who succeeded to the baronetcy in 1709, was made Vice-President in 1707, an office to which he had an obvious claim as the son of the first President. He too had already given his legal assistance when doubtful matters were occupying the Court's attention. One, which hardly sounds doubtful to modern ears, had been before them in 1694, when Dolben had just been nominated on the Court in the place of " Tobias Rustat, dec^d." The Treasurer and the Register were bidden to " waite upon Gilbert Dolben Esqr and Samuel Blackerby Esqr with a copy of the Charter,

and if upon perusall of the same they shall be of opinion
that the money belonging to this Corporation may
without breach of Trust be put into the Bank of England till a purchase can be made," then the Court are
prepared to risk with Threadneedle Street " all the
even hundred pounds lyeing dead in the Treas^{rs}
hands." Very shortly he was engaged in the task of
securing for the Charity the payment of a legacy from
his brother, John Dolben, who was a gambler and a
spendthrift, and had been sent off to the West Indies,
which no doubt interprets the reference to a will
made in " India." Returning home, he entered Parliament for Liskeard, and was the member to whom
Sacheverell owed his impeachment by the House. He
died, to the delight of the Tory preacher's supporters,
just as the trial began. A man who out of his somewhat recovered fortunes managed to enrich the Sons
of the Clergy would hardly have revoked the bequest,
even if he had lived to see Sacheverell a few years
later an active member of the Court.[1] The circum-

[1] Sacheverell was less generous. Professor Nichol Smith drew
my attention in 1913 to the fact that Thomas Burnet, the Bishop
of Salisbury's younger son, was a Steward of the Festival of 1713,
when Sacheverell preached on Dec. 10, but that the preacher,
when he came to print the sermon and to dedicate it, as usual,
to " The Stewards of the late Feast," omitted Thomas Burnet's
name. White Kennett's comment (*Wisdom of Looking Backward*,
1715, p. 325), was that Burnet " had not less Birthright, nor less
wit and Learning, than his Fellow-Stewards." The Professor
found a letter from Thomas Burnett to George Duckett, dated
November 1, 1713, saying : " I did think of staying in the country
till the middle of January, but my being in a post of Steward to
the Sons of the Clergy obliges me to go to London this month."
(David Nichol Smith, *Letters of Thomas Burnet to George Duckett*,

stances were as follows. Mrs. Dolben, it was reported, " has an account from India of a Will of her late husband . . . duely executed, whereupon the proceedings at Drs Commons in relation to two other wills had been stopt," and it was Sir Gilbert who brought the information. The upshot was worthy of the family traditions. For two years later Sir Gilbert " acquainted the Court that Madam Dolben . . . had sent the Corporation the £1000 Legacy given the Corporation by Mr Dolbens will and £100 for the interest of it whilst the will was litigating in Doctors Comons." The money was at once laid out in " Classis Lottery Ticketts " at £9 5s. each. Nor did Sir Gilbert leave the Charity out of his own will, though for all his experience he omitted to make the will legal. For Bishop Trimnell in 1722 sent a message to the Court that the late Vice-President had left £500 to the Sons of the Clergy, to be paid in five annual instalments, " but that the will was imperfect. However, Sir John Dolben [the son] declares he will pay the money according to the intent of the Will."

1712–1722 (Roxburghe Club), 1914, p. 55.) An earlier letter of Thomas Burnet to Duckett, January 1, 1713, implies that " a certain liveliness " may well have been imparted to Stewards' meetings so composed. " Dr. Sach. . . .ll," he wrote, " being to be released from the imprisonment of his Mouth, has got a Text, viz : *I was led like a sheep before the shearers, and I open'd not my mouth, but I was dumb*. Upon which I sent him in a Penny Post letter a properer Text, *And the Lord open'd the mouth of the ass, and he said unto Balaam, why hast thou smitten me these three times ?* " (Ibid. pp. 26, 27.) It is to be remembered that Burnet, whose quotations from Scripture are not precise, was qualifying, not for the pulpit, but for a judgeship of the Court of Common Pleas.

Such then were the early Vice-Presidents, men of position and of affairs, who were seldom content to be merely honorary.[1]

THE GOVERNORS

The key of the position was in the hands of the Governors of the Corporation. The first set, as we have seen, were nominated by the Crown, the subsequent appointments have been made at the annual General Courts in November. It was the body of Governors which elected the President, the Vice-Presidents, the Treasurers, and the Court of Assistants. In early days no qualification was demanded in the shape of a gift of money ; so much so that the lack of such gifts caused comment and effort to supply it on more than one occasion. In 1684 we find the Court " taking notice that there were very many worthy persons living ab^{t} Towne who were Governors of this Corporation that had not as yet contributed thereto, and being well satisfyed that they or many of them were such persons as were very forward to promote all such acts of charity and that theire not knowing where to pay in theire Charity had been the Cause they had not as yet done it." The result then was a search for " a fitt person to move them in the most agreeable manner to give something to this Corporation." Thirty years

---

[1] On the death of Earl Egerton of Tatton in 1909, the office was accepted by Lord Alverstone, Lord Chief Justice, a member of the Court of Assistants, and to him in 1915 succeeded Lord Parmoor, then Vicar-General of the province of Canterbury.

4

later, the same object is still in view. The Treasurers
are asked by the Committee of Ways and Means " to
accept of Subscripcon Rolles and endeavour what they
can to procure subscripcons at the next generall
Court," and their colleagues are " desired to assist
them therein." The fact is that men were selected as
Governors either for services rendered or for services
expected. Thus in 1712 " the present Stewards [of
the Festival] or so many of them as were not Governors
before " were elected, and the list in that instance included " Charles Talbot, Esq., now his Majesty's
Solicitor General," and afterwards Lord Chancellor,—
an instance of the class of men who help a cause by
allowing their name to be associated with it, though
they can do little more. But, on the other hand, men
were often made Governors as a preliminary to their
immediate or early election as Assistants. Their services were still to come. In any case the Governors
were the body of sympathisers whom the Assistants
could feel to be behind them in their efforts, while to
the country at large their names and numbers were
a guarantee of the need and the efforts of the Charity.
The list in the Charter must serve as typical of those
that have come after. It contained one hundred and
sixty-seven names, and consisted of doctors and
bachelors of divinity, " Clerkes," doctors of medicine,
" Gents," merchants, " Esq^{rs}," captains, and the like.
Here is " William Beveridge, B.D.," " Edward Fowler,
B.D.," the adversary of John Bunyan and afterwards
Bishop of Gloucester. " James Holman of Cajus

THEOLOGICAL LITERATURE

PUBLISHED BY

JOHN MURRAY, ALBEMARLE ST., LONDON, W.1

THE BUILDING OF THE CHURCH OF CHRIST.

BEING UNIVERSITY AND OTHER SERMONS.

By the Rt. Rev. ARTHUR C. HEADLAM, C.H., D.D., Bishop of Gloucester. Author of ' Jesus Christ in History and Faith,' etc.   7s. 6d. net.

A selection of the sermons preached by the Bishop of Gloucester during the past 20 years. The aim of the writer throughout has been the building of the Church as a great Society, representative of the religious life of the nation ; the promotion of Christian reunion and friendly relations with other religious bodies, and the restatement of the Christian faith in relation to modern knowledge.

SIMPLICITY TOWARDS CHRIST.

By HOWARD CHANDLER ROBBINS, Dean of the Cathedral of St. John the Divine, New York. With a Preface by the Rt. Rev. the LORD BISHOP OF RIPON.   6s. net.

In this age of great material progress the author feels that a study of the life and ideals of Christ, and their true interpretation, is more than ever necessary if the essential spiritual elements of our life are to be preserved. His book is alive with modern interest, and it presents sincerely a series of illuminating discussions on the value of religious concepts to us to-day.

GIVING AND RECEIVING

Six Plain Sermons on the Holy Eucharist by J. ARMITAGE ROBINSON, D.D., Dean of Wells. 2nd IMPRESSION. 2s. 6d. net.

'Few more timely or more illuminating books have appeared than this collection of sermons. They are the work of a scholar, expressed in language of exquisite lucidity and simplicity. Many will find in this book just exactly the theology that they have been groping after, the thoughts that they believe to be true.'—*Guardian.*

MEMORIES

By the Most Rev. the LORD ARCHBISHOP OF WALES, D.D. With Illustrations.   12s. net.

'Nowhere else can be found so clear and authoritative a presentation of the movement for disestablishing the ancient church of Wales, of the causes that led up to it, or of its results, as is to be seen in these pages. A narrative that cannot fail to hold the attention..'—*Times.*

THE NEW PRAYER BOOK

A Charge by the Rt. Rev. ARTHUR C. HEADLAM, C.H., D.D., Bishop of Gloucester. SECOND IMPRESSION. 2s. 6d. net.

'Should be read by all English Christians and especially by those of the Church of England who doubt the wisdom of the changes proposed. Dr. Headlam combines erudition with simplicity to a surprising degree. His argument marches forward with a balanced step, never missing a point, yet never deviating from the main issue.'—*Spectator.*

THE FUTURE OF CHRISTIANITY

Edited by Sir JAMES MARCHANT, K.B.E., LL.D. Introduction by the Rt. Rev. ARTHUR C. HEADLAM, C.H., D.D., Bishop of Gloucester: Preface by the Editor, and by various other eminent leaders in the Churches. 7s. 6d. net.

Dean Inge in the *Church of England Newspaper* says:— The essays are all good, some of them very good, and the writers are well acquainted with present conditions and recent thought, which must be our chief guides in predicting the future.'

Coll." [1] represents the Universities, and " Thomas Raymond, serjeant of Law, one of the Barons of the Exchequer," [2] stands for a profession which has always served the Charity with wisdom and generosity. Therefore from the beginning their names were printed along with an abstract of the Charter, as they are to this day. The first bill paid after the granting of the Charter was for this purpose, and at the close of the eighteenth century a Committee of Ways and Means, at which two Treasurers, three doctors of divinity, and three laymen were present, did not think it had wasted a morning, when all it had to show for its work was an entry that " the Committee examined and corrected the List of Governors and ordered one thousand of them to be printed." These early annual lists were so thoroughly circulated that there are none surviving at Corporation House, and we are left to discover the names from chance references in the records. Sometimes at General Courts the Governors attended in some force ; for instance, in November, 1711, " at which time a great Number of the generality being present Mr Vice-President [Sir Gilbert Dolben] acquainted them that this Assembly was called to meet pursuant to the Charter of Incorporation " for the annual election. The Executive deserves a chapter to itself.

---

[1] No doubt, James Halman, Fellow of Caius, 1662, Master, 1700–02 ; son of Nicholas Halman, rector of Thursford.

[2] Afterwards a Judge of King's Bench ; son of Robert Raymond, rector of Bures. Venn, *Al. Cantab.*, iii. 429.

CHAPTER III

TREASURERS AND ASSISTANTS

IT has already been hinted that the administrative strength of the Corporation's constitution lies in its Court of Assistants as set up by the Charter of Charles II. and unaltered to this day. It consists of the President, the Vice-President, the three Treasurers and forty-two Assistants. Naturally, as being chosen by the Governors, the Assistants represent the classes of which the Governors have been shown to consist. Bishops and clergy are always there. A sprinkling of the " gentlemen of the Long Robe " is never wanting. The fighting forces have their occasional representatives, such as "Captain Theophilact Bletchynden," whose very names combine the militant and the ecclesiastical, who was placed on the Court in 1693, became Treasurer in 1704, and remained active in the Corporation's service till his death in 1711. He may have been responsible for the choice in 1704 of " Sir Thomas Dilkes,[1] Rear Admirall of the White Squadron," and of " Sir James Wishart, Knt., Rear Admirall of the Blew Squadron," as Assistants, but the worthy admirals did not become effective members of the management ; perhaps they were frightened by Benjamin Hoadly, who was elected at the same time.

[1] Those who are interested in the pugnacious qualities of Lady Dilkes may refer to *Annals of Christ's Hospital* (Methuen), pp. 122–3.

Other men with little time at their disposal for active
co-operation were such as Wm. Williams, Speaker of
the House of Commons, in 1680 ; John Vesey, Archbishop of Tuam, in 1689 ; " Sʳ Richard Levett, Knight,
Lord Major of the City of London," in 1699, the first
holder of that office to take any personal part in a
work for which his successors have done so much, and
which he himself had helped twenty years before as
Steward in 1679 ; Sir Salathiel Lovell, Recorder of
London, who is mentioned in the Charter and was
Steward eighteen years later ; George Stanhope, afterwards Dean of Canterbury, who preached the sermon
of 1697 and went on the Court in 1705.   Joseph Addison became a Governor in 1706, was a Steward in
1707, and was elected to the Court in 1714 ; but he
did not attend and was " excused " in the following
year. He and Sir Joshua Reynolds, who was an
Assistant at the time of his death, and David Garrick,
who was a Steward in 1772, may serve as conclusive
examples of the men who can give money but cannot
afford time.

We turn now to the active workers, of whom the
more part were City clergy and busy laymen.   There
is Tobias Rustat, known to Cambridge men as the
founder of the Rustat Scholarships at Jesus College
for clergymen's sons, and who ought to be known to
Londoners as the man who gave the Grinling Gibbons
statue of James II. to Whitehall.[1]   He was himself a

----

[1] It has been appropriately removed to the west front of the
Admiralty.

clergyman's son, and his odd career need not detain us now. Someone described him as " a very simple, ignorant, but honest and loyal creature." At any rate he gave such capacities as he had to the Corporation. Again, there was the Sedgwick family, Obadiah, William, Francis, and Robert, men apparently engaged in the East India Company. They not only served as Stewards, but gave their time generously to Committee work, looked out for suitable investments, and for estates and property for the Corporation to purchase. William Sedgwick gives " £50 Stocke in the East India Company, provided that the Dividends may be disposed of during his and his Wives life," but his constant service on the Court and as Treasurer was worth far more than his gift. The residences of these laymen can only be gathered from the addresses of any letters of theirs that happen to be among the remaining papers. Francis Kynnesman (1692) was to be found " Att the sign of the Bell in the Upper Walk in the New Exchange in the Strand." Another (1698) is " an Apothecary in Salisbury Court in ffleet Street." Henry Rogers (1720) is addressed " at alderman Chiles house nere Tempel bar " ; Samuel Newey (1724) is a " Linnen-draper at Stocksmarket " ; Westley, who attained to high civic office, is a merchant " in Queen Streete by Guild Hall " ; Robert Glyn is " an Oil-man at the Corner of Hatton-Garden, Holbourn " ; and Thomas Fulks is a druggist in Newgate Street.[1]

---

[1] He was buried in Christ Church, Dec. 26, 1728. *Registers* (Harleian Society), p. 363.

These and their legal colleagues provided more than a quorum for Courts and committees, but they were ably supported by the City clergy, whose help was not disdained by the laymen even on the " committee of law-suits and purchases." Henry Dove, of St. Bride's, Fleet Street ; Edward Pelling, of St. Martin's, Ludgate ; Edward Lake, of St. Mary-at-Hill ; Thomas Manningham and Henry Sacheverell, of St. Andrew's, Holborn ; Thomas Whincup, of St. Mary Abchurch ; Zaccheus Isham and Roger Altham, of St. Botolph's, Bishopsgate ; Lilly Butler, of St. Mary Aldermanbury ; White Kennett, of St. Botolph, Aldgate, afterwards Bishop of Peterborough ; William Savage, of " St. Andrew Wardrobe and St. Anne Blackfryars " ; and Joseph Trapp, of Christ Church, Newgate Street, are a few representatives among the City clergy of those who most regularly took part in the deliberations of the Court in the early days of the Charity's history, and a reference to its present list would show that, though the proportion to-day is not so great, there are still several City clergy among the Assistants. Other clergy, elected to the Court, were more famous, if not more effective. Francis and Lewis Atterbury, that strangely assorted pair of brothers, were frequent attendants. Francis can be traced on the minutes from St. Bride's to the deaneries of Carlisle and Christ Church and the Bishopric of Rochester. He went on the Court in 1691, and did not retire from it till 1722. Thomas Sherlock was the Festival preacher as Master of the Temple in 1710, and in 1716 and onwards, as

Dean of Chichester, was a regular and useful adviser, perhaps more useful than he was to the cathedral of Chichester.

It should be added that almost from the first the Corporation devised a system for varying the *personnel* of the Court. A third of the forty-two went off every year for a period, being, as the phrase of 1679 runs, " discharged from their further attendance." But it frequently happened that this was only a form, the fourteen being " discharged," but some or all of them re-enlisted, if they had served well, and sometimes even if they had not. This had its disadvantages in encouraging or condoning slackness, so that in 1704 it was " resolved that for the future those of the Court of Assistants shall be first excused who have paid the least attendance, especially those that have been three years of the said Court." In 1714 this scrutiny of attendances had evidently become a fixed practice, for, when the General Court assembled in the Chapter House, " Then the List of the Names of the present Court of Assistants with an Account of the years they have served in that Court and of their attendances the last year was read, and the persons whose names are next hereafter mentioned were (upon the Question severally put) excused from their attendance in the Court this year." It may or may not have a connection with this slackness that prayer before business was specially introduced in the following year. The occasion was a Court of Distributions in the month of May, and it was resolved " that for the future before the Court enter upon business there shall be a proper Collect and the Lds Prayer read by one of the Clergy or the Senr Treasurer, and that the Lord Bishop of Carlisle with the rest of the Clergymen present or any three of them be a Committee to prepare the same." This Bishop of Carlisle was W. Nicolson, and it would have been of interest to know the sort of collect that he and Sherlock and Sacheverell, who were present, would have produced by consultation, but the books contain no trace of it. Judging by the frequency with which the signature " W. Carliol " appears in support of the petitioners of that date, one may believe that the prayer would at least have remembered the sorrows of those whom it is the privilege of the Charity to relieve. It is only necessary to add that besides attending the regular meetings of the Court of Assistants the members were expected to divide themselves among several Committees, such as " Ways and Means," " Law-suits and Purchases," " the Accounts Committee," and " the Committee to Methodize the Books." Drones were perhaps inevitable, but the honey-bees in this kindly community undoubtedly worked with a will.

THE TREASURERS

Of all those who devoted spare time and superfluous energy to this cause the Treasurers were by far the most important. The Charter of 1678 nominated three, and that number has always been maintained. Early in 1679, when they printed the list of the Governors, it was deemed necessary to print " at the end of the abstract particuler directions to the severall places of the aboade of the respective Treasurers." At the General Court of the same year one of the Treasurers was " discharged from further attendance," not for incapacity or inattention, but because someone else must have a chance to fill so important a post. Finally it was arranged that a man should serve the office for three years, rising in the third to be Senior Treasurer and then returning to the position of an Assistant or going off the Court altogether for a space till there was a vacancy. It is obvious that there was much to be said for this arrangement. It gave various members a complete acquaintance with all the branches of the business ; but the office was restricted to laymen, who were not always better financiers than their clerical colleagues. Their accounts would not balance in every case. My parishioner, Mr. Fulks, the Newgate Street druggist, afforded occupation for quite a number of meetings in 1722 before his audit could be completed, and, as he was responsible for paying out in one year some £2,400 to over 660 persons, he might be pardoned if there was some difficulty. The work of the Treasurers was always done voluntarily. The solitary exception to be traced in the books only serves to prove the rule. It belongs to 1685 and concerns Mr. Treasurer Gilbert, to whom "a present of Ten Guineys " was awarded for his great " care and paines " in the Corporation's behalf, specially in connection with Dr.

Townson's gift.   But Mr. Gilbert, it is recorded, " having resolved freely to spend what time he could spare for the benefitt of this Corporation, desired to be excused from receiving any reward for it, which he prayed might be accepted as his Contribution towards the promotion of this Charity."   The action is not less to his credit because he seems to have been a lawyer.

Considering the sums of money placed in the Treasurers' care, the Court was obviously right in demanding a bond then, though circumstances make it unnecessary now.   This was done at any rate as early as 1688, on the day that Tenison was chosen an Assistant, when the Treasurers " did each of them execute a Covenant of Indenture for discharge of their Offices with a penalty of one thousand pounds therein contained for the performance thereof."   Such security was carefully placed in the Corporation chest, and its form could be varied by permission.   Mr. Treasurer Lewis, says a resolution of 1713, is " at liberty to lodge £1,000 Classis Lottery Ticketts in the Corporation Chest as his Securitie instead of personall securitie."   But the day, in 1688, which saw this rule adopted, provided an instance of the need of it.   Sir Matthias Vincent died during his treasurership, and over £300 " of the money of this Corporation " had been in his keeping at his death and could not be recovered from the widow and the son.   It was decided that William and Obadiah Sedgwick should wait on them and, " if they nor either of them give a satisfactory answer within a weeke," then there is nothing for it but " due course of law." That, however, was avoided in an interesting way. In the following February (1689) Treasurer Sedgwick reported that Vincent was " at his death possessed of a Two and thirtieth parte of the Ship yᵉ *Modena* now in service of the East India Company." The widow and son were willing to sell Sedgwick the share and that " the Corporation should be paied out of the purchase money the £306 6s. 8d.," while " out of the greate inclinations that he had for the good of the Corporation " Sedgwick was " willing to purchase the same, soe as he could have a good Title," and he bought the share in the *Modena* for £550.

But a later case caused more difficulty though not any constructive loss. In 1728, " at the Globe Tavern in the Old Jury," Mr. Treasurer Pead's pay-book was " examined in his presence." It appeared that " there are about 46 persons paid (of which 24 are two years payments) for which no satisfactory Voucher is pro-duced, the sume whereof amounts to £350." Pead " acknowledged that there have been impositions " and asked for an adjournment " to see what further light he could give." Adjourning for two days they met " at the Three Tons Tavern in Wood Street " and reported that Mr. Pead " has not given more satis-faction than at the last meeting," but offered his own security for £400 " until he does give some further security," which implies that his bond was not better than his word. In fact he could not " answer the demand "; therefore they applied to his security, whose conduct was laid before a Committee at the " Three Tons Taverne " in the following report :—

> The Treārers being met but there not being a sufficient number to make a Comittee and the Reg^r having informed the Treārer that he had wrote a Letter to Mr House (who is Mr Pead's securitie) to acquaint him with what appeared due from him upon the ballance of his Accounts, and that the Comittee desired he would come to Towne and meet them at this time to give them satisfaccon for the said ballance, and that the Reg^r had received a Letter from Mr House from Windsor excusing his coming to Towne for that he was very ill and was going to Bristoll, and the Reg^r having also acquainted the Treārers that he called at Mr Peads at Six this evening to desire him to meet the Comittee and that his Apprentice informed him that his Master was sent for Just before the Register called to visit a Patient out of Towne, the Treārers were of opinion that both Mr Pead and his Securitie design to trifle and delay the payment of what is due from Mr Pead as much as they can, and directed the Register to proceed ag^t Mr House as well as Mr Pead with what expedicon he can.

A year passes, and in April, 1729, Mr. Pead's effects were reported as " seized by the Mercers' Company " for ground-rent of the house which he rented from the

Corporation, and it was not till the following March that his total balance, £1,131 8s. 5¼d., was duly handed to the Treasurer.

It will have been gathered from this incident that one of the duties of the Treasurers was to pay the pensions to the widows. Sometimes this work was done through the Register or the Messenger. Tyllott, of whom more presently, was specially asked in 1693 to continue the practice by which he " had for some time at the desire of the severall Treas^{rs} for their greater ease pay'd the Widdows and Children the severall summes of money allotted to them " ; but in the following year it is still arranged that one of the Treasurers should pay the pensions of the widows of " sequestered " ministers, who at that time numbered forty. Whether responsible for the annual distribution or not, the Treasurers made a point of looking after their special *protégées*. Treasurer Brent in 1713 gets a motion passed " that Mrs Susanna Treffry have six pounds paid towards bringing her out of prison," and again " three pounds for her present Releife," till in 1717 Brent is " paid what he expended for Mrs Treffry's funeral, not exceeding 40^s." As time went on it was more and more the tendency for the Treasurers to undertake the distribution, and it is easy to realise the amount of work implied for a busy tradesman in a proposal adopted in May, 1718, " that for this year the Widows Pensions be paid by One of the Treasurers for the ease of the Register," and " Mr Treasurer Glynn was desired to take that Trouble upon him,

which he consented to, and thereupon it is ordered
that publick Notice be given in the *Gazett* of Saturday
next, and also in the *Dayly Courant* and *Evening Post*,
that the Pensions will be paid accordingly by M^r
Treasurer Glynn at his house at the Corner of Hatton
Garden on Tuesdays, Thursdays, and Saturdays between the hours of 8 and 12 in the fore Noon untill
the first Thursday in August and to begin next Tuesday, And it is further ordered that the taking of Trouble
of payment of the Pensioners off from the Register
shall not be taken to prejudice or lessen " the orders
of a recent Court as to the Register's duties.

To all this must of course be added the Treasurers'
constant attendance at Courts and committees, their
waiting on the President or Vice-President for help
or advice in emergencies, their responsibility for the
investment of money, their visits to acquired or proposed estates in various parts of the country. It was
frequently the Treasurers who went to collect the rents
of tenants at a distance. I find a bill for Jacob Brent's
expenses during 1717 and 1718 in various journeys of
this sort. " Paid Coach Hire from my Lord of St.
Davids, 2s. 6d. Coach Hire to the Countess of Suffolk,
4s. Horse hire to Maidstone, 9s. Expences 3 Days
and 2 Nights, £1 2s. 6d. Spent upon ye workmen and
Tenn^{ts}, 6s. 6d." Treasurer Nicholson and the Register
have left a tattered balance-sheet giving " an Account
of a Jorney into Cambridge Shire in order to Purchase
an Estate there and to Receive the Rents of Stow
[Northamptonshire] and Sealing the Tenants Leases

there and Expences of yᵉ Jorney." Four of them were nine days on the road, and their expenses reached the modest sum of £13 18s. 8½d. ! They went by Stratford through " the Turnpike at Eping " (4d.), dined there and " att Night att Newport " spent £1 0s. 6d. Their further stages were West Wratting (the place where they were to make a purchase), Cambridge, St. Neots, Parting Hall and Northampton, and they returned through Bedfordshire. Their disbursements include 2s. for the Barber ; 5s. for the " Ringers," who were no doubt useful in summoning the tenants at Stow to appear with their rents ; " Horse-shooing," 3s. 9d. ; " A bottle Wine before," 1s. 6d. ; Tea, 6s. ; Tobacco, 2s., whether for the tenants or themselves they do not say. The Treasurer had given nine days of his time, and there was none to grudge him his modest creature comforts.

At the beginning of the nineteenth century there arose a habit of retaining the Treasurerships in the same hands, and at the present time it is the custom to re-elect them year after year, on the natural ground that their experience is invaluable. Sir E. Graham Moon, who was present at the bicentenary celebration fifty years before, was Senior Treasurer at the 250th anniversary.[1]

[1] The present Treasurers are the Bishop of Worcester, who has served on the Court of Assistants for twenty-five years ; Sir Frederick M. Fry, who has long been strengthening our immemorial links with the Merchant Taylors' Company ; and Alderman Sir Kynaston Studd, whose Mayoralty coincides most happily with our 275th anniversary.

CHAPTER IV

THE REGISTER AND HIS STAFF

WE pass to the permanent official of the Corporation, the man in whom after all the real responsibility has been always vested, and who still represents the Charity to the pensioners by his considerateness and to the public by his pleas on its behalf. We have seen that the first meeting of the Court of Assistants in Jerusalem Chamber on July 15th, 1678, resulted in the choice of a Register and a Messenger. The former, Henry Symonds, a member of the Court as nominated in the Charter, was dead before March 26th, 1679, when " Thomas Tyllott, gen^t," was " unanimously chosen Register and Assistant in the place of Henry Symmons, gen^t, lately deceased." This time their choice was more fortunate. Tyllott was a Proctor in Doctors' Commons. People who wanted to be sure of a letter finding him addressed it thus :—" These to Mr Tho : Tyllott at his office at Drs Comons or at his house in a court near Drs Comons " ; so, at least, a vicar of Isleworth wrote to him in 1702, and thereby showed more learning than another clergyman who penned " Dr Scomons." Why the title of " Register " should have been given to the chief executive officer of the Charity is not quite obvious, but I am inclined to trace it to the early and prolonged connection between the Corporation and Doctors' Commons, where Register was the title of certain officials in the depart-

ment of wills and testaments. The Charity had many
legal friends among the Stewards who served before the
days of the Charter. Nothing is known of Humphrey
Henchman, the son of the Bishop of London, and an
original member of the Court of Assistants, but his son,
also Humphrey, was a Doctor of Laws and an advocate
at Doctors' Commons, and in his day a member of the
Court of Assistants. The first Humphrey may well
have been of the same profession, and one of the letters
found at Corporation House suggests that Sir William
Wren had chambers there. The connection was of
the greatest importance to a charity like ours, which
received and still receives so much from the " dead
hand." It also led, as we shall see, to the meetings
of the Courts being held there for many years. But
on the whole Tyllott was in his day a still greater gift
of the old legal foundation to the young and unmatured
Charity. To turn out his box of papers and see the
careful marking and sorting of his receipts and memo-
randa is to feel yourself in the presence of a man of
business, and to read the letters addressed to him by
pensioners is to recognise, what the Corporation is still
able to show, that the man of business can be also a
man of sympathy. This is not the less true, because
for some years he received no salary, but only such
legal charges as would naturally arise out of the
business transactions which he carried through in the
Corporation's behalf. He was, in fact, a subscribing
and not a stipendiary official. But in 1683, when the
Palmer or Holloway estate was taken over, things came

to a point beyond which it seemed absurd to depend
on voluntary management ; and on the Register with-
drawing from the dining-hall at Doctors' Commons,
where the business was being transacted, Treasurer
Bedford enlarged upon the situation. " Mr Tyllott,"
he said, " had very industriously undergone the Trouble
of that place for above Four years, namely from Aprill,
1679, and that he [the Treasurer] had had some discourse with Mr Tyllott (upon his offering to pay his
annuall benefaction according to his subscription) about
a gratuity for him, and had proposed the presenting
him with ffourty or Fifty guineas, but that Mr Tyllott
had very kindly expressed that hee would not expect
more than Thirty guineas." The Treasurer's suggestion proved acceptable to the members, who acknowledged that the Register " had bin very industrious and
carefull and taken extraordinary paines continually in
promoting the interest of the Corporation." They gave
him the thirty guineas and waited ten years, and then
the scene was repeated but with a different ending.
Now it is Mr. Gilbert who becomes his advocate.
Tyllott, he says, has only " been gratified " for his
work up to November, 1683, and it is now November,
1693. " Having discoursed with him about a further
gratification, he found he was willing to accept of one
hundred pounds," which was readily agreed to. But
Tyllott, it was pointed out, was doing much more work
than formerly. He was relieving the Treasurers of
the distribution of pensions, and he was willing " to
receive the Rents of the Rectory of Blewberry in the

county of Berks and of all the Lands and Tenements in that County which were holden by our great benefactor Dr Townson in his life time by lease of the Bishop of Sarum." So Tyllott was called in and thanked for "his greate trouble paines and care," and was asked "what he expected annually for the future executing and performing the Office of Register and paying the severall annuities and receiving the Blewbery rents." His figure was "Twenty pounds a year which the Court readily agreed to pay him." There is still another Tyllott incident, the beginning of the end of a long and faithful career. In 1706 he fell ill, and the Court were sorry for him. They "voted that the Court of Assistants are very well satisfyed with the fidelity of Mr Tyllotts service of this Corporation and that upon passeing his Accompts they will be kind to himselfe and his ffamily and that Mr Boheme and Mr Gilbert acquaint him with this vote." Boheme, also of Doctors' Commons, was asked to become Assistant Register till further notice, but in a few weeks (January, 1707) they could recall their request, "it appearing that the said Mr Tyllott is recovered of his aforesaid indisposition." At the same time they raised his salary to £40 a year "for all manner of business to be done by him," and demanded a bond of £500 "for his faithfull performance of all business wherein he shall be intrusted." In the latter part of 1711 he died, and William Pocklington of Doctors' Commons was elected in his stead, the "sallary" remaining at £40 as before.

The term "Registrar" did not supplant the old title

of Register till 1794.   In this and other ways a distinct
change has come by the beginning of the nineteenth
century.   In the first half-century of the Charity's
work, the Register is frequently a member of the
Court, and his attendances are recorded.   In the early
part of the nineteenth century not even a sub-committee is held without the minutes stating *ore rotundo*
that it was held " in the Registrarship of John Matthew
Grimwood Esquire," as who should say *Consule Planco*.
It is a change from the furtive activity of Thomas
Tyllott.   So for the moment we return to him and to
the type of management which he set for those that
came after.   In 1679 he starts his subscription book
and delivers the money received to the Treasurers.
He suggests " the forme of Acquittance " which is
" agreed upon to be printed."   When money is wanted
to provide the purchase price of desirable properties, it
is Tyllott who writes round to the friends to lend it.
When it is suddenly realised in 1683 that the precious
Charter is in the hands of one Michael Foster, an
Assistant, it is committed to Tyllott's care " to be putt
into the Chest among the writings of concernement."
It is his business to examine petitions from widows
and present them in due form to the Court, and the
bundles of them that have lately been found at Corporation House show how carefully this part of his
work was done.   In 1691, when they could look back
on some years of useful work, the Court bade him
make a statement of the moneys they had distributed
and print five thousand copies by way of giving an

account of their stewardship. But a large part of his time was taken up with watching for the gifts of the dead, which his close connection with Doctors' Commons enabled him to do. He was " to continue an Interest with the Registers at Doctors' Commons to have an Account of all Clauses in Wills which relate to the benefit of the Corporation," and enter such clauses in a book. It is no discredit to him that after his death other books of reference were found to be necessary. Register Pocklington's duties in the way of book-keeping comprised a book of benefactors' names " with proper alphabetts to refer to them," a book of estates " with abstracts of Title, Conveyance, etc.," a book of standing orders, which still survives, a rental-book as well as minute-books for Courts and committees, " the Senior Treasurer to have a duplicate of each." He had to keep the estate-book " in some place remote from the Deeds for greater security in case of ffire or any other accident."

But the real test of the Register then, as of the Registrar now, is his way of dealing with those whom the Corporation so often calls " proper objects of charity," the widows and the children ; and for this we must look at the letters he received. " Worthy Sir," writes one old lady, " God is pleased still to continue my life notwithstanding all the hardship undergone by Reason of my low and poore condition in the world, and as long as I doe live I must make my address to you, Sir, that you would be pleased to continue your kindness and pity to me." Then she

gives him the usual information as to how her allowance can be forwarded, and closes thus : " My most
humble services to you, Sir, with my thankfull acknow-
ledgments of your pity for me and your remembrance
of me now I am at that distance from you, Sir, I
subscribe myself your poore obliged servant, Dorothy
Kennett." He was evidently liable to be sent to for
any and every purpose. His " truly affectionate
ffriend, Will. Beveridge," writes to him in 1688 to
say that if Tyllott has any money in hand for Mrs.
Smith, and will pay it to the bearer, Anthony Smith,
Beveridge will be obliged. In the same year there is
forwarded to him from " the Rev. Doctor Beveridges
house in Corbett Court in Grace Church Streete," a
letter to one Samuel Ferrers from a " sequestered "
widow named Newstead. The writer sends her
respects to Dr. Beveridge, and begs her " Cousin
Ferrers " to go and ask Tyllott " when the money is
paid for the releife of Sequestered Ministers Widdows."
To economise postage the same letter covers a commission to " Enquire what will bee the Price of a
Silver Spectacle frame of beste Princes Metle Copper
or Steele, for I have broke the horne that you sent
me ; the glasse fitts my eyes soe well that they will
last mee a long time iff they were sett in any of those
mettalls." Tyllott receives a call in 1694 from a poor
body in trouble, and the result is a receipt in his handwriting with her signature for forty shillings " towards
ye releasing me out of prison." Another appears to
be in a like case, for she writes from " Ludgatte. Sir,

I being now a close prisoner in Ludgatt because the Judge is out of toune am faine to send my Daughter to you for the mony which you ware plesed to say I should have this day and hope you have obtayned sumwhat for hir. This is all I have to troubell you with. Your sarvant Anne ffarewell." Tyllott's chambers in Doctors' Commons were in fact a cave of Adullam, and he was a recognised welcomer of those who were in trouble, paying for the funerals of some and the lodgings of others. It is hardly to his discredit that he should have obtained a Palmer pension for his sister, whom he certified to be " an object of charity." The fact may also serve to remind us that the custom long prevailed of giving a preference to parsons' sons in appointing to this and other offices. In 1803, when Henry Stebbing was elected, the Court started its proceedings with a resolution " that, as it appears to have been the usage of this Corporation to give a Preference to the sons of Clergymen before any other Candidates for the Office of Register, the same be observed in the present Vacancy." The custom that the Register should be of the legal profession, either barrister or solicitor, is certainly more important.

THE MESSENGER

The rest of the permanent staff must not detain us long, though at least one of them served the Charity rather longer even than the faithful Tyllott. When they met in Jerusalem Chamber for their first election

the Governors chose as their Messenger one Richard
Williams, citizen and Haberdasher. His duties, judging by his stipend, were hardly more than menial. The
Court fixed his fees in 1679 as follows :—" For warn-
ing a Generall Court and his attendance thereon, Ten
Shillings," so also for a Court of Assistants five
shillings, and for a committee half a crown. But
in the following year they commuted these separate
payments for an annual stipend of £12, increased in
1684 to £14, " in consideration of all sorts of services."
He was thus about a year senior to Tyllott in the
service of the Charity and he survived him by about
the same time, dying in 1712 ; but whereas Tyllott
died in harness, his subordinate had become a pensioner
some time before. His duties were evidently such as
his simple title implies. He had to summon the
members to meetings, and we have seen that he was
particularly charged to include the President when he
did so. It was evidently his business to recover the
taxes remitted to the Corporation as a Charity ; for in
1702 " the Commiss^rs for the Land Tax sitting at the
Guildhall in London " were reported by him to have
" refused to exempt two houses scituate on Snow Hill,"
and the Register had to display the deed of purchase
before they would relent. Various surviving receipts
in his name show that moneys were delivered to him
by the Treasurers for distribution to pensioners. But
with these exceptions the Messenger is an elusive
personage in the records till the day came in 1708
when, " considering the great age of Richard Williams

and the great decay of his memory, whereby he was
rendered incapable to execute the office of Messenger
of this Corporation," the Court " did discharge him
from any further duty but ordered his salary to be
paid to Christmas next." One Edward Anderton was
chosen in his place, and told to give £5 of his £14 a
year to Williams during his life. In 1710 the Court
added one of their pensions to the old man's retiring
allowance, giving him £3 a year as a clergyman's son,
" in consideration of his good services and being very
aged and poor." But in his declining years he suddenly
becomes interesting. There are suspicions at once of
his parentage and his orthodoxy. In 1711 it was
resolved to give him notice that, " an Information
being given to this Court that he is no Clergymans
Son, that he *goes to Meetings*, has given ffortunes with
his Children, and is no proper object of Charity, that
he attends the next Court of Assistants to show cause
why his sallary should not be taken of." In fact, he
is to " bring a Certificate of his being a Clergymans
Son by Lady Day next." The report may have been
due to the decreasing protection of his old colleague,
Thomas Tyllott, or to the desire of the new Messenger
to cease the handing over of a considerable part of his
stipend. Anyhow one is glad to think that it came to
nothing. The reference was discharged before Lady
Day came, and when he died in 1712 it was mercifully
ordered that " Mrs Williams bee payd her husbands
Pention due at the Court of Distributions next after
his death towards his buryall."

One detail in regard to Anderton, the second Messenger, illustrates the sort of work that might be expected of him. With his consent, in 1713, " it is ordered that he bee disfranchised and struck out of the list of Governors, To the end he may be capable of being an Evidence for the Corporation." The Register, no doubt, would conduct the case ; the Messenger must be prepared to step into the witness-box, if necessary. It is hardly likely that his wife could have done this part of Anderton's work for him, but after his death the Court gave her £15 as " a gratuity for her Husband's services and her own during his sickness."

Anderton was succeeded by Thomas Savage, whose brother, Dr. Savage,[1] was a member of the largely attended Court at which the election took place. The Messenger had now become a more responsible person, for he and the Doctor had to provide a joint security of £200 that " all the rents and moneys " shall be properly accounted for. His salary also rose to £20. But barely two years passed before Thomas Savage was a grave defaulter. He was called upon to account for £243, and blandly " declared he had used it in paying some old Debts and furnishing his House." Naturally Mr. Treasurer Pickering proceeded to " discourse Dr. Savage in relacion to the mony which his Brother the Messenger had run out of the Corporation

---

[1] William Savage, D.D., rector of St. Andrew by the Wardrobe, 1702–36 ; chaplain to Lord Keeper Wright and to Bishop Atterbury ; Master of Emmanuel Coll., Camb., 1719–36.

Cash." The Doctor, it appeared, was willing to pay interest on the principal sum, and agreed that the Corporation should " retain his [the brother's] Sallary of £20 a year till the debt is paid," but he put in a plea " that the interest might be some way moderated in regard he was at a constant charge in promoting the Subscriptions in the University of Cambridge." I have found his 1725 list of subscriptions, amounting in all to £30 ; but quite apart from this the Court would naturally sympathise with their colleague. He had been Festival preacher in 1715, he was chaplain to Francis Atterbury, and was Master of Emmanuel College at the time when his brother involved him in this trouble. Happily by 1729 the sum " run out " by Thomas Savage was all refunded, but not before the defaulter had been dead for some years. For in 1724 he was evidently known to be *in articulo mortis*. The Court met on April 24th, and fixed April 25th for the election of a Messenger, " in case Mr Savage is now dead." Apparently he was, for on the day appointed, Archbishop Wake being in the chair, they chose a certain Babington Sybbald as Messenger " during the pleasure of the Court of Assistants." They evidently meant this time to have their man under better control and in a few months they laid down his duties in greater detail. " He shall be subservient," they said, " to the orders of the Treārer for the time being, and attend the Senr Treārer every Monday and Thursday morning for the Treārers orders in any business relating to the Corporation and also call upon the Register

to know if he has any business to acquaint the
Treãrer with."

THE " SOLLICITOR "

Another official, of greater importance to the public
welfare of the Charity, was one who went by the name
of the " Sollicitor." It is obvious that he did not fulfil
the functions which are now associated with the word,
for these were clearly the business of the Register.
The need of such a functionary was felt first about
1684, when one of the Treasurers mentioned that they
were looking out for " a fitt person to be a Sollicitor
for this Corporation," and that he had himself " discoursed with one Mr Stubbs a Clergymans Sonne who
was willing to accept of that office," and who was there
and then appointed under the seal. Poor Stubbs was
dismissed in a few months without any cause being
assigned, and then came a more efficient appointment
in the person of Mr. William Middleton, whose selection
was probably due to Sir Christopher Wren. He was
a member of the Court of Assistants, and had been
Steward of the Festival in 1677. Now he " offered
himselfe ready to serve the Corporation in the quality
of a Sollicitor and brought with him a forme of deputation to be by this Court granted to him and read the
same. Whereupon the Court being very well satisfyed
of the great ability honesty and industry of the said
Mr William Middleton in the procuring and getting
in subscriptions towards the repairing of St. Paul's

Church," accepted him as "Sollicitor" of the Corporation. This entry makes it obvious that he was to be what the societies of to-day would call a collector or an organising secretary. But his work was varied. In 1687 he was the recipient of a proposal from Herbert Croft, Bishop of Hereford, with regard to a diocesan effort, of which more elsewhere,[1] and in which it appeared to the Court that Middleton had "exceeded his Commission." But they recognised that it was only a case of *trop de zèle*. A year later they were taking his "great services" into consideration. As "there was as yet noe Sallary settled upon him," they "did order seaven pounds to be given to his Mother Mrs Elizabeth Middleton besides the three pounds now given to her as a Sequestered Ministers Widdow." At the same time it was arranged that this £10 should be a first charge on "the subscriptions by him procured for this Corporation in the Counties of Kent and Sussex." This throws an obvious light on the development of his functions. He was no longer a mere London collector, but an Association Secretary for the Provinces. He had received a letter—so he reported —"from some Clergy-Men in Suffolke desiring him to come downe into the County at the Archdeacons Visitation at Easter" and was ready to go if the Court would allow him "his necessary travelling charges," —an offer which they at once accepted. There is one more reference of a humble nature to Mr. Middleton before he disappears from the scene without even a

[1] pp. 88–93.

successor being appointed. It was reported to a Court
of 1703 that he had "voluntarily sollicited the affair
of Mrs Coborns Charity" and "was now attending
without." He was called in and told that the matter
was now in the hands of a Committee and was "desired
to desist any further acting therein." But this was
not said in anger. "They would the next Court day
consider of gratifying him for what he had done."
And "thirty shillings and the thanks of the Court"
were the last of Mr. Middleton.

THE ACCOUNTANT

A society whose financial interests were of a very
varied nature was not long in feeling the need for
financial method. In 1687 it was "moved in Court
that a good Accomptant might be procured to methodize the Bookes of the Corporation and to state their
Accompts," and that "one Mr Samuel South" should
be "prevailed with" to undertake the work at a suitable honorarium. South had been a Steward in 1685,
and was then a member of the Court of Assistants,
but he leaves no further trace of himself, and the task
appears to have been left to the "Comittee to Methodize
the Bookes," which was nominated at each November
anniversary. So the office was apparently in abeyance
till 1726, when once more the Court

> took into their Consideration the nature of the
> business of the Accomptant, and are of opinion
> that he keeps a Journall and Leidger of all the

Revenues and also a Journall and Leidger of all
the Benefactions in possession or Revertion, and
that the same officer do address and make Application to all subscribers to the Corporation, and
that the same person collect such Rents as the
Treārer for the time being shall direct, and that
the Accomptant attend such Comittees as the Court
and Comittee of Accounts shall direct, and that
his Sallary be £40 a year payable Quarterly. And
that a Convenient office together with a Lodging
be appointed for the Accomptant in the Corporation house by a Comittee to be appointed for that
purpose.

Elections always brought a large attendance, and
on this occasion the Assistants included Richard
Reynolds, Bishop of Lincoln, nobly unmindful of the
fact that it would be the duty of the Accountant to
call attention to his lordship being himself in debt to
the Corporation, for he was " in arrear for his ffee farm
rents for 3 years." In any case the Court " proceeded
to recommend an Accountant and considered it should
be done by Ballotting." Mr. Valens Comyn, who was
in nomination along with two others, " upon the Ballot
had 20 votes " and was elected. And they soon showed
their satisfaction with him. In the following May they
" entered into consideration " of what he had done to
justify his election, and were " of opinion that he very
well deserves a gratuity of One Hundred Pounds for
the very extraordinary Services and Business which
he has done for the Corporation."

For the amount of work and of financial responsibility involved, it cannot be said that the Charity was lavish of salaries, even when the Register, the Sollicitor, the Accomptant, and the Messenger are taken into consideration. Notwithstanding the increase of work which the years have brought, its staff remains at the same number, though the duties may not be distributed exactly as of old.

CHAPTER V

NAME AND ADDRESS

A STRANGER coming fresh to the consideration of our ancient Charity naturally asks the meaning of its name. He finds in the present day a number of benevolent persons of all classes and certainly of more than one creed banded together as the " Sons of the Clergy." He learns that a prominent Wesleyan layman, the son of a Wesleyan, is every year a Steward of its Festival, and, if he went into its records, he would discover that at the close of the eighteenth century the Secretary of the Stewards expressed particular delight at the generosity of a gentleman called Goldsmid, whose name implies that he was one of those Jews whom commercial success had not deprived of their native large-heartedness. The fact is that from early times the name " Sons of the Clergy," however appropriate to the Wrens and the Henchmans and the Dolbens, who were mentioned in the Charter, was not interpreted to the rigid exclusion of anyone who in a practical way was prepared to wish the clergy and their families good luck in the name of the Lord. It will be seen that their officials were chosen as a rule from clerical families, but it was not long before the very Court of Assistants did not clearly know its duty in the matter. In 1719, when the second generation was being represented by men like Humphrey Henchman, Doctor of Laws and Chancellor of the

London diocese, the General Court referred it to Sir Gilbert Dolben, their Vice-President, and " such other members of the Court who are of the Profession of the Law to Inspect the Charter and consider whether any persons who are not Sons of Clergymen are capable of being Governors or Members of this Corporation." The answer is not on record, but it can easily be guessed at. The official title is " the Charity for Releife of the poore Widdowes and Children of Clergymen," and the Charter is addressed to persons " who are the children of Clergymen, *and others*." Even as late as 1789 the question was still in debate. A number of gentlemen were coming forward as Stewards who were not sons of clergy. They were all elected Governors, but could they be placed on the Court of Assistants ? So Chief Baron Skynner,[1] the Vice-President, was asked to look at the Charter once more, and a day was appointed for the special consideration of the question. In the end it was resolved unanimously " That it is both legal and expedient and will be for the Advantage of this Corporation, to elect Persons who have served the office of Steward of the Feast of the Sons of the Clergy, though not Clergymen's Sons, upon the Court of Assistants."

Thus, whether accurate or not, the name " Sons of the Clergy " came early and came to stay. It is at least one object of this story of the Charity to suggest

---

[1] Sir John Skynner, K.S. at Westminster, 1738 ; M.P. for Woodstock, 1771–7 ; Recorder of Oxford, 1776 ; Chief Baron of the Exchequer, 1777–86. Died 1805.

that in the present day, more than ever before, the title
should be an inspiration to those to whom it actually
belongs.　It is recognised to-day, and recognised sadly,
that the sons of the clergy are not pressing into the
ranks of the clergy as they once did.　They pass into
other professions, and, when their zeal in their calling
is equal to that of their father in his, they make their
way prosperous and have good success.　But they are
still parsons' sons, and our Corporation has a claim on
them in their time of wealth.　If one in ten of the
successful sons of the clergy in our midst would recognise their obligations, the Corporation would not be
left complaining that its possibilities are less than its
opportunities.

Next to a name came the need of a Seal, which, as
elsewhere stated, was produced by Sir Christopher
Wren, and the coat-of-arms was not long in following.
In 1684 " Sr Henry St. George, King at Armes had,"
it was announced, " designed to give a Coat of Armes
to this Corporation."　Sir Henry, who succeeded his
father as Garter in 1703, was naturally thanked for his
offer, and a deputation was nominated to " consider
with him of a proper Coate."　In a short time (1685)
the Court received information that " Sr H. St. George,
Clarencieux," had designed " the C^t of Armes " and
it had been sealed by him and " Sr Wm Dugdale "
without any charge to the Charity as far as they were
concerned.　All that must be paid would be " the ffees
due to the Secretary of the Lord Marshall and the under
officers," which came to £6.　It is interesting to think

THE GRANT OF ARMS.

64]

of the great compiler of the *Monasticon Anglicanum*, then eighty years of age, earning the thanks of a Charity whose very existence implied that for Anglicans monasticism was indeed a thing of the past. The Corporation, needless to say, has not changed its " coat," which is heraldically as follows :—

> Lozengy argent and sable on a chief purpure a cross patée or, between two books opened, argent, the leaves, cover and clasps gold. Crest :—The effigies of Charity standing on a wreath of the colours habited in a loose garment sable, her face, breast, hands and feet proper, her hair dishevelled or, accompanied with three naked boys, viz : one on her dexter side, and the other two in her arms all proper and crined or.

However, nothing simple would suit the first years of the nineteenth century, and we find the Stewards of 1807 improving the arms with additions. " A design for an official seal was submitted to the Archbishop and to his Grace the Duke of Norfolk adding a crest and supporters to the present Arms ; viz. for the supporters ' Faith and Hope ' from the painted Window at New College, Oxford, and for the Crest ' Charity.' For a motto the following words were proposed *Quod eorum minimis Mihi*." The supporters were indeed a poor performance, though the motto is an inspiration, and it was a wise regulation which was passed at the same time, that the improved seal should " be used by the

officers of the Charity at their Discretion on occasions
of particular solemnity, continuing the use of the
ordinary seal in the common business of the Institution." I am indebted to the Somerset Herald for the
information that these supposed improvements do not
appear to have been authorised at the College of Arms.
The Stewards, in fact, had no separate coat. Their
" Charity " crest was merely a copy of the Corporation's, and did no excessive justice to its original.
Sir Joshua Reynolds, had he lived to see them,
might have felt that much the same remark would
apply to the supporters as copied from the New
College window.

But the Corporation had to find a local habitation
as well as a name, and this came to it more slowly and
with a prudent absence of hasty expenditure on bricks
and mortar. All it required to start with was a room
where its members could deliberate ; the addresses of
the Treasurers were sufficient to secure the reception
of pensions by those to whom they were granted.
True, the Charter allowed them to have " their Hall,"
but if they could do without one for a time, there was
the more to pay out in pensions. So, as we have seen,
they accepted from John Dolben the hospitality of
Jerusalem Chamber during 1678-80, but in June, 1679,
a meeting of the Court of Assistants in Doctors' Commons inaugurated their long connection with a block
of buildings, the place whereof knows them no more
The choice of Doctors' Commons as their business
centre was no doubt due to Thomas Tyllott, their

second Register, and was acquiesced in because of
their dependence on the gifts of the " dead hand."
Another building, which they were able to use for
their assemblies in 1679–89, was " the Great Dyning-
roome at Ely House Holborne, the Mansion House of
the Right Reverend ffather in God Peter Lord Bishopp
of Ely," and, as may be imagined, Turner continued
what Gunning began. So during these ten years they
hovered between Ely House and Doctors' Commons,
which the Register is sometimes careful to describe as
" within the parish of St. Bennett Pauls Wharfe."
After Turner's ejection as a Nonjuror, their larger
meetings also were transferred to the dining-room of
Doctors' Commons, and the careful Register has left
among his papers statements of " Money Disburst on
Accompt of Holding Courts and Committees ": *e.g.*,
" 11th of January. Rec[d] then of M[r] Thomas Tylott
for three Courts of Assistants for fire Candles pens and
paper, 00[£] 12[s] 0[d]   Jos. Lampson, Comons Porter ";
" Women to cleere y[e] Roome, 1[s] 0[d]."; " Candles
1[s] 0[d] pipes 0[s] 1[d]." Probably no locality could have
better answered their purpose, for anyhow the Register's
work involved not a little moving about. He charges
for " Coach hire to Grays Inn and a Porter 0[£] 2[s] 6[d] ";
" Coach hire to Bromley when M[r] Bowerman and
myself waited upon the President [Dolben, Bishop of
Rochester] and other charges, 0[£] 15[s] 0[d] "; " Coach hire
to and from Westminster with y[e] Book [no doubt, his
minute-book for a meeting in Jerusalem Chamber]
0[£] 2[s] 0[d]." Once or twice Courts were held " in M[r]

Thos Tyllott the Registers house within the parish of St. Gregoryes, London."

In 1712, for a reason which through lack of intimation may be put down to greater convenience, they changed their meeting-place a few yards and settled for a time at St. Paul's Cathedral. On January 24th of that year they held their first Court of Assistants in the Cathedral, and thanks were ordered to "bee returned to his Grace the Arch Bishop of Canterbury [Tenison] and the Bishop of Norwich [Trimnell] for procuring the use of the Lord Mayors Vestry Roome in St Pauls Church for the meeting of the Corporation and for the more safe Keeping of the Deeds Writings Bookes and Papers and to the Deane [Godolphin] and Residentiarys of St Pauls for granting it." The matter had been already in the hands of the Committee of Ways and Means at a meeting held in Anderton's Coffee-house ; their report states that the Corporation was "to have a Key to the doore and liberty to fitt up one of the Presses there for the laying up the Bookes and Papers . . . and also liberty to sett the Chest with the Deeds relating to the Corporation estate in the same." In view of the general publicity attaching to the nave of the Cathedral, the same committee ordered that "the Messenger should for the future attend without doores for the better preventing the discovery of what is done in Court." A few weeks later they requested "the Ma^r of the Temple [T. Sherlock] to settle the Allowance to the Vergers for the Corporacon Meetings in

the Vestry and finding fire Candles and other
Necessarys."

It can easily be imagined that this was not an
altogether satisfactory arrangement, though it interests
the Committee of the Festival to-day, when they
assemble in the Lord Mayor's Vestry, to think that
they are using a room occupied for business by their
predecessors of two centuries ago and for a lunch by
those of a generation ago. Anyhow in 1714 they
moved yet a few yards further to the Chapter House,
where their first business transacted was the drawing
up of an address to George I., referred to elsewhere.[1]
The Chapter House had the advantage of providing
more than one room, and in 1721 the Stewards were
assembled in one part of the house while a General
Court was meeting in the Chapter Room. Still they
did not use the Chapter House for all their purposes,
preferring the less formal venues of the coffee-houses.
"Anderton's" in Fleet Street has been already
mentioned, and among others that enjoyed their
custom were "the Queen's Head Tavern in Pater
Noster Row," "the Greyhound in Fleet Street,"
"the Legg Tavern in Fleet Street," "the Sun
in Holborn," "the Chapter House Coffee House,"
at which long afterwards Charlotte Brontë and
her sister put up, because the very name suggested
respectability, "Nando's," and "the black Swan
in Capell Court." "A Committee at the Coffee
house" figures in the Register's petty cash at

[1] p. 266 f.

" oo$^{£}$ oi^{s} 4^{d}," so that the arrangement was hardly extravagant.

But the Corporation, having by Dr. Turner's great bequest [1] become a large landed proprietor, and having for nearly half a century saved itself the expense of a centre of its own, now had the right to secure a Corporation House. It is evident that the Treasurers had been commissioned to keep on the look-out for suitable premises ; for in May, 1725, Mr. Treasurer Rogers informed the Court that he " had agreed for a house which he thinks may be proper for the Corporation, being the late Dr Wagstaffe's house in Salisbury Court for £200 fine and £44 p. ann. for 6 yeares and 5 yeares afterwards at £50." It was a house which they must have known well already as the residence of a late colleague. Dr. William Wagstaffe, who had just died at an early age, was a celebrated physician to St. Bartholomew's Hospital. He had been a member of the Court of Assistants since 1717, and had a mortgage on their Adstone estate. Historically, it was appropriate that a society which had been wont to use Ely House, an episcopal residence in one part of the City, should find itself in Salisbury Court, once the residence of another bishop, with whose diocese the Corporation had continuous relations. But the Assistants meant business and not sentiment. They closed with the offer, and ordered " that the Register be the House-Keeper and remove into it as soon as he can." They expressed once more

[1] pp. 79-81.

their gratitude to the Dean and Chapter " for the use of the Roomes belonging to the Chapter House for the time past," and asked to be allowed still " to hold th^r Generall Court in it as they shall have occasions." Nothing remained but to request a few members to inspect the house the next day, and the following was their report :—

> The Committee having viewed the House are of Opinion that the two Roomes up one pair of Staires be reserved for the use of the Corporation, the Roome in the fore ffront for the Court and Comittee Roome and the back Room for the Compting Room, and that proper Desks and Presses be set up there both for the use of the Register and such other Clerk as the Court shall hereafter think fit to choose for the service of the Corporation and proper Cases for the Books &c., and that the Register may have the use of the fore Roome for his ffamily at such times as it is not used for the Courts and Committees, and that it be left to the Treārers to fitt up the Roomes accordingly and to provide Chaires Tables and other Conveniencys necessary for the two Roomes and what else they think proper to be done about the house.

The lease was assigned to the Register in trust, he being " indempnified by the Corporation against the Rent and Covenants." In 1726 the Register was given a companion in the person of Valens Comyn, the newly appointed accountant, it being ordered

" that the back room up one pair of Stairs in the
Corporation House together with the Closett be for
the Accomptant's office and the Room up 3 pair of
Stairs backwards be for the Accomptant's Lodging
when there is occasion." It is of course not possible
to trace the actual house, but the bills for fitting it up
have lain in a box ever since. It had " Gates and
Rails," which needed mending and cleaning, and five
guineas were paid " for making 2 Coats of Arms with
a Crest for an Iron Gate in Salsbury Court." The
" plaisterers work " involved " 1234 yards of washing,
stoping, and whiting at $1\frac{1}{2}^d$ p. yard," and was done
in time for the Assistants to meet there in September,
1725. Their faded bills enable us to see them preparing for the winter. They laid out £5 2s. " for a
19 inch fine Skelgrate tongs shovell poker and fendor,"
and November was given up to cosy upholstering ;
" 68 yards of fine Yallow Duble Camblett," " 13
Dozen of Yallow and White Silk Lace," " ticking
under ye Camblett " and " 28 Pounds of Feathers "
(at eightpence a pound) were fashioned into curtains
and window seats and " Vallances " for the four
windows of their board-room. Their table-cover may
be represented by " 9 yards Sup^r fine purple Cloath
Dyed in graine 2 y^{ds} w^d," which cost them £9, and the
attendance which they expected at the meetings held
in their new home may be estimated from their buying
" 18 Beach Chairs India Backs Coverd with Black
Leather " and " 1 Arme Chair Ditto."

They appear to have remained in Salisbury Court,

(where from 1744 onwards the Stewards also were allowed to assemble for business,) until 1756.

In 1755 Stephen Comyn, the Register, " acquainted the Court that the Dean and Chapter of St. Paul had been pleased to agree to appoint him their Receiver, and offered to let the Corporation have the Great Room at the Chapter House . . . for their Meetings and another Room to keep their Title Deeds, Books, and Writings, upon paying the Yearly sum of £30 towards the Taxes of the Chapter House, a Charge lately fallen upon the Dean and Chapter, and to be subject to no Taxes whatsoever." The Court reminded itself that the Salisbury Court house, which had been for years in bad repair, cost them £80 a year, and at once resolved to give their landlord notice and to accept the chance given them by the Dean and Chapter of saving £50 annually for the Charity. But the arrangement was not long lived, and possibly it was Stephen Comyn's resignation in 1759 which caused them again " to look out for a proper Place for the Corporation to meet at." In February, 1760, they were in treaty for a house in Warwick Court in Christ Church parish, but the necessary repairs were large and they were expected to take a seven years' lease at £80 a year. So, on a much less ambitious scale, they settled at the Temple in Mr. Chester's Chambers, which became " The Corporation Office. No. 13 in the Paper Buildings Inner Temple London," being rented at £40 a year. It is hard to resist the conclusion that from the point of view of publicity this was a bad move. General Courts, instead of numbering twenty or thirty, fell to an attendance of five or six, including the Treasurers. The fact is that the Stewards of the Festival, who at this time were occupying every year a larger place in public interest, answered to some extent the purpose of the fuller General Courts of former days ; so that the Charity could leave its affairs to the few experts and still have nothing to fear. The office in Paper Buildings was certainly inexpensive, and the sole reference to any subsequent outlay upon it is in 1776, when it was ordered that it should be " Repaired Whitewashed and Painted where wanting and that new Windows be put in the Court Room and . . . that the Pictures be cleaned and put into a neat plain genteel Frame." These would doubtless include the picture of Charles I.'s children, a copy by Walker of Vandyke's famous canvas, which hangs to-day, apparently in the same " genteel " frame, in the Court Room at Bloomsbury Place, as a perpetual reminder to the Assistants that their work sprang from a desire to relieve those who had suffered for their faithfulness to the Royal Martyr of " Blessed Memory."

But the Corporation, having committed itself to maintaining a Corporation " Office " rather than a " House," began to find that its address could easily be changed. In Thomas Wall's old age, the Court nominated a Joint Register to do the work and to succeed in due course to the sole charge of it. So the headquarters must follow him, and in 1788 they moved " to a sett of Chambers at No. 5. Coney Court Grays

Inn provided by Mr Topham the Joint Register for
that purpose," and transported thither their " Books,
Muniments, Papers, Pictures, Furniture, and other
matters," paying Topham £50 a year rent.   In 1790
" 5 Coney Court " had become " 5 Grays Inn Square,"
where they continued till 1795.   In that year Register
Topham informed the Court that " he had engaged
a House in Bedford Row (No. 10) which would be
more convenient for transacting the business of this
Corporation than the present Chambers are," and the
Treasurers, having inspected it, agreed with Topham
for £100 a year.   In 1804, having chosen Henry Stebbing as their Registrar, they again moved their office
to his house, No. 64, Chancery Lane.   It was he who
in 1805 rented from the Duke of Bedford for his own
purposes No. 2, Bloomsbury Place, the lease of which
the Court acquired at a valuation on Stebbing's death
in 1808, and thus the wanderings of one hundred and
thirty years came to an end one hundred and twenty
years ago.   But before the next Festival our present
lease will have expired, and the future is again
obscure.

CHAPTER VI

BENEFACTIONS

WE have now seen the right by which the Sons of the Clergy set about their work, the method by which they organised their deliberations, and the officials whom they chose to do that routine work for which, as busy men, they themselves could hardly be expected to find time. But it would all have been visionary or impossible without the necessary funds, and in a general way, then as now, funds are not secured by the mere willingness to receive them, and the task, as modern "collectors" discover, is not easier as time passes and other causes spring up with similar desires. What the friends of the Charity had done in this way before the Charter was granted it is impossible to say, and I incline to think that there were no funds except those gathered by the Stewards of the annual Festivals. But the very first Court held under the Charter of 1678 settled among other things the "preamble to the Subscriptions." Money must be raised, and the first requisite is a good statement of your case to the benevolent public. The next is to spread your net as widely as possible. So they soon secured helpers in the provinces, and May, 1679, found them sending "Copyes of the Letters" of appeal to "the Deputy Receivers in the Country." Soon afterwards they had agreed on a form of deputation, a word which we apply to the person representing the society in the country, but which they used of the formal written authority by which he did those things. Along with the written deputation they composed a letter of appeal, printing a thousand copies of each, and these were sent to " severall persons in divers counties for to promote this charity." Also they printed two thousand receipt forms " for annuall subscriptions " and one thousand " for an intire sum," evidently in the pious hope, which the Corporation still fondly entertains, that it may be given more of the former than of the latter. The deputation, being a legal document, was to be signed and sealed by the Treasurer (until the Corporation could get its own seal), and the " charges of carriage " for all these papers were " to bee paid here and allowed of the Stocke."

Attention was next turned to various classes who might be expected to be specially sympathetic. In January, 1680, there is a resolution that " such of the Lords the Bps. as are members of this Corporation be humbly desired to promote the Charity . . . amongst the rest of the Lds the Bps." At the same time several clergy were selected " to move the rest of the Clergy in and about London to contribute." When they were about to make their first purchase of landed property, within the provisions of the Charter, it was thought well, instead of borrowing, to " write to the severall Deputyes in the Country " to tell them what was proposed, and to bid them send in " An Accompt of what Subscriptions or ready money they have by

7

them." In 1684 they bethought them that there might
be some comfortably circumstanced pluralists on the
provincial chapters, and resolved that " a forme of a
Letter bee drawne to be sent to the severall Deanes
and Chapters in England, and Dr Dove is desired to
peruse it." Possibly these provincial efforts languished
for a while after their first energy was somewhat spent,
for the Assistants of 1695 were again desired " to
inquire after such persons in every county as were
able and willing to promote the Charity by getting
subscriptions." This time they decided to promote
continuity by instituting a Committee " to consider of
Wayes and Meanes for promoting of the interest and
benefitt of this Corporation by subscriptions or otherwise." It was " to sit every Wednesday att three of
the Clock in the afternoone att Jonathans Coffee house
in Exchange Alley neere the Royall Exchange " and
to report from time to time " what they shall doe
herein." One-and-twenty clergy and laymen, or half
the Court of Assistants, were asked to serve on this
committee, but I have not been able to find their
minute-book. The point is that they began the collecting work all over again. They drew up and presented an " instrument or Deputation " as if none had
ever been drawn before. They had it " fair wrote,"
and submitted it to Tenison before they affixed the
seal to it. There was a reason for this revived
effort, for in 1699 " considering the State of the
Corporation it is agreed that noe new petitions
bee taken in."

And again the work languished, and again they tried
to galvanise their Ways and Means Committee into
something like activity, calling upon it in 1707 to
' meet Thu rsday next at three of the Clock in the
Afternoon at Anderton's Coffeehouse in Fleet Street
and on every Thursday till further order." This time
the result was more permanent, and the committee
showed some enterprise. In 1713 it suggested to the
Court " that the sending Subscripcon Rolles to the 2
Universities in order to procure Subscripcons from the
Heads and Fellows of Colleges may be a great Advancement of the Charitie." The Court was delighted.
Sherlock, then Master of the Temple, had already
" waited upon the Bp. of Norwich [C. Trimnell] to
desire him to waite upon the Ld. Arch Bp to begg his
Graces assistance " in the matter, and could report
that " his Grace was pleased to approve of the design."
The project was hardly on foot before the Corporation
was enriched by a residuary legacy of over £18,000
from Dr. Thomas Turner,[1] President of Corpus Christi
College, Oxford. It fell to Sherlock to announce this
splendid gift to his colleagues on May 19th, 1714, but
they were cautious men, and not unduly elated. There
was a whisper about a " pretended codicill." In the
meantime they contented themselves with suggesting

---

[1] A son of Dr. Thomas Turner, Dean of Canterbury. He held
a prebend and the precentorship of St. Paul's from 1682 till
his death in 1714 ; he was also Archdeacon of Essex and rector
of Fulham. In 1688, the year of his appointment to Fulham, he
was made President of his college, Corpus Christi, Oxford, and
retained both offices till his death. See further, p. 283.

an advertisement " in the publick Prints " of a reward
of twenty guineas " for the discovery of the Contriver
of the pretended Codicill," and with asking Mr. Boheme,
one of their Proctorial colleagues, " to take care to
search the Prerogative Office and to give notice to M^r
Treasurer Lewis from time to time of any Caveat."
But it was a false alarm, and the great gift came safely
to hand. John Rogers,[1] the preacher of 1718, who
was a former Fellow of Dr. Turner's college, might
well apostrophise his memory in the Cathedral pulpit.
" Let us magnify the Name of our GOD, Who has
raised up among us a glorious Example . . . who has
shewn us how the Bounty of a Prince may be imitated
in a private fortune." Rogers goes on to say " with
what care and wise Frugality " Turner " manag'd the
sacred Treasure, long set apart and devoted to God."
In a footnote he adds that " this excellent person
(whom I am obliged to mention with particular Honour)
made this Disposition of his Estate several Years before
his Death ; all which time the whole Improvement of
his Fortunes was in effect annually applied to this
Charity, by which Method he had the Satisfaction of
doing Good every Day of his Life, together with the
Concealment his Modesty desired in doing it." It is
noteworthy in connection with this legacy, first, that
on being asked by Turner's executor to place him in
communication with one of their number to represent

---

[1] John Rogers, son of John Rogers, vicar of Eynsham, was Fellow
of Corpus Christi Coll., Oxford, 1706–16 ; canon of Wells, 1719 ;
vicar of St. Giles, Cripplegate, 1728. Died 1729.

them in negotiations the Court should have nominated not a layman or a lawyer, but " the Ma^r of the Temple " (Sherlock) ; and, secondly, that it was the great size of this bequest which made it necessary to apply to the Crown in 1714 " for granting a Charter to enable the Corporation to purchase £3000 p. ann. more " ; thirdly, that the Corporation kept the memory of their great benefactor before the eyes of the public by pictures of his tomb first engraved and printed in 1716. In 1725 they were still spending £9 10s. 8d. for six hundred " Prints of Dr. Turner's Monument " upon " large strong Paper."

But in smaller ways the Dons had not been unmindful of the Charity. Among the Governors elected in 1702 was " Charles Roderick, D.D. Provost of King's Colledge in Cambridge," who, as its historian reminded us,[1]

> " . . . labour'd more his worth to hide
> Than others to have their's descri'd,"

and who was, no doubt, brother to the Rev. Richard Roderick, D.D.,[2] of St. Michael Bassishaw, elected the

---

[1] A. Austen Leigh, *History of King's College*, p. 160.

[2] " He was brother (I think) to Dr. Rodderick, Schoolmaster of Eton " ; Hearne, *Collectanea*, ii. 71. Charles was Provost of Eton, 1689–1712 and Dean of Ely, 1701–12. Richard, a K.S. at Westminster, was rector of St. Michael, Bassishaw, 1701–30 ; on his institution he became a tenant of chambers in Sion College at £9 a year, and resided in the college, of which he was President in 1722, for the rest of his life (cf. E. H. Pearce, *Sion College and Library*, pp. 101, 347). The two were sons of the Rev. Richard Roderick, of Wem, Salop.

same day, and for very many years an active collector
of funds for the Charity. In 1703 came "Arthur
Charlett.[1] D.D. Rector of University Colledge in
Oxford," and in 1710 "Robert Shippen.[2] D.D. Principal
of Brazen Nose Colledge in Oxford," who lived to be
a Steward of the Festival a quarter of a century later.
The immediate result of this latest raid on the Univer-
sities was seen at the General Court of 1716, when
"Bardley Fisher,[3] D.D. Master of Sidney Sussex
Colledge" and "Daniel Waterland. B.D. Master of
Magdalen Colledge," Cambridge, were made Governors.
Waterland proved a very close friend to the Charity.
He preached the Festival sermon at St. Paul's in
December, 1721, and, being rector of "St. Austin and
St. Faith," he was not obliged to leave his parish in
order to do so. "The Rev. M[r] Archdeacon Water-
land" headed the Stewards of 1732, and he was by
no means infrequent in his attendance at the Courts.

But a stray subscription list among the papers at
Corporation House gives us Dr. William Savage's
Cambridge subscribers of 1725. It is headed "The
Names of those Persons in or near Cambridge who
have subscrib'd to the Clergy Sons Corporation in
order to the advancing the poor widows' Pentions."
There are twenty-seven names on the list, one sub-

---

[1] Son of the minister of Collingbourne Ducis, Wilts.

[2] Principal of Brasenose, 1710–45 ; rector of Whitechapel, 1716–
45 ; Gresham Professor of Music, 1705–10.

[3] "The portraits of this comfortable-looking divine and his
handsome wife . . . still adorn the Master's Lodge." G. M.
Edwards, *Sidney Sussex College*, p. 159.

scriber belonging to " Lestershire," and another to
" Huntingtonshire." The amounts are variously two
guineas and one guinea. The list is headed by Snape,
the Tory Provost of King's, and it says much for the
comprehensiveness of the Corporation that he should
be a supporter of a Society which counted Benjamin
Hoadly and his son, the doctor of medicine, among its
zealous helpers ; for Snape fell into disgrace at Court
through his attacks on Hoadly—attacks in which the
Provost had the support of Thomas Sherlock, Master
of St. Catherine's College, whose services to the Corporation meant the devotion of a lifetime to its interests.
Other heads of houses on Savage's subscription list
were Robert Jenkin, Master of St. John's College, who
refused to take the oath under William and Mary but
submitted on the accession of Anne, and William
Towers, Master of Christ's College, a Whig henchman
of Bentley, and therefore an opponent of Sherlock and
Snape. " Mr. Washington " [1] (£2) was Fellow of
Peterhouse and incumbent of Little St. Mary's, and
his gift connects the Corporation with the hero of the
American Republic. But the interesting point in the
list is that there is a guinea from each of the Esquire
Bedells. For William Savage was Vice-Chancellor in
1725, and one can think of him pressing the claims
of the Corporation on the gentlemen with the silver
wands in the course of a stately procession to the
Senate House or the University Church.

---

[1] Godfrey Washington. For the circumstances of his election
as Fellow, see T. A. Walker, *Admissions to Peterhouse*, p. 192.

But the Court flew at still higher game. Tenison
had approved of their design of appealing to the Universities, but soon after it was decided that a deputation
should " wait upon his Grace the President and give
him a Copy of the new Charter and endeavour to
obtain another Benefaction from his Grace." Of their
actual success on that occasion I have found no record.
But Tenison's name appears on a list compiled in 1733
of " the severall Bishops and clergymen " who " gave
each of them One Thousand Pounds or upwards."
Another of these large donors was Godolphin, Dean of
St. Paul's and Provost of Eton, who, as we shall see,
played a not inconsiderable part in the history of the
Festival. I find it entered on the minutes of September 4th, 1724, that he " hath given £500 to the
Corporation," and that Roderick of St. Michael Bassishaw and Joseph Trapp of Christ Church, Newgate
Street, who were nominated to " wait on the D^r "
with the thanks of the Court, were " kindly received."
The gift is worth mentioning as having been made
during the giver's life ; in that sense it is comparable
to the earlier donation of Lewis Burnet,[1] " rector of
ffaringdon in the County of Devon," one of the
" deputyes " in the country, who not only collected
money with great success, but took, as various stray
papers show, a personal interest in the pensioners.
Here, for instance, is a scrap of paper bearing a widow's

[1] Prebendary of Exeter and Sub-Dean. He incorporated from
Aberdeen (Foster, *Al. Oxon*), St. Andrews (Venn, *Al. Cantab.*) at
Oxford and Cambridge, but there appears to be nothing else to
connect him with Gilbert Burnet.

ARCHBISHOP TENISON.
Reproduced by permission of the Vicar and Churchwardens of St. Martin's-in-the-Fields from
the picture in their possession.

receipt for money which the good man had paid her
in Devonshire, no doubt without waiting to receive it
from Mr. Tyllott :—" July 3rd. 1694. ffrom Bishops
Nimton. Then Recd from Lewes Barnett the summe
of forty shillings By order of the Governrs of the
Charity for Relife of poore Widows and Children of
Clergy Men and ye appointment of Mr Thomas Tyllott,
Regr to that Corporation, I say Recd by me Mary
Potter." And it may be guessed that he had himself
nominated her to receive the pension without telling
her that his own gift was the origin of it. For in 1693
he had given £300 and promised £200 more, but
suggested that special consideration should be given
to Devonshire widows. The Court, fully alive to his
generosity and zeal, sent him a joint letter, undertaking to allocate the proceeds to the local applicants,
"and especially all as shall be recommended by your selfe
without any other certificate. Yor affectionate ffriends."

But as the Corporation became by degrees a considerable landed proprietor, it was natural to regard
it as capable of receiving money at interest. In plain
words it became a bank, though with this difference,
that at the lender's death the principal was turned to
charitable uses. The earliest case of this sort occurred
in 1682. " A certain person," so Mr. Treasurer Bedford reported, " (whose name he did not now at
present knowe) had proposed to give Fifty Pounds to
this Corporation Provided that this Board would allow
to two poore Ministers Widdowes by him to be named
twenty shillings a peice during their lives." This offer,

which was at once accepted, complied, at the then
rate of interest, with a resolution passed in 1679.
" Whereas," it ran, " the President and Court of
Assistants are informed that divers persons who give
charitable Annuityes and Pensions to the Widdowes
and Orphans of Clergymen would be ready to pay the
same into the hands of the Treasurers of this Corporation to be by them issued forth . . . and *would also
give some overplus* yearly to the Treasurers to bee by
them disposed of to the use of the Corporation," the
Court was ready to accept such gifts if they complied
with the above condition. So in 1685 " Dʳ Townes-
end "—no doubt an error of the minute-writer for
" Dʳ Townson," a munificent benefactor,—gave £2,000
" with this Condition that one Moiety of the profitts
thereof or of the Lands purchased therewith should be
at his disposal." More elaborate conditions were
attached to the gift in 1691 of Mr.—after Sir—John
Johnson, " a Goldsmith in Cheape Side," who " would
give ffifty pounds to the Corporation under these
conditions, Viz That yᵉ Intereste thereof after the
rate of 5 p. centum p. annum should be paid yearely
to the Widdow of any Rector of the parish of St ffosters[1]
London whereof he is a parishioner that should be in
want, and till there should be such an object of Charity
there should be paid every fourth yeare towards the
binding out the Son of a Deceased Clergyman that
should be an object of charity Ten Pounds." This,
too, they accepted with only the delay necessary to find

---

[1] *i.e.* St. Vedast, Foster Lane.

out what security the good goldsmith wanted, and in the
following year he doubled the principal sum.   To-day
one hardly thinks of the widows of City clergy as proper
objects of charity, but it is a fact that in 1709 a certain
Mrs. Hopkins received a pension under this bequest.

Sometimes the conditions attached to gifts were
only remotely connected with the proper work of
the Charity.   Mr. Edmundson, for instance, gave the
Corporation " a Classe Lottery Tickett of £125, they
giving their Bond for payment of £2. 10s. to the vicar
and churchwardens of Sparsholt," a Berkshire parish,
which still receives an annual cheque from Bloomsbury Place, while the " Classe Lottery Tickett " is
represented by an equivalent in the general funds of
the Corporation.   Sometimes there was a tendency
to regard the Charity not merely as a bank but as an
insurance society, this being of little consequence as
long as either business resulted in ultimate profit to
the cause.   The following instance—with due allowance for the fall in the rate of interest—is no bad
example for modern benefactors.   In 1719 " a friend
of Dʳ Roderick," who proved to be " Mʳˢ Mary Fel-
stead, of St. Brides in the West, widow," proposed to
give the Corporation £1,000 on condition of receiving
at the rate of 7½ per cent. annually during her life,
and owned to being fifty-two years of age.   The Court
replied that the interest asked for "was too much,"
but " agreed to accept and to pay 7£ p. ann. for it
during her life Quarterly."   Roderick consented to
this on her behalf, and Westley, one of the Assistants,

"was so kind" as to borrow the money at 5 per cent.
Still it was perhaps as well that the demands of others
were more modest, such as "a proposall on the behalf
of a Gentlewoman for paying in to the Corporation
the sume of £500," the Corporation to give "Interest
for the same at the rate of 4 and ½ p. cent during her
life and the principal to sink to the Corporation after
her death"; or the still more extensive gift of the
same year, 1725, of the Rev. Thomas Dunbar, who
proposed to sell his brother William's "Stock in the
Severall Companys and to take the Corporation
Security for payment of the Common Interest for his
life for what it produces."

But conditional benefactions of another sort were
compassed with greater difficulty. What, for instance,
was to be the attitude of the Corporation to diocesan
efforts on similar lines, or to benefactions for the sole
advantage of a particular diocese? The latter came
into acute discussion in 1687 through a proposal made
by Herbert Croft, Bishop of Hereford. Croft is
another instance of men whose zeal on behalf of the
distressed goes far to modify opinions formed as to
their want of zeal in other directions. The modern
historian [1] is apt to sneer at him as a Restoration
bishop who thought it not "wise to be zealous for the
surplice," but at least he had interests at heart which
are not to his discredit. He made his suggestion to
Middleton the "Sollicitor" in a letter which has not
survived, but its purport can be gathered from the

[1] H. O. Wakeman, *Hist. of the Church of England*, p. 409.

answer which the Court ordered " to be wrot thereto,"
and which was as follows :—

My Lord,

The contents of your Lordships Letter was this
day communicated to us by Mr Midleton and Wee
are extreamely well satisfyed with your Lords^{ps}
pious and good intentions and to the intent the
same may be effected in your Lords^{ps} Life time and
to your Lords^{ps} full satisfaction Wee thought convenient to send the Bearer on purpose that yor
Lords^p may be the better informed of our proceedings, and how impartially the moneys from time
to time have been distributed, and the difficulties
some have mett with have not proceeded from
any remissnesse or Neglect of the Governors but
for want of Benefactors suitable for ye number of
the poor distressed Widows and Orphans. Your
Lords^p therefore may rest assured if the £500 be
pay'd into our Treasury the utmost that it will
purchase shall be yearely distributed to poore
Widows in y^r Lords^{ps} diœcesse, and that others
may be encouraged to follow y^r Lordsh^{ps} great and
good example £10 p. Annum shall be added
more to the same for the terme of five yeares.

And Wee are of Opinion Severall of the
Reverend Clergy of ability in yor Lords^{ps} Diœcesse
will contribute, and if they shall not thinke fitt to
give a sume of money yet may subscribe for a
terme of yeares (as Severall have in other Diœcesses)
and tho many Subscriptions are but small yet
being in proportion to the abilitys of the Donors,
they will be kindly accepted, for a considerable

number of small sumes will make one great sume,
and that will help towards the support of many
poor Widows and Orphans.

Wee Conclude with our Prayers for yo[r] Lords[ps]
good health and happinesse and y[t] yo[r] Lords[ps]
eyes may see this good worke finished and that
GOD will be pleased to add some longer time to
the number of yo[r] dayes to see the good effects of
your Lords[ps] piety and charity and in the meane-
while remaine

> My Lord
> Your Ldships humble Servants
>
> > > Fra : Ely
> > > W[m] Wren.

There are one-and-twenty other signatures to this
letter in order to mark the Court's sense of the importance of the matter, which was not destined to run
smoothly. Three weeks passed, and on March 30th,
1687, Middleton brought a form of agreement with
the Bishop, which the Court did not like on constitu-
tional grounds.   By June 30th they had not established
a *modus*, and were informed that his lordship was
" very urgent to have his Charity of £500 to be settled
to the uses by him designed," for the capital sum had
been in Middleton's hands since April. So they appointed a sub-committee " to meete at Lyons Coffee
House," and the result was the following letter, dated
July 13th, 1687 :—

May it please your Lordship.

Wee have considered of the Draught your Ld-
ship caused to be sent to us, and Wee have returned

to yo[r] Lordship another draught somewhat differ-
ing from it, that being contrary to our Constitution,
for wee cannott binde our selves to pay the money
to any but poore Widdowes and Children of
Clergymen, but yet wee can confine our selves and
successors to distribute your Lordships Charity to
such Widows and Children as your Lordship and
after you the Deane and Chapter shall nominate,
Which wee conceive to be the maine thing your
Lordship aimes at, And this wee have effectually
provided for in our draught and that your Lordships Charity may be for ever preserved and
distinguished Wee intend to lay out this mony
in a seperate purchase which occasions the other
alteration. Hoping your Lordship will accept
hereof and will be pleased to favour us with an
answer because M[r] Middleton does not thinke fitt
to pay the £500 to us till your Lordship hath
executed this intended Deed or agreed to it.

Wee remaine
Your Lordships most humble Servants
William Wren Vicepres[t]
[and eleven others.]

My Lord
'Tis the humble request
of the
Court of Assistants
that your
Lordship would be
pleased to
returne an Answer to me
at my Chamber at Doctors
Commons.

The footnote is perhaps Tyllott's, but it failed of its effect, for the matter lapsed till the following February, when the Court were informed that " the said Bishop had altered his mind herein and ordered the said money to be returned back to him." His reasons were, first, " that it will at best prove a trouble-som buisiness unto poore Widdowes in his Diocess to send to London for that small Charity which they may with more ease receive from the Deane and Chapter of Hereford," and, secondly, " that he designed to add £20 per Ann to two poore Cures in his Dioces and that it would not be fitt to divide that matter." So Middleton returned the money, and we are left to decide why so desirable a scheme could not become part of the Corporation's work. The two reasons given by the Bishop seem to be the real explanation. He wanted to carry out two necessary objects, the sustentation of the poor clergy and the pensioning of poor widows in the same scheme and with the same capital, but clergy sustentation was then no part of the Corporation's work. Before this matter came up in the negotiations, the Court had hesitated whether they would accept a capital sum on condition that the interest should go wholly to a particular territory. They were willing to promise preferential treatment to Herefordshire widows, but may have questioned the wisdom of confining a portion of their income to them on the ground that a given supply of pensions might very well tend to create an unreal demand. By the kindness of the late Bishop of Hereford [1] I learned that, in making his will in the year following, 1688, Bishop Croft left a sum of £1,200, now invested in a rent charge of about £45 a year, to pay £4 yearly " to six poor Widows of Ministers, who have been beneficed, or served Cures, within the County of Hereford," such pension to cease if they should have " any further maintenance, rent, or estate of £10 per annum at the least " ; also to pay £14 a year to the incumbent of Yarpole, which was no doubt the part of the trust which our Corporation could not undertake ; and, thirdly, to devote the balance to paying apprenticeship fees for the sons of clergy. In the present lapse of the apprenticeship system there is a balance of over £200 to the credit of this part of the fund, and the trustees, who are and must be members of the Hereford Chapter, have accordingly increased the six widows' pensions from £4 to £8.

Another scheme was more fortunate. It dates from 1700, when Mr. Entwistle,[2] Archdeacon of Chester, and Mr. Taylor made a proposal " setting forth that they desired a Deputation under the Seale of this Corporation for them to receive *and dispose* of such money as they should collect for the releife of poor widdows and children of Clergymen of that Archdeaconry and that they would annually give an account of their receipts and disbursements to this Corporation, or to that effect." But the Court were not satisfied that this idea came within the terms of the Charter, and took counsel,

---

[1] Dr. John Percival, who died in 1918.
[2] Edmund Entwisle, Archdeacon of Chester, 1695–1707.

8

as we have seen, with their colleagues " of the Long Robe," and especially with Lord Keeper Wright. Their verdict was favourable to the project, which would, in their view, not involve any breach of trust. So the deputation was issued and the county of Chester proceeded to look after itself. In the preliminary instructions to the Court of Distributions of 1719, which can hardly be the first actual instance, it is laid down that " no Petitions be received from the Diocess of Chester in regard they have collections among the Clergy of that Diocess for the widows of their own Clergy." Nor is it easy to establish a consistent course of action in the matter ; for a minute of 1722 implies that both parties had wavered from their purpose. The Register, it says, is to " apply to the Arch Deaconry of Chester to render and transmitt an Account of what they have collected and distributed in Charity " pursuant to the deputation, which is natural enough ; but it is added that no Chester petitions were to be received in London till the account came, whereas no such petitions should have been received in any case.

It is idle to speculate whether the support extended to the Charity in the shape of annual subscriptions would have been more extensive if the organisation had been more diocesan. The signs of such efforts in the records are few and fitful ; such, for instance, as the suggestion in 1722 of Sherlock, then Dean of Chichester, to send a deputation to the " Clergy and Gentry of the Diocess of York." At that time the Court had so far forgotten their own history that the

Register was ordered to " search the Books to see if any Deputation has been formerly granted to any particular Body or persons to receive Contributions towards this Charity in the Country."

But before a charge of slackness of organisation is brought against the Court it has to be remembered that the " dead hand " had treated them with a generosity which, if not wholly independent of organisation, at least tended to make them leave a man alone during his life, in the hope that there would prove to be something for them out of his will after his death. In the revival of Church life after the Restoration the Corporation seemed to make a natural appeal to those who had any goods laid up and were conscious that they could carry none away with them when they died. This, indeed, was the only prominent Church Society that was of anything more than local significance, till the efforts of Dr. Bray and others produced the S.P.C.K. and the S.P.G. These soon asserted their place in testators' interests. Among the papers at Corporation House is a sheet of discoloured foolscap, forerunner of those testamentary intimations on blue paper which gladden the heart of the modern Registrar, and the first instance I could find of another society being thus associated with ours. It is dated 1721, and is headed " E Regro Curiae Praerogativae Cantuar extract," and deals with the will of Mary Hales of Teddington. The operative clause is, " And I further Will that Two hundred pounds be paid to the Society for propagating the Gospel in fforeign parts and fifty pounds to the Governours of the Charity for the Relief of the poor Widows and Children of Clergymen." In the same way there is a note in the records of 1724 that under the will of Samuel Saywell, by which the Corporation benefited considerably, the Christian Knowledge Society and the Society for the Propagation of the Gospel could each put in a claim to a fourth part of the Willingham rents.[1]

It might have been expected that such *post-mortem* benefactions would not come into the account for some years after the incorporation ; but the royal patent gave an immediate opportunity to trustees of private charities to amalgamate with the Sons of the Clergy, and this could be done at once. In November, 1679, Mr. John Bucanon announced to the Court that " he had discovered a considerable charity long time given to the Widdowes and Children of Clergymen." The trustees were dead, and " Sr Thomas ffanshaw . . . is consenting to a Decree in Chancery for the settling the said Charity to the use of this Corporation " ; so the Treasurer was authorised to advance money for the necessary legal costs. The result was at least the nucleus of an income. Presently, in 1681, there is another little cost of the same sort by reason of a resolution to " give Three Guineys to Mr Sheppard, the Scrivener, who wrott Mr Bowles his will, for his good Services done this Corporation in this affaire,"

---

[1] Queenholme farm, Willingham, Cambs., was sold in 1918. Under an order of the Charity Commissioners, Nov. 1, 1918, the S.P.C.K. and the S.P.G. received their proportionate shares of the proceeds.

which resulted in a legacy of £300. Next year came
the quaint bequest of " Mr Ralph Davenant,[1] late
Rector of the Parish Church of St Mary Matfellon al^s
Whitechappell," who bequeathed to the Corporation
the £100 owed to him by Mr. Henry Loads, one of
the original Treasurers. He let his friend off the
interest due, and bade him pay the money to the
Treasurers, who promptly distributed it to others.

But the first bequest of any size was that of one
Mr. Palmer.[2] It was not a direct gift to the Sons of
the Clergy, for " he hath by his will given £100 p.
annum for ever to twenty poore Ministers Widdows,"
and, as " some of the Trustees appointed for the
Management of the said Charity are willing to trans-
ferre that Trust to this Corporation," the Court were
naturally willing to negotiate. This was in 1683, and
twelve years passed before they could have on the table
before them " the writings relating to the assignment
of Mr Palmer's Charity," together with the names of
Dr. Dove and the other trustees. The estate connected

[1] Son of Rev. Edward Davenant, vicar of Gillingham, Dorset,
who was nephew of John Davenant, Bishop of Salisbury. The
Bishop made the nephew prebendary of Torleton, 1623, Ilfra-
combe, 1624, and Chute, 1632, Archdeacon of Berks, 1631, and
Treasurer of Salisbury, 1634. (W. H. Jones, *Fasti Eccles. Saris-
beriensis*, pp. 153, 348, 375, 397, 426.) See also Walker, *Sufferings
of the Clergy*, pt. ii. 63. Ralph Davenant was made Fellow of
Trinity Hall, Camb. (by royal recommendation), 1664–5, and a
Canon of Exeter. He was rector of St. Mary Matfellon, Whitechapel, from 1668 till his death in 1681.

[2] James Palmer, of Magdalene Coll., Camb. (B.A. 1601–2 ; B.D.
1613), was vicar of St. Bride, Fleet Street, from 1616, till he surrendered in 1645 (D.N.B.), or died in 1660 (Hennessey, *Novum Repertorium*, p. 113, where his Christian name is wrongly given as Thomas).

with it will come before us in another chapter. But
in 1692 they had the delight of fighting a will case.
Dame Mary Huddleston had named as her executor
one " Richard Cock als Cokke," who, " being a recusant
convict," could not get probate from " the Right
Worshipful Sr Richard Raines, Knt., D^r of Lawes
and Judge of the Prerogative Court of Canterbury."
The niece of the charitable dame was given letters of
administration and the " recusant convict " appealed,
which appeal was reported at the November meeting
to be " now depending in their Majesties Court of
Delegates." Being liable to " reap the benefitt of the
charity disposed of by the said will," the Corporation
agreed that it was worth while to spend money " towards bringing the said Cause to a sentence." In the
result the " convict " was defeated, and the Sons of
the Clergy secured their £500 less costs. The fact that
£25 was given to the " discoverer of Lady Huddleston's
charity " recalls another case of the same sort which
occurred in 1696. " The Rev. Mr Richard Hill,[1]
deceased, late one of the Cannons of the Cathedral
Church of Sarum had by will given fforty pounds of
lawfull money of England to this Corporation," which
his executor " refused or at least delayed to pay."
Naturally he must be prosecuted. But it appeared
that " one William Wallington a very poore man who

---

[1] He held the Sarum prebend of Alton Borealis, and died Mar. 20,
1695. He was buried near the door of the Consistory-court in Salisbury
Cathedral, to which church, as to us, he was " larga manu bene-
ficus." (*Fasti Eccl. Sarisb.*, p. 354.)

is a Clergymans Son and sexton of the Church of
St Nicholas Coleaby London first gave the Information
of the said Legacy, which had beene for neere two years
concealed." So they promised him £5 when the legacy
was received " for his and others encouragement in
the like cases."

Another bequest, which caused some difficulty and
occupied the attention of a special committee sitting
for the nonce at " Garraways Coffee house," came in
1697 from Mr. Edmund Burroughs, citizen and Vintner.
His will contained a definite bequest of £300 for building almshouses, but the matter which caused trouble
was that he also bequeathed £1,000 to the Corporation,
being money due to him from " Erasmus Smith Esq
and Richard Loder, Scrivenor." It was reported that
" the Master of the Rolls who sat for my Lord Chancellor had decreed three hundred pounds only with
interest and without charges should be paied, for that
it did not appear to him that M[r] Smith had received
more." The incident is of interest on account of one
person involved, for Erasmus Smith was one of the
great and wise benefactors of his generation both to
London and to Dublin. In the latter his name remains
attached to the school he founded, while his unique
services to Christ's Hospital after the Great Fire show
that he was not one to grudge a few hundred pounds
to a Charity like ours, if it were his legal duty to pay
them.[1] Among conditional benefactions mention ought

---

[1] Cf. *Annals of Christ's Hospital*, pp. 50–54. His portrait hangs
in the Hospital's court-room.

to be made of that of " John Millington,[1] Doctor in Divinitie," who in 1726 gave the Corporation £200, and at the same time bequeathed £100 " toward erecting a new Steeple to Kensington Church, Provided the old Steeple bee taken downe and a new ffoundation laid within 12 Months after his death, and if not done gives the 100^s to the Corporation."

It would be of interest, if it were possible, to trace some of these gifts of the dead to the encouraging influence of a book which the Court thought it useful to circulate. For many years the Assistants had as their colleague a divine called William Assheton,[2] Fellow of Brasenose, whose biographer and neighbour, Thomas Watts, of Orpington, thought sufficiently well of him to introduce his memoir as " The Christian Indeed and Faithful Pastor impartially represented in a Practical Way and Historical Account of the Exemplary Life and Works of the late Eminent," etc., etc. Assheton, who was rector of St. Antholin's, London, and of Beckenham, and whose negotiations with the Mercers' Company about pensions for the widows of clergy showed his real interest in our cause, published in 1696 a book " Intituled a Theologicall Discourse of last Wills and Testaments," and it was

---

[1] Fellow of Magdalene Coll., Camb., 1673. Senior Proctor, 1700–1. For many years he was concurrently vicar of Kensington, rector of Stoke Newington and prebendary of St. Paul's.

[2] Son of William Assheton, rector of Middleton, Lancs., Fellow of Brasenose, 1663. D.D., 1673. Chaplain to James, Duke of Ormond. Rector of St. Anthony with St. John, Walbrook, 1674–7; rector of Beckenham, 1677–1711. Prebendary of Knaresborough in York Minster, 1673. Died September 1711.

resolved by the Court to circulate one hundred copies " as shall be most for the benefitt of this Corporation." The unpretentious little volume contains a deal of sage advice, and at its close, after suggesting as suitable and safe recipients of legacies the colleges of Oxford and Cambridge and the Royal Hospitals of the City of London, the Doctor proceeds to commend " another late Foundation," " as yet not so generally known," and the rest of the " Theological Discourse " is made up of the Corporation's usual abstract of its Charter and its gentle suggestions of the way in which the benevolent should phrase their wills.

It is an easier task to say a word in praise of benefactors " which have no memorial," and whose gifts could not be directly acknowledged. All that the Court could do in their case was to order " that an Advertizement be inserted in one of the Publick Prints that the severall Gifts to the Corporation from unknown hands have been brought to the Account of the Corporation by the Treasurers."   Such secret givers would have been more than satisfied if they could have read the following minute of a Committee of Ways and Means held in 1729 : " The benefactions from unknown hands within the last year is the Chief Reason for the Admission of more Widows this year." Their secret joy at the result would certainly pardon the committee's grammar.

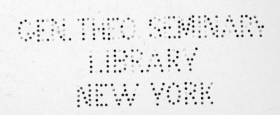

CHAPTER VII

LANDS AND INVESTMENTS

A CHARITABLE society of to-day would hardly expect to find its investment of the funds committed to it affording any particular interest to the historian. It may, and probably will, have its romantic reminiscences of the wonderful ways by which funds come into its hand, of the reasons which prompt the rich to make bequests or inspire the poor to give out of their penury. But it hardly hopes to find any lively interest excited by the funding of the gifts in some safe and not very productive stock. However, the early years of our Corporation were remote from the humdrum security of Consols and Local Loans. The first Assistants based their hopes of financial stability on the permission which the Charter gave them to purchase land to yield them not more than £2,000 a year. Their investments in any other form of security were of the nature of temporary expedients, and can be dismissed in a few words. They began with one of their own number. In 1680 " Mʳ Nicholas Carey, a member of this Court," announced himself to be " willing (if it might be of any service to this Corporation) to allow after the rate of Fiue pound per cent. per annum " for any sums of money that might be " left with him." But more public concerns were soon under consideration. In 1681 there was a suggestion of " a purchase of some shares in the New River Water,"

and this was followed by another of greater moment
to the Corporation, and no doubt due to the presence
of the Sedgwick brothers among the Assistants, " ab^t
buying some Actions in the East India Company with
considerable advantage to the Corporation " and
sending " the present cash " to the same concern " till
a purchase can be made." But there was at once
some hesitation about it. Was it " practicable " ?
Might it " legally be accepted " ? The only way was
" to advise with Councells," and Sedgwick, as the
maker of the proposal, took the decision of " M^r
Moses," [1] who was " of opinion that this Board cannot
legally accept of " any such stock. It was characteristic of Mr. Moses to earn the thanks of the Charity
" for his advice given in this particular gratis," and
given with the more grace because he was the official
counsel of the East India Company. He did them
the further service of causing them to get a " By-
Lawe " passed by which they could place their money
upon good security, pending a purchase of land or
houses. Money being once entrusted to " John
Company," equivalent sums could be raised on the
strength of it. " Whereas "—they record in 1683—
" there is due to this Corporation from the East India
Company One Thousand Pounds upon one Bill and
this Court haveing present Occasion for Money, It is
ordered that Any sume not exceeding three pounds p.

---

[1] No doubt Mr. Serjeant Moses, a munificent benefactor to
Christ's Hospital and Pembroke College, Cambridge. Cf. *Annals
of Christ's Hospital*, p. 270.

centum be allowed to any person that will pay in One
Thousand Pounds to this Corporation and take the
said Companyes Bill for the same." Indeed, William
Sedgwick combined business with generosity in this
matter. For in 1686, having already been " a considerable Benefactor," he gave the Sons of the Clergy
£50 stock in the East India Company, and certain
Assistants were asked to take the Corporation seal to
the East India House in order " to be present at his
transferring the same." The Corporation, it may be
added, remained faithful to " John Company " as
reconstructed, resolving in 1700 " that what money
can bee got in bee lent to the new East India Company
upon their Bond." For the rest, the Court put their
funds into such Government securities as would commend themselves to faithful and wise stewards, such
as " Specie Exchequer Bills " (1698), " Tallyes and
Orders on the Land Tax " (1707), and " Classis Lottery
Ticketts " (1712, etc.). Sometimes, of course, even
" Government securities " proved a misnomer. It
was announced, for instance, to a Court in 1701 " that
this Corporation has Tallyes for 500ᵉ upon the Duty
for Marriages Births and Burialls and that the same
are worse now than Par by 2ᵉ 10ˢ per Cent," and the
Treasurers wanted to know if they should sell out.
The Court decided to hold them for the moment, but
for the moment only. For general confidence was
falling and William III. was dying, and there arose
almost immediately a determination " that the money
lent upon publique funds bee disposed of with all

convenient speed." In the Public Lotteries [1] the Corporation, like other institutions, invested to a considerable extent. Two "Lottery orders" were sold in 1721 for £3,019 12s. 6d. These lottery tickets became a favourite form of gift. In 1719 Mr. Treasurer Westley gave three tickets "in the present Lottery now drawing for the benefitt of the Corporation and offered to give them others instead of either of them which shall appear to be already drawn Blank." They were deposited in the chest, and in due course were "delivered him to examine if any Prize hapned upon the same." To modern ears it sounds strange that the same benevolent Treasurer should at the same time inform the Court "that Bank Stock was sinking" and should propose "to Transfer 2,000$^£$ Capitall Stock into the South Sea Company in lieu of Bank Stock." This happened just a year before the famous bubble burst, but South Sea Bonds were still being put into the chest along with East India Bonds in 1727.

However, all such investments were a mere *parergon.* The necessary task was to accumulate real property. Within eighteen months of the signing of the Charter the Sons of the Clergy were preparing in a tentative way to make their first purchase. At a meeting in Jerusalem Chamber in December, 1679, it was resolved "that a purchase in land or Houses not exceeding the value of Two Thousand Pounds and not less than ffifteene Hundred pounds be with all convenient speed

[1] Cf. Ashton's *Lotteries* (1893) and *Annals of Christ's Hospital,* pp. 240–2.

made." They have neither the money in pocket nor the property in view, but they must make a beginning. Subscriptions are invited, and, if they fall short, security can be given under the seal to those who lend money for the purpose. "All the Members of this Court are desired to enquire after such a Purchase and report to this Court." So within three months they have resolved to buy " Justinian Pagitt Esq his estate in Kent," if it is ascertained that " the title be good." The Treasurers do their part by procuring " a surveior to goe downe and view the lands belonging to the said Purchase and the condition of the Houses," and the Register does his by writing to those who had promised donations " to pay in theire money," and before writing he is to " showe the draught of the said Letter to some one of the Court of Assistants and take his Appro-bācon therein." Exactly a year later, March 4th, 1681, this property at Newington in Kent was being held by Mr. Treasurer Jackson for the Corporation. He had paid £770 for it, and " the value of halfe a yeares rent " was £23. He was thereupon freed from his trust, and the Sons of the Clergy had thus become landed proprietors. But their possibilities were not exhausted, and other proposals were soon before them. Sir William Russell's estate at Takeley, Essex, was considered. It had a rental of £123, but inquiry must be made " whether that Estate be Abbey Lands." It proved so to be, and in consequence the Court did " not think fitt to Meddle with it." They went further in their negotiations for the " Mannour of Queenborough,

Essex," which they had agreed to take on a lease for three lives, but they changed their mind ; " an Estate in fee," they thought, " is more proper for this Corporation than any other Estate " ; so instructions were given to " wave the bargaine," if possible.

Next they turned their attention to City property. In November, 1681, Sir Christopher Wren and others purchased a house in " Pancrasse Lane, London, of the yearely value of 70£ p. Annum " for £1,050. Within five days other Assistants were named to " treate about yᵉ Ground Rent in the Strand near Temple Barr," but the project came to nothing. In 1682 they were still more enterprising. " A Ground Rent in Water Lane London of fifty pounds p. annum . . . the improved rent being One hundred and twenty pounds p. annum " was going at " two and twenty yeares purchause with twelve pounds for a gratuity." They secured this, and it is represented by a large rental[1] to-day. More important still was the acquisition in the same year of some ground rents in Bartholomew Lane (margin, " Capel Court "), for which they paid £2,832 5s. This property was a constant subject of pleasant anxiety to the Corporation, and of course proved a splendid investment. It has been gradually disposed of to great advantage ; the last portion of it remaining in the hands of the Corporation was sold to the Alliance

---

[1] The Water Lane ground-rents are still retained by the Corporation, with the exception of part of a warehouse in Oram's Yard, which was sold in 1920. The gross rents amount to £4,260, but from this there are considerable deductions for rates, taxes, etc.

Assurance Company (1 and 2, Bartholomew Lane) in 1892 for £35,000. In 1684 one of the Capel Court leases fell in, and it was decided to let the house to "M^r le Count," a watchmaker, for fifteen years at £30 a year, allowing him " 3^£ 10^s. towards repaires," which " they were the more willing to doe for that he is accompted a substantiall man and like to make a good Tenant and was laying out a considerable sume of money upon the said House." Another house in the same property, tenanted by Mr. Maurice Moseley in 1690, at £9 a year, he receiving £26 per annum from his sub-tenant, was relet to him for twenty-one years for an additional pound a year in rent and a fine of £100. Some years later there was battle-royal in Capel Court about " ancient lights." Mrs. Levett, " tenant of the house called the Swan . . . complained that there were lights struck out of some houses adjoyning to the yard of the aforesaid house," and wanted " leave to proceed to the stopping them up or to lett leases of them as shee shall think fitt according to a coven^t in the lease granted to her of the said house by Sr Robert Clayton and Mr Morris." Apparently these two gentlemen held the house from the Corporation, and sub-let to her. If so, the Court were to be congratulated on their tenants. Sir Robert Clayton [1] was Lord Mayor in 1679–80, and provided, along with Daniel Morris, his partner, large sums for the rebuilding of Christ's Hospital after the Great Fire, Sir Christopher Wren supplying the plans for a block, of which in 1904 only

[1] Cf. *Annals of Christ's Hospital*, p. 55.

a few bricks were left.[1] There was some reason for Mrs. Levett's complaint, as the Assistants ascertained. For they took with them " an able workman " and found ' eleaven lights or Windows made out into the said Yard " without consent. Of course even in early days the possession of house property was attended with risk about rent. In 1683 a tenant appeared before the Court, " desiring some abatement of Rent, alleadging that his House was too deare." As might be supposed, he was in arrear. If he paid " the halfe yeares rent due at Michaelmasse last," the Court told him, they might consider what he asked. But " if hee did not pay the said Rent within ten Dayes (it being first demanded three times at his House, which the Court ordered Richard Williams their Messenger to doe) Hee shall be proceeded against." They soon got rid of him, but there must have been others of the same sort to justify the contemporary complaint that it was " very prejudiciall to the Corporation to lett tenants run in arreare, especially att this time when the Corp^n is soe much indebted." One other City purchase should be mentioned. In 1687 they acquired " two houses scituate on Snow Hill of the cleere yearely value of 50£ holding rents, for which neare 900£ was demanded." Mr. Trewlocke, the owner, asked £870 for them, but " being a Clergyman's sonne did give to the Corporation 20£ of the said money." He also served as a Steward of the Festival in 1688 and became a Governor. Nor was he the only generous person

---

[1] The whole site is now covered by the General Post Office.

9

in this transaction. Mr. Serjeant Leake for perusing the title and drawing the deed would take no fee, except a consideration to his clerk.

By the gift of Dr. Townson, " our great benefactor," as they affectionately called him, the Sons of the Clergy became possessed of an estate called Saltagh Grange, which they held till 1919, and of rents at Blewberry in Berkshire, which brought them into contact with the Bishops of Salisbury. This " great benefactor " was John Townson, or Tounson, the eldest son of Robert Townson, Bishop of Salisbury (1620–1), nephew of Davenant, Bishop of Salisbury, who left him £10, and brother-in-law of Humphrey Henchman, Bishop of Salisbury. The last is a name which occurs not infrequently in our story, and shows how John Townson's interest in the Corporation may have arisen. I am indebted to the Rev. E. P. Eddrup, vicar of Bremhill, near Calne, for the information that Townson was incumbent there from 1639 to 1687, having been collated to the benefice by his uncle Davenant, and that he was buried there in the chancel. He was ejected under the Commonwealth, returning at the Restoration. During the stay of Charles I. at Oxford he remained with the King till the city surrendered to Fairfax, and he paid for his loyalty to the Crown with a fine of £320.[1] He was therefore entirely of the spirit that characterised the early Sons of the Clergy, and, if John Davenant took care, on King James's

---

[1] For his difficulties in raising this sum, cf. *Wilts Archæol. and Nat. Hist. Magazine* for December, 1889.

advice, to put his fatherless nephews into comfortable benefices, it cannot be questioned that in this case the Church received her own again with usury. His gifts to the Corporation are stated by his will to have been already made " by Indenture Tripartite."

The Saltagh Grange property is described as " in the parishes of Kenningham and Ottringham in the County of Yorke," and its nature may be imagined from the conditions under which young Townson, the doctor's son, was appointed " Agent for the Corporation " for five years. He was to pay them £100 a year " cleere of Taxes (saving that if in any yeare of the said Terme the King-Tax for the Landlord shall exceede ffive pounds, in that case the Corporation is to pay the Surplusage)." He also undertook to " build up a Barne upon the premeises large enough to containe twenty-five loads of Hay " and to " Keepe and maintaine the Bancks of the Homber in goode repaire." The barn suggests tithes, even if it was not actually concerned with them, and in the course of a few months the Assistants were in argument with Henry Guy, who " hath as hee pretends a right to the Tythes of Saltagh Grange." So they put the question into the hands of a *rota*, who " are to desire the right Reverend ffather in GOD Thomas [Sprat] Lord Bishop of Rochester to assist them." But the question remained unsolved. In 1702 it recurred on a further demand for payment, and a request was made to one of the numerous lawyers on the Court to give his

opinion " whether the said Estate which did once belong
to the Monks of yᵉ Cistertian Order were freed from
paying of Tythes. To which he redily consented, and
the said writings were ordered to bee sent to his house."
His opinion was unfavourable to the Corporation. So
Sir Thomas Meres and Mr. Mallory were asked to
intercede with Mr. Guy " to show some favour to the
Corporation." They saw him, they report, but " they
could not prevaile with him therein." So the tithe
question settled itself adversely, but the river was more
capricious. There are occasional references to " damage done to the Clough of Saltagh by the Spring
Tydes " and to the immediate necessity for repairs.
Directions are given for laying in " such Timber as
shall be necessary for a fresh supply upon any such
like occasion." Something induced the Committee of
Lawsuits and Purchases in 1729 to express the opinion
that " it will be highly conducive to the advantage of
the Corporation to sell the Saltagh Grange Estate and
vest the purchase money in another Estate," yet this
former appanage of the celibate Cistercians long remained to us [1] as a means of assisting the widows and
children of the English clergy to the extent of some
£900 a year.

The Blewberry property is chiefly of interest by
reason of its having brought the Court into frequent
communication with the Bishops of Salisbury. Apparently Dr. Townson had held the manor on a copyhold
lease from the see, and the first mention of it in the

---

[1] The Corporation sold the estate in 1919.

minutes is in the shape of a complaint from the Bishop
that " Witherby the Tenant of the Rectory of Blewberry in Barkshire . . . had suffered the Parsonage
house thereto belonging to run to ruine and that it
was ready to fall and that he had likewise cut down
timber off the gleab and sold the same." It was
considered of sufficient seriousness for "the Lord
Bishop of Lincoln [Tenison] and Sir Thomas Meeres
to attend the Bp. of Sarum about it." So the Bishop
of Lincoln and the Member for Lincoln went off to see
Gilbert Burnet, Bishop of Salisbury, about a rectory
in Berkshire. In 1694 we come to the first of various
periodical negotiations for renewal. William Lloyd,
Bishop of Coventry and Lichfield, then President of
the Corporation, " had spoken with the Bp. of Sarum
about renewing the Lease of Blewberry . . . and he
demanded two hundred and fifty pounds as a fine . . .
and would not abate anything of it but out thereof
he would give this Corporation thirty pounds." Burnet,
in fact, was a Scotsman in matters of business, and
was generous withal ; and Lloyd was the natural
person to negotiate with him, for the two had almost
collaborated in the famous " History of the Reforma-
tion." Burnet disapproved of these constant renewals,
and in 1695 " came into Court and proposed to change
the Lease of Blewberry holden from the Bishopps of
that See from lives into yeares, and the Court considering of this proposall unanimously resolved that
it would not be for the benefitt of the Corporation to
accept of the same." They agreed to pay the £250,

and they put in the lease the life of a boy of fifteen,
the son of Captain Theophilact Blechynden's " carpenter and servant," of " Barton Stacy in the County
of Southampton." Among the papers I came upon
one of Burnet's receipts, dated December 13th, 1704.
It is signed with a bold " Gi Sarum," and witnessed
by " John Macknay," whose name suggests that Burnet
may have brought an Aberdonian factor with him.
He has received " of Thomas Tillet the sume of thirty
one pounds sixteen shillings In Money which with the
allowance of seven pounds sixteen shillings for two
quarters Tax makes the sume of Thirty nyne pounds
twelve shillings, and is in full for two Quarters Rent
due to me out of the Mannor of Blewbury at Michās
last." The next renewal was not achieved without
some smoothing of the learned Bishop's feathers. One
of the Assistants reported in 1711 that he " had
waited upon the Bishop of Salisbury who seemed to
resent the Committees not waiting upon him at his
coming to Towne and that he should expect £300 for
putting in a New Life in the Blewberry Estate." So
a sub-committee was nominated, both to explain why
they had not waited upon him before and why they
preferred £250 to £300, and the life of Thomas Tyllott,
Junior, went into the lease for £250 and " ten guineas
to the Bishops Steward for fees." But there were
other troubles in store at Blewberry. In 1713 the
tenant was £450 in arrear with his rent and had written
about it. His explanations were considered " trifling,"
while the state of the Corporation required " all the

money to be gott in that can possibly be had agst the next distribūcon." So, if he did not send in £200 before then, " an Accōn at Law shall be cõmenced for his Arrears or distress shall be taken for the same." Secondly, in 1715, there was " consideracōn of sending out Soldiers for the Estate at Blewberry," and a few days later the tenant told them " that the Estate was likely to be charged to the Militia," and a Treasurer was desired " to use his interest to gett the Corporation excused by such applications as he shall think proper." Thirdly, after a long interval, in 1772 there is a reference to " the claimes made by Mᴿ Smythes as Vicar of Blewberry agᵗ the Corporation and their Tenants in relation to certain Tyths " and to " the Bill brought by him in the Court of Exchequer on that Accᵗ." Of course, in the process of years it happened that the see of Salisbury was occupied by other bishops who were devoted friends of the Charity. The Sons of the Clergy, for instance, never had a more industrious colleague than Thomas Sherlock, but the fines for renewal did not diminish on that account. In 1737 Sherlock, somewhat to the Court's chagrin, asked £350 for the insertion of another life, and at that price the Court inserted the name of Thomas Potter, son of the then Archbishop of Canterbury and a member of their own body.

Another country estate, not the less rural because it was at Holloway, came to the Sons of the Clergy in 1693. The trustees " for the Disposition of Mᴿ Palmers Guift of one Hundred pounds per annum to Twenty

clergy-mens widows for ever" appeared before the
Court and " declared that they were willing to transfer
the said trust to this Corporācon." It seemed that
this property was " Copyholden of the Mann^r of
Clerkenwell, which is the estate of the right honb^{le} the
Earle of Northampton but at present in Joynture " to
the Dowager Countess. Therefore the Register was
bidden to put the case before the Bishop of London
and Sir Thomas Meres, that they might intercede with
" the aforesaid honble persons," and beg them " to
enfranchise the said estate." It may have been
noticed that the Bishops of London, in whose diocese
the Charity has had its home, do not so far figure in
its story, either as Assistants or as benefactors. It
was only after a century or so of work that the Bishops
of London came in and joined it actively, and the
change was due to Thomas Sherlock, whose long
services to the Charity were continued with his occupation of Fulham. Since his day every Bishop of London
has been on the Court of Assistants. But in the case
of this Holloway estate there was special reason for
appealing to the then Bishop. For Henry Compton,
who had recently been through moving times, was a
cadet of the House of Northampton, being a son of the
second earl, who fell at Hopton Heath. As a man who
gave much of his income in charity, his absence from
the Courts was due to no hostility, and he no doubt
exerted the desired influence in this case. The Register
was soon able to say that the Lady of the Manor of
Clerkenwell was " inclineable to admitt the persons

nominated by this Corporation into the Copyhold estate
. . . out of which Mr Palmer's Charity is maintained,
if the Corporation would allow her to nominate a
Widdow every sixt vacancy successively dureing her
life." The property consisted of a " house, Barne, and
Lands " in Holloway, and in 1705 the tenant, having
the choice of a new lease of twenty-one years at the
same rent as before, £100, with £100 fine, or an increased rental of £110 a year, chose the latter. No land
in the possession of the Corporation has gone through
such a change as this Holloway Estate. We pass over
rather more than a century and find in 1811, in the
Treasurership of John Bacon, great searchings of heart
in the Court about a Bill before Parliament for a road
from Kentish Town to Holloway. The special committee may be found protesting against " the clause
imposing a Toll on Foot Passengers " and against that
" for Fencing the Road against Fields &c." They are
also very anxious " that nothing in this Act shall extend
or be construed to extend to compel the Owners to sell
any more Land than shall be necessary to make the
intended Road or for the purpose of Toll houses and
other necessary Buildings." And they are justified by
the present state of the property. As I used to sit
in Sir Paget Bowman's room at Corporation House,
the chances were that among his visitors would be
someone interested in this estate or engaged to watch
it. Maps would come out, and the value per foot of
frontage would be discussed. Mr. Palmer's £100 a
year has multiplied about seventeen-fold, and a quarter

of a century hence there will be rack-rents and a still greater harvest.[1]

It was only when the Sons of the Clergy came into possession of Dr. Turner's legacy of over £18,000 that they were in a position to make a considerable purchase. Some time in the summer of 1715 it was suggested to them that what they wanted was to be had in " the Mannor and Demesne Lands of Stow with Nine Churches in the County of Northampton." It consisted of

> " some Quit rents and 1493 Acres of land divided into 14 severall farms let to so many severall tennants amounting in all to 673 15 00

	£	s.	d.
" some Quit rents and 1493 Acres of land divided into 14 severall farms let to so many severall tennants amounting in all to	673	15	00
120 Acres of Woodland *Communibus Annis*	50	00	00
Some Cottages and 10 Acres of Land belonging to them let at	9	16	11
Quit rents and tyths at	2	4	2
In all p. annum	735	16	01
Out of which is payable for four acres belonging to Stow Church p. ann.	1	00	00
And for Certainty Money	1	13	00
So that the Clear Rent is	733	03	01

There is a great deale of young thriving Timber and the rents are holding rents and improveable and the Committee is of opinion that the estate is

---

[1] The approximate total value of the Holloway estate in 1909–10 was £405,000 ; but some parcels of it have since been sold.

DR. TURNER'S MONUMENT AT STOWE.

in every respect a suitable estate for the Corporation and is a cheap Purchase at £15,500."

This is the official account of the property in the minutes, but there are papers surviving which evidently provided the Assistants with the necessary information. The Rector of Stowe was to receive, according to these documents, £100 a year in tithes. They also give details of the acreage. There were about 150 acres of " Arable," about 70 of " Meadow," and over 500 of " Pastures," in addition to " a piece of Ground upon the Heath of about 11 Acres for taking Brakes and Furzes." But, as those who recommended it were careful to note, it had one considerable disadvantage from the Corporation's point of view. They could agree with the Rector " for the Composition for Tythes," but, if possible, they must " avoid buying the Advowson, that being judg'd improper for the Corporation." This, however, did not appear to be practicable. Evidently they had to take the advowson with the rest, but they had no desire to keep it, and on January 31st, 1717, the Court resolved that it should be " put up to Sale to the best Bidder this day fortnight." The Register was to " prepare a Particular to deliver to such Persons as shall be inclinable " and to each member of the Court. The day fixed was a Court day, and they were their own auctioneers. The conditions were settled as follows :—

That each person have liberty to bid 3 times and that any member of the Court have liberty

to bid and that the severall proposalls made by
any Bidder be delivered in Writing into the Court
and that all the Bidders be called in after the first
and second Bidding, and acquainted with the
highest summ which is bid at each Bidding and
that the Person who Bidds most the Third time
shall be the Purchaser, making a Deposit of 100$^£$
and signing a Minute of the Agreement and paying
the residue of the money within a Month. . . .

Then comes the result of the auction :—

Severall Persons having delivered in their Bid-
dings and Mr John Loyd bidding 1,055$^£$ at the
Third Bidding which was more than any other
Person was allowed the Best Purchaser.

Considering that the Corporation alone was under an
obligation to pay the incumbent £100 a year in tithes,
the purchaser may be said to have made a fair bargain.
The first avoidance took place by death in 1720, and
one William Lloyd was appointed, being no doubt the
relative for whom John Lloyd intended his purchase
[*vide* Appendix, pp. 283–5]. But, even so, the Corporation did not get rid of all responsibility for the
higher welfare of the inhabitants, for in 1720 came a
legacy from Lloyd's predecessor of £120 to provide " a
Sallary for a Person for teaching the poor Children at
Stow to read, knitt, &c." In the same year, having
acquired the neighbouring estate of Adstone, they were
once more met with a question of patronage.

The Comittee being informed that some of
the Inhabitants at Adston are willing to make a
Contribution towards paying some Neighbouring
Clergymen a Stipend for reading Prayers and
Preaching in the Chappell belonging to the Mannor
house every other Sunday at least are of Opinion
the Corporation should allow 5£ p. ann. towards
Incouraging so good a work during the pleasure
of the Corporation only.

The matter was so far in hand that Mr. Fulks, the
Newgate Street chemist, who had been down in
Northamptonshire with others on a "view," brought
back with him a recommendation as to the particular
clergyman to be appointed. But attention was soon
turned from the chaplain to the chapel. The bailiff
informed them in 1725 that "Adston Chappell was
so much out of Repair that neither the Minister nor
People can sitt dry at Divine Service and the Committee
are of opinion that the necessary Repaires ought to
be done, having first an account of the charge thereof
from their Bayliffe."

We must not leave Adstone without a reference to
John Bacon's visitation in 1811. In his old age, after
a lifelong service to the Festival,[1] he threw himself into
the routine of the Treasurership, and went the round of
the estates—Braintris, West Wratting, Willingham,
Wisbech, Stowe, and Adstone. His report, dated from
"Fryern House, 13 Nov^r, 1811," occupies six folio
sheets of the Court Book, and is in his characteristic

[1] Cf. Chapters X.–XII.

manner. He tells you of his "most hospitable welcome" by the vicar of Steeple Bumpstead, and how
he was "greatly gratifyed in the contemplation of
many most curious and valuable antiquities in the
Church." He called at the Palace before he left Ely,
and thence "bent our way to Peterboro', where we
attended Divine Service and were invited and most
kindly entertain'd at Dinner by the worthy Prelate of
that diocese."[1] Arriving at Adstone, Bacon "view'd
the Chapel, which was covered in and in part repair'd."
He thought himself "very fortunate in arriving there
before it was finish'd as the Workmen were proceeding
very awkwardly in the interior parts, not allowing a
proper Seat for the principal Tenant of the Manor
Farm or placing with propriety the Altar, Pulpit, and
Reading Desk, which I hope I have now properly
arranged." He adds that the "aggregate expence" of
the necessary improvements would not be more than
£70, "and the recompence and reward will be the
Civilization of reclaiming from a wild and savage Life
a Population of 185 Males and Females. Surely this
is a Praiseworthy Undertaking." Then he turns to the
chaplain's stipend, and reminds the Court that they
were still paying only £5 voted in 1720, which for value
should in 1811 be represented by £30. If they would
rise to this figure, the inhabitants would give £10 and
Worcester College, Oxford, who formerly subscribed
to the stipend as local landholders, might do so again.
"These together will make," said Bacon, "a fair and

[1] Spencer Madan. Died 1813.

adequate allowance for a Stipendiary Curate doing single duty every Sunday throughout the year." At his suggestion "A Bible and Prayer Book, Pulpit Cushion, Cup and Salver for the Communion Table and Surplice for the Minister " were sent down to the care of the Chapel warden, and the Adstone service was once more started on its weekly round.

The advowson of Adstone, for which there is now a small endowment, remains the property of the Corporation, but the Registrar no longer pays his kindly visits to the two estates.[1] Still, we like to think of the 1715 Register receiving the Court's instructions that in collecting rents he is " not to trust any one upon the place," and " that it would be of service to the Corporation to have all the rents paid upon one certain day and that the best way to bring the Tenants to comply would be the giving them a reasonable time after each half year. . . . They must pay their Michās Rent at Candlemas and their Lady days Rent at Lāmas Day Constantly, to which the Tenants are agreed "; or that the bailiff is to be told to " forthwith build a Lime Kilne and as soon as finished to give Notice to the Tenants that they must repair with Mortar made of Lime instead of Clay "; or " that the Minister and Churchwardens be put in Mind of going their yearly perambulations "; or that one tenant

[1] The greater part of the property at Stowe-Nine-Churches and Adstone was sold in 1916. All that we retain is the Tanborough farm, which is let to the Northamptonshire County Council, and some meadows and cottages at Weedon. The little benefice of Adstone is held with the neighbouring rectory of Maidford.

may " have a Tree allowed him for making a new Pump," but another must " bring back the doors of the house which he lived in, which he had taken away."

With one other small responsibility (still existent), this chapter may conclude. A certain Mr. Lee had left us a property at Wraysbury, near Staines. It carried with it the appointment and maintenance of a lecturer at £26 a year. In 1705, Tenison being in the chair, the Court " agreed that Thomas Jenkinson curate of Datchett Clerk [1] bee and is hereby chosen Lecturer of the parish of Wirardsbury in the County of Bucks and Dioces of Lincoln for Sundays in the afternoon according to the Will of Mr Lee the Donor. His Grace the Lord Archbishop of Canterbury in whom the jurisdicōn of the Dioces of Lyncoln now is [between Gardner's episcopate and Wake's] orders that hee shall have a Licence to perform the said Lectur."

[An additional Note on Dr. Turner's gift and monument is placed in the Appendix.]

[1] Thomas Jenkinson, of Magdalen College, Oxford, was chorister, clerk, and minor-canon of St. George's Chapel, Windsor, and was vicar of Datchet from 1687 to 1742. Foster, *Al. Oxon.*

CHAPTER VIII

WIDOWS

THE most patient of readers will have long since remarked that he has not been given the information he expected to obtain. Clerical poverty is almost the chief problem of the Church of to-day, and the records of the Corporation, he will naturally reason, ought to supply us with details of its extent in former times and with experience and suggestions in the way of a remedy. The disappointment is inevitable. Such records as there are in Corporation House of the trouble as it presented itself to the Assistants during the first half-century of their work will be dealt with in this chapter. But the records, it must be remembered, describe the daily work of men whose benevolent business it was, not to estimate the extent of the suffering, but to palliate what they saw with their eyes. They made the best use of their property that they could devise, and they gradually fell into fixed and formal methods. Annually in the early spring they held their Court of Distributions, having previously gone through their list of petitioners and made a rough estimate of what they could afford to distribute. Ardent benefactors like Sir Gilbert Dolben in 1713 might sometimes add £50 to the available amount. All that the good men could do otherwise was to give out what was entrusted to them, and the records only stray from the bare lists of beneficiaries when some widow has managed to evade the rules and to be paid twice, or when another has not managed to be paid at all. Anyone who wants estimates of the amount of poverty needing to be relieved when the Corporation started must construct his figures out of standard works such as John Walker's *Numbers and Sufferings of the Clergy* (fol. 1714). It is true that when Philip Bisse, Bishop of Hereford, was President, he prepared in 1718 a paper " containing a Short Acct of the State of the Corporation and answering some Objeccons in relacon to the Widows relieved by the Corporation." It was ordered that 2,000 copies should be " distributed as there shall be occasion," and in 1728 the same paper was brought up to date and reprinted. It is probable that this is the origin of the appendix to the Festival sermon of 1718, entitled " The Present State of the Charity applied to the Relief of the Widows and Children of Clergy-Men." After explaining about King Charles' Charter, the President there goes on to plead, as we still plead to-day, that the revenue of the Corporation (then about £2,000 a year), " great as it is, and greatly redounding to the Honour of pious Benefactors . . . is nevertheless far insufficient to answer the pressing Wants for the relief of which this Corporation was erected." He then proceeds to give some such estimate as the practical reader desiderates in this volume. " There are usually near six hundred Widows of Clergymen, who have been left so entirely destitute of all Subsistence as to apply yearly for Relief to this Corporation ; and the Number . . . hath hitherto encreased." It is evident that this number had led to unfavourable comment, but the President goes on to urge that it was inevitable.

> The number of Clergymen in *England* may be computed to be about twelve Thousand, their Widows applying for Charity about six Hundred, which is about One in Twenty. But when it is consider'd that there are five Thousand Livings (including Donatives and perpetual Curacies) not exceeding fifty Pounds a year; and of these two Thousand, not exceeding ten Pounds a year; it will not appear so strange that of Clergymens Widows One in Twenty should come to want; as that from among the other Clergy (chiefly) in fourty Years time a Subsistence for them should be raised of two Thousand Pound a Year.

After reckoning the number of poor children at about two thousand, he goes on to suggest a rough estimate of the amount that ought to be placed yearly to the credit of the Corporation.

> In order to allow each of these six Hundred Widows, with their Family, for their whole Subsistence, but ten Pounds a Year, it would require an Annual Revenue of at least six Thousand Pounds: That of two Thousand Pounds, wherewith this Corporation is at present endowed, tho' applied with the greatest Care and Fidelity, not being hitherto capable of affording to each more than three Pounds yearly; a Sum much lower

than many of the meanest Parish-Poor receive, especially if they have Families depending upon them.

There the estimates of the Corporation may be said to end, and the fact that the President was asked to produce this appeal goes to show that the Assistants felt they had other work to do, which had been theirs from the beginning and remains with their successors of to-day. In 1679, before they had begun to gather in subscriptions, we find the Earl of Longford proposing to the Court in Jerusalem Chamber " two persons as great objects of Charity," and the Register was ordered to " sett downe their Names in this daies order." They would get help when there was the wherewithal to give it.

But that soon came. In 1683 they were able to call a Court " on some convenient day in next Trinity terme in order to the Distribution of a sume of Money not exceeding One hundred pounds," and on July 4th, Sir Christopher Wren and Dr. Tenison being present, they allotted £98 10s. to various applicants, and agreed that the Treasurers and the Register should allocate the residue " as they thinke fitt to give itt." It may be that some sentimental interest was considered to attach to this first distribution, for I found in a miscellaneous bundle a sheet of paper, folio size, giving the whole details. Its front page contains the full minutes of the meeting, which of course were copied into the Court Book ; but the other three pages are

filled with " the Names of the severall persons to whom
money was ordered to be given and their Severall proportions." There are on it eighteen gifts of £2 each,
twenty-one of thirty shillings each, and twenty-nine of
£1 each. The lines are occupied with the date when
the gift was paid out, the signature of the person
receiving it, the name of the person to whom the gift
had been granted, and the amount. They are all
widows, except two cases where " (a daughter) " and
two where " (a son) " is added to the name. Four
persons on the list never received their " proportion."
Twenty-six obtained it through others, either their own
representatives or kind members of the Court such
as William Wren, who saw to its safe delivery.
William Middleton, the " Sollicitor," signs for a gift
to his mother. Of the widows who came in person,
twenty-eight were able to sign their own names, and
six could only make a mark—either a cross or a bald
capital letter.

Almost at once there arose the trouble that was inevitable in the prevailing conditions of communication.
In the October following it was reported that some of
those to whom gifts had been assigned had not come
to claim them nor sent anyone on their behalf, and so,
" itt being supposed that some of them might be dead,"
the rest were given till Lady Day to claim their awards.
All through the early stages of the Charity the continued existence of the persons named in the yearly
lists had to be left undecided. What could a Register
with an office in Doctors' Commons know personally

of the welfare of widows scattered about the country ?
If they were Londoners, he could send the Messenger
to investigate, and a paper now before me implies that
this at any rate was fitfully done. It is a " List of
Widows in yᵉ City and Liberty of Westmʳ," and is
dated 1728, the Jubilee of the Charter. It contains
twenty-two names. Only three were found to be living
at the address " in yᵉ Book." One " has been in Scotland 3 years," another " Lives at Lewisham in Kent,"
several were found at new addresses, and seven are
marked, " Not to be heard of." But not a few were
beyond the use of pensions altogether. One " dyed
on Xmas Day 1724," another, " dead above 2 years,"
another, "Dead about 3 months. Bury'd at St. James's
Church yard, a fine ffuneral." All this was not mis-
management ; it simply could not be avoided, and it
may easily be imagined how much less the Court could
know of their *protégées* when the majority were scattered
over the English and Welsh shires.

What the Assistants could do, however, was to
classify their applicants, and the first requisite was
a special list of those whose pitiable needs first called
the Sons of the Clergy charity into existence—the
widows of those who had been faithful during the
Rebellion. Early in 1684 the Register had orders to
" peruse the petitions he hath by him or shall be
brought to him and give an Accompt at the next Court
what Petitions he hath of Widdowes whose Husbands
were sequestred or plundered in times of the late
Rebellion for theire Loyalty to his late Majesty of

Blessed Memory." This was on January 25th, and
the 30th of that month probably found the Register
obeying an order which the day would make appropriate. Anyhow by March he had a list of twenty-
eight such widows, " all or most of them ancient,"
who received £3 apiece. In the following year there
were already some gaps in their ranks. Two were
dead ; another, who had been dead for some time,
" was personated the last year by another woman who
had got her certificate "—a not infrequent occurrence ;
while Dr. Ashton's widow had been " married to a
layman and therefore was not qualified to enjoy the
benefitt of this Charity." There were thirty-four fresh
applicants ; indeed, " the Register acquainted the
Court . . . that some of them came daily to his
Chamber enquiring when the Court would make any
distribution." So ten " sequestered " widows were
added to the list. In 1686 the number has risen to
fifty, and the reader must refer to the note (p. 153 f.)
for the development of the numbers. He will there
see that the beneficiaries fell naturally into three
classes—" sequestered " widows, other widows, and
children—and that the first dwindled, the second
rapidly increased, while the third remained fairly
stationary and is hardly worth giving, because to make
it of any value we ought to reckon in the number of
apprenticeship fees provided, which cannot be done.
For the moment we are concerned with the " sequestered " widows, whose numbers rose to fifty-three in
1688 and then steadily dwindled till they disappeared

with Ann Lightburne, who, being the last survivor, had
her allowance raised to £6 in 1719 and to £7 in 1721.
After that she appears no more, and if we take 1655
as the date of the Cromwellian ejections, and she was
then the wife of a sequestered minister, she must have
outnumbered the years of Anna the prophetess. John
Walker, whose *Account of the Sufferings of the Clergy*
is the main authority on this subject, has hardly any
information about the " sequestered minister " of this
name. Westfield in Kent, he says, " is, if I mistake
not, the Living which he left. When his Death happen'd I know not ; but after it, either his Widow or
some other of his Family were forced to beg the
Publick Charity of the *Corporation for Ministers
Widows*." [1] In fact, Walker's only reason for including
Lightburne or Lightbourn in his list is that he found
the name on our books. Indeed, persecution in any
form was a sure passport to the Corporation's sympathy, as may be gathered from a gift in 1691 to the
widow of " a late beneficed Minister in Ireland deceased
nd th ence forced into England upon the late persecution," or from another of £10 in 1718 to the daughter
of a " Sequestered Minister," who wrote " setting forth
her deplorable condition as being dead on one side by
the Palsie and otherwise become helpless."

But the second class of widows, those who fell into
poverty after the Restoration, were a permanent and
an increasing body. For their sakes the Charity was
bound to try to go on and prosper. It must have been

---

[1] Walker, *Sufferings* (1714), pt. ii. 294.

difficult after a time to find " Sequestered " widows.
The difficulty with these others was to have satisfactory
regulations for their admission to the Corporation's
benefits. One way was to lay upon the several
Assistants or benefactors the burden of responsibility
for the worthiness of their nominees. Thus, in 1691,
they resolved that " noe more Widdows of Clergy Men
be admitted to receive the Releife of this Corporaćon
but such as shall be recomended by some one of the
Benefactors," unless there should be a vacancy by
death or by a pensioner ceasing to be " an object of
charity." The number of cases in which they were
imposed on was exceedingly small. For instance, in
1699 the Court was told " that Mrs Styles who received
the charity of this Corporation has Eighteene pounds
p. Annum of other Charityes " ; so it was " ordered
that shee be discharged from receiving anything
more " ; she had done well, for she was one of those
who made " her marke " in the 1683 list already described. Or again, in 1702 it was discovered that Mrs.
Judith Edwards " is one of the Widdows that are in
Bromley Hospitall in Kent and likewise has a Lease
of a considerable estate holden of the Church of
Rochester " ; so she too was dismissed from the
Corporation's care. The reference to Bromley Hospital
brings up a matter upon which the Court kept a careful
eye. No widow living in any of the various homes
for poor gentlewomen connected with the English
Church was eligible for a pension, so the Accountant
of 1728 was ordered to keep lists of the widows " in

the severall Hospitals of Winchester, ffrogfield, Salisbury, and Bromley," and also of those " who receive
Pensions from the Crowne." And, to show how carefully they tried to prevent unnecessary pensions, there
is an entry in the list of 1723 of " Sarah ffern of the
Cathedrall Church of Ely " giving her address in the
College (which would elsewhere be called the Close or
the Precincts), who was admitted to a pension " if the
College be not a place of Charity." There was also
the danger of impersonation. Take the case of Ann
Taylor, of Blandford, who had perhaps been recommended by some member of the Wake family. She is
an " admitted Pensioner," but " her Pention has been
received for 2 years past by another Person of the
same name who never was admitted, who alleadged
herself to be a Clergyman's widow and pretends that
she was informed that she was admitted." The
rightful Ann Taylor was to be paid her arrears, but
" the other Ann Taylor who received the Pention
shall not be admitted till she does right to the Cor-
poraĉon in respect to the 6ᵍ which she has already
received without having any right to it." So in 1728
Alice Thorne " of Bampton in Devonshire and Skilgate
in Somersetshire " is struck off the list, " she being
the same person and having received a double Pension
for severall yeares past," while Susan Denham was at
the same time suspended, " she having received Anne
King's pension for some Years and not pay'd her the
whole." Perhaps the case which is most typical at
once of the Court's difficulties and of its sympathies

was that of a certain Mrs. Bishop, who, in 1729, had
been " receiving Pensions by false Certificates."   " The
offence," said the Court, " is punishable as ffraud by
Indictment," but they agreed " that the prosecution
be deferred till her husband is better recovered of his
Indisposition, there being no one else to take Care
of him."

So justice was done in one way, and in another it
was not lacking, for the good men would always make
up arrears to any widow who had been neglected in the
yearly ministration through any misadventure.   They
did what they could to secure worthy pensioners.   They
printed lists of their names, the sums given them, and
" the places whereof their Husbands were Incumbents
. . . with a Postscript desireing all persons to give an
accompt to the Reg^r whether they are alive or married
againe or any other waies provided for."   After that
they felt they had nothing to do except distribute their
money as much as possible.   There were sometimes
circumstances of stress, and they had sorrowfully to
resolve that " considering the state of the Corporation,"
they " could not make any augmentations this yeare."
There were sometimes fat years in which they could
gladly decree that " an additional allowance of twenty
shillings be paid to such new Petitioners as are of the
age of seaventy yeares and upwards."   They did not
even confine themselves to the annual allowances, for
the pension that would have been paid but for the
poor body's death was often handed over to her
relatives for her burial.   Thus, in 1694, " A Minister's

widow to whom twenty shillings was ordered the last
distribuc̄on dyed before she received the same and
Isaac Webb, her landlord, who was a very poor man
and buryed her at his owne charge, did humbly pray
that the Court would allow him the said twenty
shillings towards the said charge," which of course the
Court did, and I doubt if a resolution passed in 1719
that all such posthumous payments must cease was
kept to the letter. If no one else could see to it, the
Register would evidently arrange for the funeral of a
pensioner himself. The following voucher has no date
attached to it, but is in Tyllott's handwriting :—

an account of ye burying of Mrs Dobson

	£	s.	d.
for a Coffen and Shroud . . .	01	00	00
paid Mr Marten for ale . . .	00	05	00

ye goods was sold for two pound seven shillings
which was laid out in paying ye nurs and dis-
charging ye parish duties.

More than once there are records of small charitable
payments, such as twenty shillings " to Mrs Chapman
for attending Mrs Granger a Clergymans Widdow in
her sickness and for the money she lent her," and the
same sum in the same year (1698) to Mrs. Barbara
Smith, " a poore Minnister's Widdow," who came
" setting forth that she had expended the same upon
Mrs Mary ffolks a poore Minnister's Widdow deceased."
When the poor were kind to the poor, it was not for
the Corporation to send them away empty.

But their main business was to provide pensions and to see that worthy folk received them, and it would be doing them an injustice to imply that they were not business-like as well as benevolent. The basis of their work in this matter was the certificate. Every applicant must be provided with a formal petition duly attested. As time passed on, the certificate naturally became more careful in its requirements. It must state on the authority of the witnesses—so they decreed in 1728—that " her circumstances are such as she cannot subsist with out it " ; and two years later even this was felt to be not sufficiently definite, and the witnesses were asked to say : " It doth appear to us after a very carefull and strict Inquiry and Examination into her Ability and Circumstances that She &c &c." When they had got in their pile of certificates, they proceeded to draw up a list of those which they approved. Sometimes the list contains nothing but the widows' names and their " proportions," but for some reason that of 1722 is more elaborate. It is drawn up in five columns headed thus : " Widows Name and Age," " How many Childr^n," " Husbands Name and Abode," " When dyed," " Who recomended by." Ten have the support of Mr. Treasurer Westley, six of Mr. Fulks of Newgate Street, three of Dr. Sacheverell, two of the Bishop of Peterborough [White Kennett], besides a number of individual nominations. Behind this careful list were the certificates that had been sent in and examined, and a small number of them which have somehow survived at Corporation

House are the only real authority which can be adduced for the actual forms of distress relieved by the Corporation. It will therefore be fair to give some instances.

> Dorothy Pope's " Husband [Curate of Hallwell, Devon,] was a person of honest Character and well esteem'd off in his parish, and tho' no further preferr'd than to that Curacy of between 30^g and 40^g per Annum, yet had a Competent Temporal Estate sufficient to support himself and Family in a decent and comfortable manner, but being unwarily drawn into an engagement for the Debts of a Knavish Relation, he was so harrass'd with frequent Arrest and Suits of Law as at last forc'd him to Mortgage his Estate almost to ye value of it for ye paym^t of ye others debts. Under which circumstances it pleas'd God to take him from me, now about four years since, having little left me besides five children, two of which were young, one decrepit, and another an Ideot and dumb, which last has been not only ye greatest Trouble, but Charge to me also ever since. They are still living, two of 'em work at Husbandry, with whose small Assistance and my own labour, together with what little was left me, I have hitherto made a hard Shift to provide for ye rest a wretched maintainance. But that little being now wholly spent, I had thoughts of applying myself to the Parish for some Subsistence."

However, some kind friends suggested the Corporation, and her petition came before the Court signed by

Nic : Kendall,[1] Archdeacon of Totnes, Wm Roberts, Proct^r for the Clergy of the Diocese of Exon., Tho. Lynford,[2] Archdeacon of Barum, A. P. Champernowne, M.P., and a number of local clergy. It was posted to Dr. Lynford at Westminster Abbey.

Susannah Lawson applied in 1709 as " the Relict of Mr John Lawson [3] late Minister and Chaplain of Her late Majesty's Ship the Rumney . . . and was left without any Provision or Meanes of Subsistence, tho' her said husband was eleven Years in the Sea Service as Chaplain of Severall ships of War, but sustained such losses by his being five times taken prisoner by the Enemy that he could not save anything for the support of this his distressed widow. . . . She has been very Industrious for the Obtaining an honest Livelyhood, but being of a very weakly Constitution and grievously afflicted with bodily distempers, which with a decay of Sight makes her incapable of working for her bread as she has done heretofore in the Parish of St. Margaret West^r, Where she has Lived these ten Years past."

[1] Nicholas Kendall, a Cornishman, of Lostwithiel ; Fellow of Exeter Coll., Oxford, 1678–81 ; Prebendary of Exeter, 1688–1740 ; Archdeacon of Totnes, 1713–40   Venn, *Al. Cantab*. iii. 7.

[2] Thomas Lynford, son and grandson of Bedfordshire clergymen, was rector of St. Edmund the King, Lombard Street, 1685, Prebendary of Westminster, 1700, and Archdeacon of Barnstaple, 1709 ; and held all three offices till his death in 1724. He was buried at St. Edmund the King.   Venn, *op. cit*. iii. 87.   At Westminster his vote was generally given against any project of Atterbury's. Cf. H. C. Beeching, *Francis Atterbury*, pp. 202–208.   He was President of Sion College, 1706.

[3] A man of this name was Chaplain R.N., 1691–1708.

Her supporters were the curate and churchwardens of St. Margaret's, and Dr. Strahan,[1] of Doctors' Commons, signed her paper as an Assistant.

The Mayor and twelve aldermen of " Kingstone upon Hull " and the " Master of the free schole, Beverley," were witnesses in 1716 for the widow of " Mr Simon Oxnard, late Vicar of Waun a Little Country Town between Hull and Beverley." She

> ever had a very ffair Character amongst her Neighbours. She was left (between ffour or ffive years agoe) with six Children all unprovided for. . . . She has putt Robert and Joseph Apprentices One to a Barber and the other to a Glover, one at Eleven the other at Twelve Yeares old. Ralph and Hannah Maria being slenderly putt to service and not so ffortunate to meet with such as are good and profitable falls upon your Petīcon^r for help. Dinah getts her own living. The Two which are Apprentices are to be found with Cloaths and the Youngest wholly to maintain. Your Petitioner went to service herself being ffour and ffourty years old, but by reason of badness of sight and other bodily Infirmities is not able to continue.

We pass to Bedfordshire and take up the plea of " the Relict of the Reverend Learned and Orthodox Divine Mr John Price Deceased late Vicar of Stotfold," who had been left with

> three Daughters ; two of Which tho' married are Unable to relieve her, the Other a Constant care

[1] William Strahan, LL.D., Advocate-General. He was a Steward in 1713, when Sacheverell preached.

and charge to her, Subject to Epilepsies and many
other disorders, notwithstanding the triall of Many
learned Physicians ; [the petitioner] is truly become a due Object of Charity and has hitherto
honestly and frugally endeavoured to support her
self and family for some years past by teaching
some poor Children whose parents were not able
to reward her Care but in the Lowest Degree and
but few of them, and the rather now because her
sight begins to fail and Shee is almost uncapable
of teaching any Longer.

A Wiltshire widow, whose husband had been Minister
of Titcombe, stated

that her circumstances are very strait and narrow,
having only a little cottage and keeping a little
shop, her stock being about three pounds value,
and endeavours by industry to maintain her children by working with her needle and sometimes
spinning.

The widow of the Vicar of Bampton, Westmoreland,
rejoiced in the name of Pentecost Knott, and she
humbly shewed

that, whereas the Annual Income of your Petitioner's Husband did not exceed the sum of
08$^£$ 13^s 08^d for y^e maintenance of Himself, his
Wife and children, and He dying sixteen years
ago in so much Debt, that all His Goods and
Parsonal Estate (wch was all He had) were sold
towards the Payment of it . . . that for about
nine years, whilst it pleas'd God to allow her
Health and Strength, she labour'd as an hired

Servant, and, as those fail'd, taught a petty [1] School, the income of w[ch], through her Age and feebleness, is now so very mean and inconsiderable, that she cannot any longer subsist," etc., etc.

There is a note to her petition, dated April 20th, 1715, " I know the petitioner and believe the contents of the petition to be true. W. Carliol." [2]

In spite of Bishop Croft's [3] benefaction, there was an application in the same batch from Herefordshire on behalf of the widow of John Wyllym, curate of Pencoyde,

> a graue sober aged poore woman, and hath only a smal estate of aboute seuen pounds p. annum to maintaine her selfe and two daughters (tho' grown up yett unprovided for) and that she hath a right to but one third of the said estate, but her three sons to whome it is descended, it being gavel kind, doe consent that their aged mother (being seuenty yeares old) shall enjoy it during her life (they being put to ordinary trades and able to gett their own livelyhoods) which however is so little that without some assistance will not afford her bread.

A covering letter from a clergyman to " the Reuerend D[r] Dwight [4] at Fulham neare London," who evidently

---

[1] Called in still earlier days " a Schoole for the Petites or Petties." Cf. *Annals of Christ's Hospital*, p. 26.

[2] William Nicolson, Bishop of Carlisle, 1702–18.

[3] Cf. pp. 88–93.

[4] Philip Dwight was vicar of Fulham 1708–29. He and Samuel Dwight, M.D., who practised at Fulham, were possibly the sons of John Dwight, the potter. (*D.N.B.*)

had undertaken to see the case through, explains that the sons " can just gett their own bread as journey men, not being able to sett up ; one is a black smith, another a joyner and y⁸ third a currier or dresser of leather." " My service," adds this friend in need, " to y⁸ good Doctors who have promised their helping hands."

The case of Mrs. Tench, of " Hartyn," in Sussex, has other circumstances of interest attaching to it. She had the authorisation of the vicar and church-wardens and overseers of the parish for her not very syntactical statement that her

> husband by having a numerous family and being oblig'd to contend with a Rich and Powerfull Adversary for the Rights and Dues of his Vicar-idge ; And tho' after a long and expensive Suit He recover'd a very considerable Addition to his Vicaridge, yet He was thereby so impoverish'd that He could not appear abroad by reason of the Debts he had thereby contracted. And Dying in July last [1718] He left me . . . and ffive poor children wholly unprovided for. Wherefore in Consideration of the poverty of me and mine and that the Caus thereof was chiefly occasion'd by my Husbands being oblig'd to sue for the Rights belonging to His Church, your Petitioner humbly hopes," etc., etc.

Martha Pym, widow of the former rector of Litton, in Dorsetshire, had the emphatic testimony of Fr.

Roffen (Atterbury) and P. Hereford (Bisse) to her statement that

> she was left with eight Children, and so far in debt, that all ye effects of her deceased Husband were not sufficient to discharge it . . . That her Misfortunes have been much increased by the small pox, which the last Summer passed thro most of the Children, and deprived her of two daughters, wch were most assistant to her, and that this hath reduced them to the greater necessitys.

Nor were the applicants found merely among the families of poor country clergy. Henry Owen, minister of Naunton, Gloucester, was made Prebendary and Canon of St. David's,

> who enjoying that preferment so little a while and leaveing his Widdow with Seven Children all now living [she] is become through the narrow circumstances she was left in the object of the Wonted goodness of the Charitable Society of the Sonns of the Clergy. She has by her Care and Industry for these five yeares since her husbands death endeavoured to support her numerous family and is now engaging her selfe in the business of a School to Instruct young Children. She is exemplary virtuous and well affected to the Church of England. She was left in a very low condition through the great expences her husband was at in rebuilding the Parsonage house.

It was, of course, sometimes the case that Assistants brought forward the needs of poor relations. My predecessor at Christ Church, Dr. Joseph Trapp, puts at the foot of the petition of " Mrs Elizabeth Trapp, ye Relict of Mr Nathaniel Trapp, late Rector of ye Parish of Middleton Scriven," Salop, this statement :—" I am fully assured of the Truth of the Certificate above ; and do earnestly recommend the Petitioner's Case to the Court of Assistants. J. Trapp."

Sometimes the influence of a powerful member of the Court would be sufficient to secure a widow's admission without the formality of a certificate. Thos. Lutwyche,[1] afterwards Treasurer of the Inner Temple, writes in 1716 to Sherlock, Master of the Temple, in regard to a case over which the two had evidently had a talk.

> " You told me," he says to Sherlock, " that there was no meeting till Easter and you were pleased to say you would then do what you could for her . . . I hope you will be an instrument of support to her in her necessityes. If there be anything more that is required by ye rules and methods of this Charity please let me know. I had intended to have waited on You my self, but that I was obliged to go the Circuit before yor return to Town. If you'l please to leave a Line at my House in Lincolns Inne ffields it will be sent to me. I should not have given you so much

---

[1] Admitted K.S. at Westminster, 1688 ; son of Sir Edward Lutwyche, Judge of Common Pleas. M.P. for various Tory boroughs. Buried in the Temple Church, 1734.

trouble but that I know you delight in doing good
and therefore I will make no excuse."

The necessary details are recorded on the back of
this letter, which Sherlock countersigned and passed
on ; so the widow received her proportion without
more ado.

And it must not be supposed that only the families
of country clergy came up for assistance. " The
Minister of Hammersmith and sole Church warden of
Fulham on Hammers[th] side together with the Overseers
of the Poor of the s[d] Hamlett of Hammers[th] " testified,
in 1717, that Sophia Musgrave's

> Husband [late Reader of Hammersmith] was a
> very worthy Clergyman of the Church of England,
> but during the whole course of his Life having
> but a very small Income he was not able to make
> any provision for your petitioner, who hath no-
> thing to support her self with but only by letting
> of Lodgings in a House which she rents.

If it be urged that Hammersmith was still rural and
agricultural, we may pass into the City itself and
take the case of the widow of a " Minister of All
Hallows on the Wall in the City of London."

> She is a Person of good reputation, and upon
> her Husbands not complying to take the Oaths to
> the Government at the Revolution he was obliged
> to resign his preferment, and being thereby ren-
> dred incapable of making provision for his family

left his Widow and Son in very deplorable Circumstances.

Indeed, a man might be employed at the very core of the State and still leave his family in poverty, for in 1716 the clergy and churchwardens of " St. James's Parish in the Liberties of Westminster " asked help for " the Bearer Sarah Key, Widow and Relict of Francis Key, clerk, Master of Arts and Presbiter of the Church of England, who at the time of his Decease in the moneth of June last and for about the space of 5 or 6 years before was one of the Readers at the Chapel Royal in White Hall."

It will have been noticed that hardly any two of the above instances belong to one county or diocese, and it is one of the surest signs that the Corporation had arranged its work on good methodical lines, that its benefits were so widely spread. It happens that the county (not the diocese) is added in the cases of eighty-eight new pensioners admitted in 1721, and any one who analyses them will find that no less than twenty-six English and four Welsh counties are mentioned. The Court could hardly be more ubiquitous in the days of the Penny Post. Indeed, there were at least two cases, the widow of " Augustine Wallbank, late Minister of Philadelphia," recommended by Dr. Sacheverell in 1711, and the widow of " Alexander Duncan of South Carolina " in 1721, in which England was too small to limit their possibilities. In other ways also the change between then and now is by no means as great as might be lightly supposed. The increase in the number of clergy has not been accompanied by an increase in stipends or by a decrease in the number of " objects of charity " whom they leave behind them. If it were possible—the kindly secrecy with which modern petitions are treated at Corporation House makes it quite impossible—to give extracts from the pleas which the widows of to-day urge in their favour, it would probably be found that in some instances we have not improved on the inequalities of social station that separated the poor parson of the seventeenth and eighteenth centuries from his more fortunate brethren. To-day we should hold up our hands in horror at the idea of a parson's widow leaving the rectory of her late husband for the kitchen of anyone who would give her employment, or apprenticing her boy to a blacksmith, when, according to our notion, he ought to be a Bachelor of Arts. The Corporation comes in to remind us that our horror ought to have its practical counterpart in some effort to meet the needs of her case, if we lack the courage to make her case less inevitable.

This chapter ought not to close without a reference to the now quite forgotten fact that the Corporation was once able to give certain widows not only a pension but a home as well. Mention has been made of the will of Mr. Edmund Burroughs,[1] who in 1697 left £300 " for the building of six houses for six Ministers Widdowes," and also a debt of £1,000 due to him, which, however, only brought the Corporation £368.

[1] Cf. p. 99.

Tyllott has left behind him a scrap of paper detailing
his " expences at yᵉ 3 Tunns receiving Mʳ Burroughs
legacy," as follows :—

	£	s.	d.
Bread and Beer	00	00	06
Wine	00	09	00
Lobsturs	00	03	06
Buttur	00	00	08
Pepper and vynegar . . .	00	00	06
	00	14	02
yᵉ Drawer . .	00	00	04
	00	14	06

So unusual a trust necessitated a sub-committee, which
was at once appointed " to inquire after the building
of six houses for the aforesᵈ Widdowes and to treate
with the Owners of the ground for the same and with
workmen for the building." One would think that the
task was no sooner mentioned than completed. Five
months later came Dr. Assheton—he of the discourse
on " Last Wills and Testaments "—with a suggestion
that " the Deane and Chapter of Westminster had
some ground neer new Chappell in Westminster which
would be convenient for the Building of six houses,"
and Sir Thomas Meres was " desired to treat." Apparently the Dean and Chapter were not of the same
mind, for in another month the Court had heard of a
" ffee " belonging to Mr. Hewer, an Assistant, and
consisting of " some ground in Clapham adjoining to
the Churchyard on the East side thereof." Mr.

Hewer, it was reported, " is come to this resolution to
sell to this Corporation a rude of the said ground ffor
thirty pounds." This was a tangible offer, and orders
were given to go on at once with the work of con-
struction. But still nothing happened. The bequest
was apparently engaging the Court of Chancery, and
the ultimate result to the Corporation disappointed
their hopes. And then appeared a *deus ex machina* in
the person of Dr. Leach, who had heard about the suit
and " asked whether the Corporation would accept of
a house which would hold six Widdows." Mr. Mallory
and the Register were soon sent to " veiw three houses
in Plumtree Streete near the Church of St. Giles in
the ffields. . . . They conceived that the biggest of
them would be convenient for six Widdows to inhabit
there." So this house was accepted, and Dr. Leach
was thanked. By January, 1700, the house was ready
for three widows, and in subsequent years there are
frequent references to this strange establishment. " A
Question being put [1709] whether the Widdows in
Plumtree Street should have any Coals it past in the
negative," but in 1712 the Ayes had it, and the good
ladies received " halfe a Chaldron of Coles." Alas !
between the two votes about fuel there had been sad
doings in Plumtree Street. In October, 1711, the
Court minutes contained a resolution that Mrs. Smith
and Mrs. Oard " be turned out of the house in Plumtree Street within such time as Mr Treasurer Brent
shall think sufficient for them to provide themselves
a lodging," and the other four were " summoned to

answer severall objections made against them by the Court." No details of the tragedy appear in the minutes, but the immediate context contains a request to Brent " to mend the rails before the House in Plum-tree Street and to make such repairs as he shall see convenient," and this, in the absence of an official account, must be left to speak volumes. A tiny bill now before me " for mending ye house in Plumtree Street " favours a hope that the damage did not exceed 3s. 4d., but it mentions " ye joyner for a board," " ye Shutter mending," " ye Smith for ye Latch and hinge for the doore," and " 2 scruse and one pin for ye windowes," all of them significant of a considerable engagement, which was perhaps not confined to the house, for the damage necessitated the payment of a shilling " to the Gardiner." In these circumstances the Court was merciful. It is true that " Question being put whether Mrs Smith be restored to her Room . . . it passed in the Negative," but " extenuating circumstances " were represented by a rider that she could stay in her room " till such time as Mr Treasurer Brent shall see an occasion to turn her out." For the rest the history of the almshouse was uneventful, save that in 1716 one of the inmates was found to have " married a Lay Man since her first Husbands death," and was " put out."

It was not the internecine struggles of the inmates, but the system on which the house was held, that decided the Court to abandon it. Before Dr. Leach's death there had been efforts made to induce him to

" assȳne his interest in the house in Plumbtree Streete to this Corporation." When he died in 1707 they made the same request to " the Relict and Executor." In view of their failure they made up their minds in 1717 to " resigne the possession of it to them [the executors] unless they think fit to assign it to the Corporation." So the Messenger was sent to " give Notice to the Widows in Plumbtree Street that they must provide themselves of other Lodgings ag^t Christmas, for that the Corporation are to throw up the house at that time." And for the time being that was the end of Mr. Burroughs' design. A committee brought out his will in 1732 and reminded themselves of his intentions, but after all the Corporation is fortunately without almshouses, and its beneficiaries are happier among their own folk.

Another fund for the pensioning of Widows brought the Corporation into active connection with the City Clergy and Sion College. In 1765 a society had been established at Sion College for the relief of the widows and children of those clergy who were within the bills of mortality or the County of Middlesex, and who should subscribe during their lives one or two guineas annually under certain restrictions.[1] This society had a capital consisting of £2,000 South Sea Stock, but it had no great success, and towards the close of the eighteenth century was in difficulties owing to the decease or growing incapacity of its surviving members.

[1] Cf. *Charity Commission—Report on the Corporation*, 1835, pp. 826–7; E. H. Pearce, *Sion College and Library*, pp. 61 f., 85.

Therefore, in 1790, an agreement was come to for its being handed over to the Corporation. The rights of the widows of original members remained for the time being, till there was but one such widow left. She had an indefeasible claim to the whole of the income arising from the stock, to which £1,000 was added at the time of its transfer to the Corporation. She therefore enjoyed a pension of about £90 a year till her death in 1830. The proceeds of this endowment, now about £130 a year, are given in annual grants of £5 to various Corporation pensioners who come within its terms. The matter is worth mentioning as a good instance of overlapping, for the Clergy Widows' Society has exactly the same constituency, and the pensioners of the one are frequently also the pensioners of the other.

NOTE

The following list represents the progress or otherwise in the number of pensioners, from 1684, when the first list occurs in the Court Book, down to 1721, when the last payment was made to a sequestered minister's widow, after which the Court Book ceases to give full details.

	"Sequestered" Widows.	Other Widows.	Children.
1684	28	62	6
1685	34	98	—
1686	45	106	26
1687	50	131	43
1688	53	156	60
1689	52	161	59

	"Sequestered" Widows.	Other Widows.	Children.
1690	45	168	53
1691	44	176	37
1692	40	215	36
1693	40	245	36
1694	40	244	36
1695	41	262	37
1696	39	270	32
1697	30	248	30
1698	28	258	30
1699	24	244	30
1700	22	276	31
1701	19	273	28
1702	21	285	27
1703	17	291	23
1704	16	294	22
1705	15	314	20
1706	14	322	20
1707	12	337	20
1708	11	404	22
1709	10	327	20
1710	10	402	19
1711	9	386	18
1712	8	331	12
1713	8	349	13
1714	7	397	12
1715	No details.		
1716	7	496	14
1717	4	464	12
1718	2	—	—
1719	1	517	10
1720	1	563	10
1721	1	620	8

SUMS OF MONEY DISTRIBUTED, 1684–1702.

(From Appendix to White Kennett's Sermon, 1703.)

	"Sequestered" Widows.	Other Widows.	Children.	Total.
1684 . .	£84.	£101. 10.	£100.	£285. 10.
1685 . .	£99.	£129.	—	£228. 00.
1686 . .	£135.	£179.	£20.	£334.
1687 . .	£144.	£170. 10.	£29. 10.	£344.
1688 . .	£147.	£206. 10.	£45.	£398. 10.
1689 . .	£138.	£257. 10.	£43.	£438. 10.
1690 . .	£135.	£258.	£57. 10.	£450. 10.
1691 . .	£141.	£296. 10.	£74. 10.	£512.
1692 . .	£132.	£289. 10.	£64. 10.	£486.
1693 . .	£120.	£339. 10.	£52.	£511. 10.
1694 . .	£120.	£414.	£55. 10.	£589. 10.
1695 . .	£123.	£438.	£55.	£616.
1696 . .	£117.	£465. 10.	£61. 10.	£644.
1697 . .	£90.	£425.	£68.	£583.
1698 . .	£78.	£397. 10.	£51.	£526. 10.
1699 . .	£60.	£402.	£41. 10.	£503. 10.
1700 . .	£60.	£420.	£42.	£522.
1701 . .	£51.	£444.	£47.	£542.
1702 . .	£63.	£525.	£52.	£640.

CHAPTER IX

CHILDREN

IT must not be hastily assumed that, because the last chapter dealt with the widows, while this mainly concerns the children, the clergy themselves were wholly untouched by the work of the Corporation. It is true that at first they were not assisted, and we have seen Bishop Croft's legacy declined on the ground that clergy sustentation, as it is now called, lay outside the limits of Corporation activity. But time and the terms used by testators altered this. In 1779 Mistress Cam's fund led the way, followed by the will of Mr. John Stock, which took effect in 1782. I mention him *non sine honore* as a generous benefactor both to my old school [1] and to my parish. What he did for the Corporation was to leave a sum of money sufficient to pay £10 a year each to ten curates, who must be of good character, with a preference for those who are married, and with an income of not more than £40 a year. From this time onward the clergy themselves came more and more within the purview of the Sons of the Clergy, and the report of 1903 shows the extent to which operations under this head have increased. During 1902 assistance was given directly to 274 clergy, of whom 158 were beneficed, 61 were curates or chaplains, and 53 were without regular duty. The well-known delicacy with which our society's opera-

[1] Cf. *Annals of Christ's Hospital*, pp. 132–3.

tions are conducted conceals their names from the public, but the total sum thus expended was over £4,500 in that one year.[1]

Nor should it be forgotten that as the Sons of the Clergy led to the formation of the Clergy Orphan Corporation, to be referred to later,[2] so they were in some sense the real instigators of the Queen Victoria Clergy Fund. For in 1887, at a time when glebe farms were often unlet and tithes were falling away, the Corporation, at Archbishop Benson's request, set on foot what was called the Clergy Distress Fund and raised some £50,000, which they distributed in grants to distressed clergymen, giving, if need required, as much as £250 to an individual case.

It is obvious, however, that when we turn to the younger generation of sufferers there will be less to record in the way of permanent beneficence on the Corporation's part. True, the title conferred upon it by King Charles II. put the two branches of the work side by side. It was to aim at " the Releife of poore Widdows and Children of Clergymen." But the amount of effort required in the latter case would naturally not be as great in the mass, or as continuous in each instance, as it would in the former. Still the work for the children developed as time went on and

[1] If during 1927 the number of clergy helped was 208, and the total sum disbursed, £4,038, it must be remembered that in twenty-five years there has been a marked diminution in the number of names in *Crockford*, as well as a notable effort to raise the stipends of the poorer benefices.

[2] Cf. pp. 169–71.

12

appropriated charities came in. At once there would
arise the question, How much elasticity may there be
in interpreting the word " child " ? In 1684 they
consulted " Mr Baron Gregory " whether the word " as
is expressed in the Charter did extend to Children in
generall of any age or to such as are in theire Minority."
His answer is not on record, and ten years later they
put their own interpretation on it, but not without a
shrewd saving-clause, agreeing " that no Children of
dec'ed Clergymen who are above Twenty one yeares
of age shall for the future bee releived by this Corporation unles where they come recommended by
considerable benefactors." In 1695 they made a further
restriction to " noe children . . . above eighteen . . .
saving such as are already being relieved." But even
the Sons of the Clergy may make rules and break
them. So in 1714 " Mr Stockton's son " is " struck
out of the List of Pentioners being of full Age and
using the Trade of a Pattenmaker in Baldwin's Gardens " ; whereas in 1705 they readmitted to a pension
" George ffoxcroft a Minister's son," who

> had been formerly admitted a Pentioner to this
> Corporation, and had for severall years received
> twenty shillings successively, but going into Ire-
> land and staying some time there he had neglected
> to receive his said Annuall pention, so that in
> course it ceased to be longer paid, and *being now
> seaventy yeares old* was by sickness and other mis-
> fortunes reduced to a most deplorable condition
> even to the frequent want of Bread.

The general uncertainty is well illustrated by a notice of motion intervening in 1708 between these two instances " to consider at what ages children under eighteen years admitted in the Corporation shall be discharged from receiving their charity." In fact, it was impossible to stick to rules as long as your rules were liable to be upset by some testator involving you in a trust, say, on behalf of elderly maiden daughters. In the end they left the decision—where it still remains —to circumstances, and we must follow their operations as well as we can.

The children of " sequestered " clergy were no doubt treated with special generosity. Some of them became pensioners for life just as much as the widows. Take the petition of Anne Swayne, 1718, which states that she

> was Daughter of William Swayne,[1] Vicar of Cranborne in Dorsetshire, who was sequestered under the usurpation of Oliver Cromwell and she was Niece by ye mother's side to the late Right Rev^d : Bishop Stillingfleet, and sister to the Revd Mr William Swayne, Vicar of Tyshurst, in Sussex . . . being sixty three years of Age and having the stone always upon her and the use of one side wholly taken away from her by the palsy and has

[1] When William Swayne, afterwards vicar of Ticehurst, 1681–1718, was admitted to St. John's Coll., Camb., he was described as the son of William Swayne, deceased, clerk, of the Isle of Wight, Venn, *Al. Cantab.* iv. 191. No doubt the brother had helped the sister, and his death in 1718 caused her to make application that same year.

not been able to go to bed or dress or undress her
self these four years last past.

It is obvious that the Court could only help her to
any purpose by doing so for the term of her natural
life.   So with a petitioner from across the Border, who
was supported by the signatures of Lords Marchmont
and Binning, and who

> was Daughter to Mr George Davidson late Minister
> of Whitsum in the Mars in Scottland and Grand
> Daughter and Great Grand Daught^r to Clergymen
> who all Dyed and left your Petičon^r an Infant with
> sever^{ll} other Children in mean circumstances un-
> provided. . . . She has taken true care and paines
> to get her living and is now Grown infirm by
> Slauish business and being in years is very neces-
> sitated.

It was cases like these that the bequest of Mistress
Dutton was the first to take into its special care, and
it would appear that the Court was in some doubt
whether it ought to undertake the trust.   So at least
I gather from a letter of one Robert Style to Mr.
Michael Hillersdon " in Bush Lane, London," which
procured a pension without further formality.

> S^r, (he writes) So large an Interval has pass'd
> since I made a request to you in behalf of an
> Indigent Relation y^t ye variety of y^r own Business
> and ye Publick Station which I find by ye Prints
> you still adorn has made a repetition of it abso-
> lutely necessary.   'Twas in Behalf of an old Maid

a Clergymans Daughter above ye age of Fifty. . . .
She lyes under a Double incapacity both of Mind
and Body so far as to be incapable to furnish her
self with a competent subsistance. . . . When I
last saw you ye Society was undetermined whether
they should take ye Maiden Ladies estate who left
the Benefaction into y^r Hands. I presume by y^s
Time they are come to a resolution.

This letter is not dated, but it belongs to the years
1715–20, to judge by the bundle in which it was found,
and by that time the Corporation was committed to
the task of caring for " children " of any age, if their
circumstances warranted an exception being made to
rules.

It is one of the commonplaces of such work as ours
that those who beg for aid are not infrequently related
to generous benefactors. Take a petition, undated but
during Tenison's presidency, which is not marked as
" admitted." The petitioner says she

is the unfortun Daughter of Mr Edward Larkin,[1]
late Rector of Limpsfield in Surrey, and her
Grand ffather, uncle, and kinsman dec'd were all

[1] Edward Larkin or Lorkin, son of John Lorkin, Prebendary of
Rochester, 1625–54 and rector of Limpsfield, 1622–54, was admitted to King's Coll., Camb., from Eton, 1639. Fellow of King's,
1642–53 ; rector of Limpsfield, 1654–5 ; rector of Tatsfield, 1667–
87. Venn, *Al. Cantab.* iii. 105. The " uncle " referred to was
John, son of John Lorkin, above. Admitted to Clare Coll., Camb.,
as a pensioner, 1636. Rector of Woldham, 1660–7 ; Prebendary
of Rochester, 1661–6. The " kinsman " was Thomas Lorkin, son
of Hezekiah Lorkin, chandler, of Southwark, who was brother of
John Lorkin, the elder. Vicar of Stockbury, 1639–70 ; Prebendary of Rochester, 1667–70. *Ibid.,* 106.

Prebends of Rochester. She is the last of her ffamily and has been forced to work for her bread . . . had a tedious fitt of Sickness and Lameness, whereby she became indebted for three Quarters Rent and Daily threatened to haue her Goods seized and . . . is Distitude of the Necessaries of Life . . . Therefore most humbly prays the Honble Court in Consideraĉon that her late ffather was a Benefactor to the Hob^{ble} Corporation . . . that you will be pleased to admitt her to Partake of the yearly allowance lately left for Clergymens Daughters.

But it is still more remarkable to find relatives of Dr. Townson himself, to whom the Corporation owed the Saltagh Grange and Blewberry estates, throwing themselves on the charity of the Court. One of the Dutton pensioners admitted in 1729 was grand-niece " to the late Rev. Dr John Townson, vicar of Bremhill, Wilts, a very considerable Benefactor to your Corporation." Many years earlier, in 1698, " a certificate being produced well-attested on the behalfe of Theobald Townson, Cozen German of Dr Townson deceased, setting forth his great age and his poore and miserable circumstances," the Court gave him £5, and practically admitted him to a pension of that amount.

Such pensions were not often needed in the case of men, nor are they any oftener now. But the maiden daughters of the clergy in their old age are a natural object of sympathy, and this part of the Corporation's work has grown and is capable of further growth without becoming greater than the needs of the case.

Mistress Dutton's bequest has been followed by several others ; when a bequest of £23,000 from Vice-Admiral Sir Peter Denis [1] came to the Corporation in 1794, the Court at once resolved to increase these maiden pensioners to one hundred and their allowance from five guineas to seven ; to-day pensions of from £10 to £30 [2] a year are given to over three hundred maiden ladies.

But the young children of the poor ministers were felt to have equal claims. Life lay all before them, and it was then, as now, the first step which cost. Somehow they must be given a good start. And the wisdom of our forefathers provided in apprenticeship a system which our less patient age has almost discarded, to the great disadvantage of our commerce. When the Corporation began its work this system was in full vigour, and the Court turned to it instinctively as a means of helping without pauperising. So natural did this course seem that we find " Madam Mary Reynolds," widow of Edward Reynolds, the saintly Bishop of Norwich (1661–76), leaving £100 in her will " To the Company at London for binding out Ministers Children Apprentices." Her son, Archdeacon Reynolds,[3] made no difficulty about paying the money to the Corporation ; and, indeed, the very Court at which the legacy was announced (June 10th,

---

[1] This son of a Huguenot refugee minister fought at Quiberon Bay in 1759 and died a Vice-Admiral of the Red in 1778.

[2] The amounts should now be stated as " from £20 to £40."

[3] Edward Reynolds, born 1630. St. Paul's School and Merton Coll., Oxford. Fellow of Magdalen Coll., 1650–60. Prebendary of Worcester, 1660–98. Archdeacon of Norfolk, 1661–98. Venn. *Al. Cantab.* iii. 444.

1684) proved the Corporation's right to it. For it
spent that day £80 in binding out the children of rural
clergy. One was bound to Nathanael Ferriby, a wax
chandler in Bow Lane, and a good friend of the Charity ;
another to a "Writeing Master" of "Castleyard in
Holborne " ; and a girl was committed to a sempstress
" of St. Martens in yᵉ Feilds." In the goodness of
their hearts the Assistants did not stop at the fees.
For in 1685 John Tovey, an apothecary in the Strand,
was willing to take a parson's son as his apprentice
and at present had him " upon likeing," but he insisted
on the fee of £15 " being pay'd in hand," and also
" Clothes after the Rate of foure pounds a year all the
time of the said Apprenticeship " (eight years). One
after another the members of the Court then present
offered the cost of a year's clothes for the boy till the
whole sum had been raised in the room. In the same
connection we come upon the only mention of Archbishop Sancroft in the records. William Sancroft,[1]
his nephew, announced to the Court in 1690 that as
executor to " one Mʳ Benjamin Maldon late Rector of
Sundrith " [? Sundridge] he had to pay over £10 to
the Corporation. He asked for £5 in order to apprentice a boy, and was given this sum on the understanding
that " My Lords Grace of Canterbury would ffurnish
him with Clothes."

It was not the least of the benefits of apprenticeship
that it enabled a generous person who had provided

---

[1] Probably son of Thomas Sandcroft or Sancroft, of Ufford Hall,
Fressingfield. Admitted as pensioner to Emmanuel Coll., Camb.,
1665. Died 1713. *Ibid.* iv. 12, 13.

the fees to keep a friendly eye on the 'prentice himself. Unless the boy ran away, the patron always knew where to find him. This accounts for the anxiety of the Corporation's benefactors to be allowed to administer some of their gifts themselves. Archdeacon Reynolds, in paying over his mother's bequest, asked permission to dispose of £10 himself for the same object. Sometimes subscribers had a subscription returned to them in order to use it in binding a *protégé*; for instance, in 1683 Mr. James Paul, one of the original Treasurers, " who hath subscribed Ten pounds per Annum," was " allowed his last annuall subscription due at Michaelmasse last past towards putting out a poore boy (being the Son of a clergyman) by him recommended to this Court," provided that the Court approved the trade and the master. It was the same Mr. Paul who, having had a boy bound to him by the Court among the batch of apprentices in 1684, took the boy without fee, and set £5 at liberty for the binding of another. If other funds of the same sort failed, the Sons of the Clergy came to the rescue. Dr. Dove, of St. Bride's, was granted £3 10s., which he had advanced towards the apprenticing fee of Widow Ayscough's daughter " upon the promise of Sʳ Thomas Fitch, one of the Trustees of the Right Revᵈ ffather in God Lancelot [Andrewes] late Lord Bishop of Winchester to allow him five pounds out of the said Charity last Christmas, which he did not performe."

This apprenticing work brings us to the first mention in the Corporation records of the Stewards of the

Festival.   It is in the year 1680, and there is a petition
before the Court " on the behalfe of one Charles Gosse,"
who is at once " recommended to the Present Stewards
of the Feast as a great Object of Charity and worthy
of their Favour."   I have found no definite arrangement between the Court and the Stewards that the
latter should devote themselves to this work of providing the parsons' children with apprenticeship fees.
Certainly the arrangement was made, and it need not
be doubted that this was what the Court meant when
they recommended this boy to the Stewards.   Twenty
years pass, and in 1700 there is a resolution of the
Court " that all the preceeding Stewards bee desired
to give an accompt of what Child^n have been put out
by them and to whome, and that one bee employed att
the Charge of the Corporation to attend the Stewards
and that the Stewards for the time being bee applyed
to upon the same accompt and Mr Williams the
Messenger is ordered to take care thereof."   The two
bodies, however, were so interlaced that the work of
one was in effect the work of both, and the enormous
apprenticeship work done by the Stewards may as well
have its recognition in this place.   The early details
are not forthcoming.   The Stewards' books have been
either lost or burnt, till we come to John Bacon's books
of 1774 and onwards.   Then we can take a view of
a succession of years, 1774 to 1814, with the exception
of 1799 to 1802 inclusive, whose results for some reason
are not given.   These thirty-seven years provided the
fees of 1,450 children, or an average of rather less than

forty each year, at an average annual outlay of about
£1,000. The lists give the names of the children,
the name and occupation of the tradesman and his
residence. All parts of the country are impartially
represented ; London is by no means predominant ;
and the trades are of every description. " Mantua-
makers " and milliners and " Black Milliners " abound,
for quite as many girls as boys received the benevolence
of the Stewards. There are mentions of a " mistress
of a Boarding School," an " Attorney at Law," a
" Schoolmaster of Soho Square, Middlesex," " William
Clowes, Mathematical Master, Chichester " ; " Luke
Herman Coleridge,[1] to John Kestell, Surgeon, Ottery
St. Mary," in 1779, and Ann Coleridge [2] to some Exeter
milliners in 1781, brother and sister of the " logician,
metaphysician, bard " ; a Scrivener ; " William Hudson, Musician, York " ; and surgeons in plenty ; but
naturally the professions are not as much to the front
as the trades. John Bacon, of whom more will be
heard later, could look back with natural complacency
on the fact that there had passed through his hands
for this work of apprenticing no less a sum than
£30,000 up to the year 1799, when he ceased to be
Secretary of the Festival. Of course, like many other
things, the cost of binding apprentices tended to rise.
In the early days £5 or £10 mostly sufficed, but in

[1] Father of William Hart Coleridge, Bishop of Barbados (died
1849). Luke was at the London Hospital under Sir William
Blizard, set up practice at Thorverton and died in 1790, aged
24. Lord Coleridge, *Story of a Devonshire House*, p. 54.
[2] She died unmarried.

the middle of the eighteenth century it was necessary to rearrange some of their charities. Thus in 1761 Miller's charity for binding two children yearly at a cost of £20 was found to be accumulating " for want of Proper Objects offering on Account of the Smallness of the Consideration," and it was decided to assign £20 instead of £10 in each case. But at the end of that century £50, £60, and even £100 were paid by the Stewards as single fees.

Nor were they wholly addicted in their operations to trade and commerce. The universities claimed their quota of the parsons' sons, and, if the claim could not have been met, the Church would have had to face then her present problem of the shrinkage in the number of candidates for Holy Orders. But there are no early signs of this educational part of their work having been done to any systematic extent. There may have been more of it than we know, for the books do not specify the object of the gifts to " children." For instance, the munificent Seth Ward, who himself collected or provided £25,000 for the repairs of Exeter Cathedral at the Restoration, and who died Bishop of Salisbury in 1689, left a legacy of £200 to be distributed among children, and his wife, Aletheia, in paying in his gift, " desired that Ten pounds thereof might be given to the Two Children of Mr William West,[1]

[1] He was Succentor of Salisbury Cathedral, 1675–83. On his appointment Bishop Seth Ward assigned a " preaching turn " to the Succentor, and recorded West's promise either to preach or to provide a preacher each St. Barnabas' Day. *Fasti Eccles. Sarisber.*, pp. 272, 444.

late sub chanter of the church of Sarum and Rector of Boscomb in the county of Wilts." Such gift may well have had an educational purpose. But here also the Stewards had to some extent made themselves responsible in the Corporation's stead. Their Constitutions of 1749 empowered them " to raise a fund for *Educating* such of the said Orphans as are not of a proper Age to be bound *Apprentices*." For lack of authorities I am unable to bridge the time between 1749 and 1774, the year when John Bacon's minute book begins ; but in his list of apprentices for the latter year an asterisk against one child's name points to the following note :—

The child marked thus hath been maintained and educated since the death of her Father, at the school in *Hoxton Square*, for some years past (to the great relief of her distressed Mother) by the *Society* of Stewards and Subscribers for maintaining and educating *Poor Orphans* of the *Clergy* till of Age to be put *Apprentice*.

This note is repeated next year with an additional explanation to the effect that

this above-mentioned (formed in 1749) is a preparatory Institution, supported by the annual Subscriptions and Benefactions of Ladies and Gentlemen, to educate, cloath, and maintain the Sons and Daughters, *Orphans of distressed Clergymen*, till of Age to be recommended to the said Stewards to be apprenticed.

In 1776 " the school in Hoxton Square " is replaced by " the School at Thirsk in Yorkshire." In 1779 the two schools are given side by side, and it becomes clear that girls were sent to Hoxton Square and boys to Thirsk. After 1780 there are no more asterisks, and the children apprenticed have therefore no apparent connection with the " Preparatory Institution," but it continues to be described, and its Treasurer's name is given at the foot of the annual list as usual till the end of the eighteenth century. But the list of 1809 contains the following addition :—

There are now near One Hundred poor Orphans under the care and protection of that Society, who are educated in a Manner to render them useful Members of the Community ; but from the great increase of Numbers of late admitted into the Schools of the Institution, and the vast Advance in every Article of Consumption, the Society has lately been under the painful Necessity of limiting the Numbers to be elected into their Schools on Account of their Finances, whereby several poor deserving Objects have been delayed from being admitted under their Patronage.

And then, to mark the close connection between the Sons of the Clergy and this " Preparatory Institution " of the Stewards and their friends, it is added that contributions " are thankfully received by J. M. Grimwood Esq. No 2. *Bloomsbury Place*, Registrar of the

Society." Grimwood held the double office for no long time, but we cannot pursue the subject further without trespassing on the ground of other folks. For this " institution," to which our Stewards gave birth, flourishes in our day as the Clergy Orphan Corporation, and the connection is shown in the frequent presence of our Registrars upon its Board. The existence and work of this society may at any rate be held to absolve our Assistants from any charge of having neglected the needs of young children.[1]

Higher education and exhibitions to the Universities formed no part of the Charity's regular operations till special benefactions made it necessary. This is not quite what might be expected from the presence on the Court of Tobias Rustat, the founder of the scholarships for sons of clergy at Jesus College, Cambridge. Strangely enough, the first benefaction of this kind brought the Corporation into relations with the same college. It came from Dr. Gatford,[2] who had been a

---

[1] I regret that in the interval I have gained no fresh light upon the origin of the Clergy Orphan Corporation, which was incorporated in 1809, the year of the extract last given. It is quite clear that the activities to which the new Corporation then succeeded were the outcome of the labours of the Stewards of our Festival. Exactly when, and exactly why, there was a severance about 1800 is wrapt in mystery.

[2] Lionel Gatford was the son of Lionel Gatford, who was of Sussex origin, a Fellow of Jesus Coll., Camb., and rector of Dennington, Suffolk. There is a long account of the father's arrest by Oliver Cromwell and his subsequent privations in Walker's *Sufferings*, ii. 255. The son was a scholar of Jesus Coll. ; rector of St. Dionis Backchurch, 1680 ; Archdeacon of St. Albans, 1713 ; Treasurer of St. Paul's, 1714 ; and held these offices till his death in September, 1715. He was President of Sion College in 1703.

member of the Court of Assistants, and was announced
to a meeting in October, 1715 :—

> Dr Gatford had given two Annuitys of £50 p.
> ann. each payable out of the Exchequer for the
> remainder of a term of 99 yeares to the Corporaĉon
> Upon the following Trusts, Viz^t :—As to one £50
> p. ann. . . . that the Corporaĉon do yearly pay
> the same to ten poor Widows of Clergymen who
> had lived in good repute for their learning sobriety
> and firm constancy in the Principles of the Church
> of England as by Law Established, the Widows
> themselves being of a grave and unblemished
> Conversation and of agreeable ffortune and Parent-
> age before they were marryed, And as to the
> other £50 . . . that the Corporaĉon shall yearly
> pay £20 part thereof to such two of the Sons of
> deceased Clergymen as are placed in Jesus Colledge
> in Cambridge, vizt to each of them £10 half yearly
> from the time of their taking their Batchellor of
> Arts to their Master of Arts degree if they reside
> in the Colledge so long, The Master and ffellows to
> approve of such Clergymens Sons as they usually
> do the Schollars of the house, And that the
> Corporaĉon pay the remaining £30 equally yearly
> for putting out 3 Clergymens Daughters Appren-
> tices or for setting up their Trades after they have
> served their times honestly and carefully.

A rule was passed by the Court a few months later
that no pensioner should hereafter be " admitted into
Dr Gatfords or any other appropriated Charity of

greater value unless they relinquish their present
Pention "; but it can hardly be supposed that this
refers to University exhibitioners, for whom no endowments were hitherto in the hands of the Corporation.
The bequest was soon doing its proper work. In
July, 1716, nine months after it had been announced,
there came a letter to the Register from "D[r] Ashton [1]
Ma[r] of Jesus Colledge Cambridge acquainting him that
they had fixed upon the schollars pursuant to D[r] Gatfords will and desiring payment of their Sallarys."
Thereafter, these gifts became a matter of routine and
were mentioned no more.[2]

There were evidently other funds from which the
Court could provide exhibitions if they saw fit, for in
1723 an allowance of £10 is mentioned as being made
to the son of Dr. John Broughton [3] "out of D[r]

---

[1] Charles Ashton was Master of Jesus Coll. and Prebendary of
Ely, 1701–52.

[2] The income of Gatford's fund is about £190 a year. The Charity
Commissioners issued a scheme for its use in 1856.

[3] John Broughton, son of Rev. Thomas Broughton, vicar of
Bishop Wearmouth, was of Christ's Coll., Cambridge. D.D. 1716.
Chaplain to the Duke of Marlborough. The allowance was evidently needed for his son Thomas, who passed into college at
Eton, 1716–20, from the schools of St. Andrew, Holborn ; thence
to St. Paul's School, and a sizarship at Caius ; vicar of Bedminster
and Prebendary of Sarum, 1744–72.

That egregious gossip and place-hunter, Edmund Pyle, D.D.,
Chaplain-in-Ordinary to George II., has a characteristic paragraph
in a letter to Dr. Kerrich, which bears, I think, on this case. The
letter is dated, " Xmas Day 1756 " and is franked " B. Winchester "
[i.e. Hoadly] :—

" A London clergyman, whose name I can't recollect, to whom
the Archbishop [Herring] took a liking, as Secretary to the Cor-

13

Cave's [1] charity to enable him to follow his studies at
the University." In 1729 came another appropriated
charity in the shape of £100 a year from Mr. Edward
Pauncefort.[2] There came to be an accumulation of
£300 on this bequest, and the Court ordered £180 to
be handed " to such person as the Dean of Christ
Church College in Oxford shall depute to receive the
same for the benefitt of poor Servitors in the said
college according to the Directions of the Will." It
will be noticed that here, as in the case of Dr. Gatford's
bequest, it was the College, not our Corporation,
which selected the beneficiaries, but it can hardly be
doubted that in both cases the Corporation had a
chance to assist those whom it knew to be deserving

poration of the Sons of the Clergy (or, that of 1st fruits and tenths,
or some such fraternity) is the person to whom Shuckford's living
in town was given (by the Church of Canterbury)."

Now, " Shuckford's living in town " was All Hallows, Lombard
Street, to which in 1755 the Archbishop (not, as Pyle says, " the
Church of Canterbury ") appointed the Rev. Thomas Broughton,
who was secretary of S.P.C.K. 1743–77, and who is not to be
identified with the man whom the Stewards helped out of Dr.
Cave's charity. Pyle's Thomas Broughton was eleven years old
when the other was entering Cambridge. A. Hartshorne, *Memoirs
of a Royal Chaplain*, p. 283. Hennessey, *Repertorium Londinense*,
lvii., confuses the two by making Broughton of All Hallows,
Lombard Street, a Prebendary of Sarum.

[1] William Cave, D.D. (1637–1713) was the son of Rev. John
Cave, a " sequestered " minister. He graduated from St. John's
Coll., Camb., in 1656, became chaplain to Charles II., vicar of
Islington, 1662–69 ; rector of All Hallows the Great, 1679–89 ;
canon of Windsor, 1684, and vicar of Isleworth, 1690. He held
the last two till his death on August 4th, 1713. He published in
two folio volumes *Scriptorum Ecclesiasticorum Historia Litteraria*,
re-issued with his own corrections in 1740.

[2] Of the parish of St. Margaret, Westminster.

among its particular *clientèle*. An instance of this
comes to hand in the shape of a letter to Mr. Michael
Hillersdon, an Assistant :—

> S[r]
>
>   I am directed by a Friend of mine in London to
> apply to you for the Payment of an Exhibition
> due to me from the Corporation of the Sons of the
> Clergy, Be pleas'd S[r] to pay it to the Bearer of
> this who is a Friend of my Tutor Mr. Arnald to
> whom the money is due and you will highly oblige
> S[r] your very Humble allready oblig'd Servant
>   GILBERT WALTON.[1]

This letter is dated " Finedon, Aug. 18, 1729," and
Finedon is the ancestral home of the Dolben family,
to whose interest young Walton would doubtless owe
his exhibition.

In regard to the subsequent history of this department of the work, it is impossible to suppress the
notion that it hardly received its full measure of attention.   Thus, in 1787, they found that there had been
no application since 1781 for Dr. Cave's exhibition of
£10 for a parson's son at the University—which would

---

[1] Gilbert Walton graduated from Emmanuel Coll., Camb., in
1729.   His father, Rev. John Walton, was schoolmaster and curate
of Finedon.   Venn, *Al. Cantab.* iv. 327.   His " Tutor Mr. Arnald "
was Richard Arnald, Fellow of Emmanuel, 1720, who in 1733
accepted the college benefice of Thurcaston, Leics. (the birthplace
of Hugh Latimer).   At his death in 1756 he was succeeded as
incumbent by Richard Hurd, afterwards Bishop of Worcester (cf.
E. H. Pearce, *Hartlebury Castle*, pp. 282–4).

hardly have occurred had it been duly advertised. So
they funded the arrears, making the £10 into £13,
and arranged to give half to a scholar at Oxford
and half to one at Cambridge. The same system
prevails to-day, but the income has just doubled
itself, each exhibitioner receiving £13. The first
Cambridge recipient under this scheme was a Sizar
of St. John's College, Cambridge, in 1789. To-day
the Sons of the Clergy are doing a splendid work in
this direction, on a scale which would be called large
if it were not capable of infinite increase. During
1901 they spent £4,868 in apprentice fees, educational
grants to students, both boys and girls, at the Universities and at schools, and outfits to enable them to
make a start in some employment.[1] The total number
benefited was 420 (267 boys and 153 girls), of whom
93 were orphans. About 80 of these were students
proceeding to a degree at some University, and others
were at theological colleges. A moment's thought will
show the importance of increasing these possibilities
at the present time. For it has hitherto been most
frequently the prophet's son who has taken up the
prophet's mantle and gone into the Church's work
with the heir's double portion of the prophet's spirit.
To-day the prophet has fallen on evil times; his very
mantle is scarcely worth handing on, and his son
cannot be prepared for the exercise of the father's
spirit because the father cannot afford to give him the

[1] The sum thus spent in 1927 had risen to £7,991 and the number
of young recipients to 603.

necessary education. The times require a strong effort in this direction, and the Corporation has all the experience and all the machinery that are needed to give such effort the fullest scope. There could be no better memorial of the 275th Festival than a great addition to these educational activities of the Sons of the Clergy.

CHAPTER X

THE FESTIVAL AND ITS STEWARDS

THE annual service of the Sons of the Clergy is the feature of the life of the Corporation which appeals most to the public at large. For one person who knows anything of the multifarious benevolence of the Charity there are hundreds who know that such a service is annually held and thousands who have been present at it in our own day. It has been held without interruption [1] since 1674, but the first known service of the kind took place in 1655, when " Mr *George Hall*,[2] Minister at St Botolph's Aldersgate, Preached at St Paul's, to the Sons of Ministers, the 8th of November, 1655." [3] That sermon was printed the same year " at the Gilded Lyon in St *Paul's Church Yard*," very much as the great majority of the annual sermons have been printed ever since, and, as we shall see, there is nothing about it to suggest that it is the first of its series. It throws a flood of light on the tolerance of the Cromwellian administration that it should be possible for an orthodox minister, himself deprived of several preferments, and the son of a

[1] Except by the General Strike in 1926.

[2] Son of Joseph Hall, Bishop of Exeter and Norwich (deprived 1647). Born at Waltham Abbey ; Fellow of Exeter Coll., Oxford, 1632–8 ; vicar of Menheniot and Archdeacon of Cornwall (deprived). His appointment to St. Botolph, Aldersgate, is a mystery. Bishop of Chester, May 11th, 1662 (consecrated at Ely House, Holborn). Died August 23rd, 1668. Stubbs, *Reg. Sacr. Anglic.*, p. 123.

[3] Freeman, " Compleat List," 1733.

deprived bishop, to plead in the chief church of the
capital before the sons of orthodox ministers the cause
of the widow and the fatherless among their order. It
was only in March of the previous year, 1654, that
Cromwell had set up his commission of " Triers " for
" the approbation of public preachers," who were to
be in permanent session in London, and without whose
certificate no one was to be " able and fit to preach
the Gospel." To these were added in August, 1654, a
commission of " Ejectors," distributed throughout
England with a view to the removal of " scandalous "
ministers. They were to take account, not merely of
morals, but of predilections ; they were to eject not
only Papists but Prayer-book men as well. Triers and
Ejectors alike were to " discern something of the grace
of God " in a man before he could be nominated to,
or confirmed in, his benefice. Anyone who considers
that these commissions were composed of Presby-
terians, Independents, and Baptists, as the recognised
" three sorts of godly men," and of any others who
had " the root of the matter " in them will not need
to be told that they went about their work with a will
and not without animus. " Many thousands of souls,"
said Richard Baxter, who was not inclined to be partial
to the new administration, " blessed GOD for the
faithful ministers whom they let in," and he is perhaps
justified in his statement that there were " ignorant,
ungodly, drunken teachers " among those whom they
expelled. But, when all was said, the cause of the
expulsion was not their drunkenness or disorderliness,

but their disaffection towards the new Government,
and while the Church may have been the purer for the
loss of some of them, those who expelled them did so
not to purify the Church but as a matter of conscience,
and equally as a matter of conscience the ejected submitted to ejection. Now, when conscience is in question, men's hearts are harder than at other times ; but
still George Hall was allowed to plead the sad case of
the widow and the orphan in St. Paul's, and the Cromwellian soldiery, who at least knew the inside of the
Cathedral, did not stop him when he gave out Numbers xvii. 8 as his text—a challenge in itself—and spoke
of the expelled ministers as " Venerable Wanderers,"
" who ill became their condition, and the Relicts of
worthy servants of GOD (sufferers for a good conscience)
eating Ashes as Bread and mingling their Drink (if
they had any) with Weeping . . . their Children in
worse case than the young Ravens which God feedeth
when they call upon Him." These are not the words
of a man who was afraid to speak, and the fact that
they were then and there uttered is creditable alike to
preacher and Protector.

But, indeed, George Hall's sermon, which occupies
thirty pages of close print, is worth a closer inspection.
It has a quaint address to the reader. " My comming
forth," he says, " into this open light, who have
rejoyced in my close retyrednesse, is as if the Batt
should stare the Sun in the face at noon day." The
service " fell unexpectedly upon me by Lot " : " I was
not a little tempted to decline the employment." " I

was ingaged betweene opposite Parties, which I was to
Speake unto ; the rigid Punctilio-men, both of the
right hand and of the left ; unto whom to speake of
anything tending to Moderation is the same thing as
to bring severall swelling mountaines together to grow
into one even ground." But charity was his object,
and charity in its two senses. Though the whole sermon is well worth reading, we are only concerned with
the light it throws on the circumstances under which
it was delivered. It is, he notes, an " extraordinary
occasion." It is " a Meeting not of Vanity but Piety " ;
not " that it may be spoken how many of the Lords
people are Sons of the Prophets," but because God
" hath given us this occasion of a free and solemne
Convention." But the preacher clearly considered it
an occasion for plain speaking. " To the stopping of
the mouthes of our Vilifiers and Contemners we will
plead the high dignity of our Office." " And here to
all Antiministeriall Spirits (perhaps some may be
within hearing) unto whom we are such eye-sores, and
who would insinuate us to be such Cyphers, I offer
this to be chew'd upon." " Because I see . . . our
Ministry is hard beset by Papists on the one hand and
Sectaries on the other, I cannot but borrow a few sands
of my houre to Apologize." " Our Brother Anabaptist
—(St Francis was so mannerly that he used to call
every Beast Brother, as our Quakers now are pleased
to call us Fellow-Creatures)." Again and again he
makes it obvious that his audience is composed definitely of the sons of the clergy. " Next to the debaucht

scandalous Minister, which I acknowledge to be the greatest eye soare in the World, . . . is the scandalous Son of a good Minister, he throwes dirt in his Fathers Face." Hall states that benevolence " is indeed the grand motive and inducement of our summoning one another this day," and hints, as Manton did after him, that the feasting should be kept in a subordinate place. What he never does is to say or imply that this was the first sermon of its kind or its series.

But, stranger still, we find a statement in Manton's life, that " the custom of preaching to the Sons of the Clergy began in Dr. Manton's time ; Dr. Hall preached the first Sermon to them, as Dr. Manton did the Second." This sermon [1] from Psalm cii. 28, which is printed in his works, is headed, without any date, as having been " preached before the Sons of the Clergy," and the internal evidence is conclusive on the point. When we look into the external circumstances, there are facts which help out the notion. Manton was ordained deacon at Exeter by Joseph Hall, the father of the first Festival preacher. At St. Paul's, Covent Garden, he succeeded his father-in-law, Obadiah Sedgwick, who was almost certainly a relative of Obadiah and the other Sedgwicks, who afterwards became earnest members of the Court of Assistants. His connection with the work was therefore not remote. It is true that Dr. William Harris, Manton's biographer, is no Isaak Walton, but, accepting his record in this particular, we appear to start with three facts : first,

[1] Vol. iii. 116 (folio) ; Complete Works (Nisbet, 1873), vol, xv. 463.

that Hall's sermon was actually the first of the series
(though Hall himself does not say so) ; secondly, that
there was some regularity about the effort, the natural
conclusion from the statement being that Manton's
sermon followed in 1656, the year of his appointment
to St. Paul's, Covent Garden ; thirdly, that the Charity
was not confined to orthodox clergy (and so presumably not to orthodox laity), for Manton, though not a
regicide, and subsequently chaplain to Charles II., was
still a member of the Westminster Assembly and was
a convinced Presbyterian to the end of his days.   There
is therefore nothing inherently improbable in the sup-
position that during the three succeeding years of the
Commonwealth the anniversary was continued by the
preaching at St. Paul's " to the Sons of Ministers, then
solemnly assembled," as the phrase runs on the title-
page of George Hall's sermon.   But that is guess-work,
and to guess-work we are left till we come to the
evidence supplied by a little book " printed for William
Mears at the Lamb on Ludgate Hill " in 1733.   It is
called " A COMPLEAT LIST of the Stewards, Presidents, Vice-Presidents, and Treasurers belonging to
the ROYAL CORPORATION, for the Relief of the Poor
Widows, and Children of Clergymen, from the time
their Charter was granted . . . together with the Names
of all the Preachers, and at what Churches the Sermons
were preached, and which of them were printed to this
present time. . . ."   Written in ink on the copy in the
possession of the Corporation, along with many other
notes, is the name of the compiler, " Wm Freeman.

A.B. Lecturer of St. Butolphs Aldersgate," who may
have been attracted to the subject by an Aldersgate
man's interest in Dr. Hall, and whose object was
certainly to draw attention to the worth of the Charity.
But he could have done that and still have told us
from what authorities he compiled his list of preachers
and his record of each year's Stewards, and why it
is that there are no details of any anniversary between 1655 and 1674. There is not the slightest
reason to doubt his information, but I have come upon
practically no means of confirming it, except that of
referring to the sermons stated by him to have been
printed.

The first of these after Dr. Hall's was Thomas Sprat's,
preached in 1678, and published by him in a volume
of *Sermons Preached on Several Occasions* in 1697. This
particular sermon is described as having been delivered
" at the Anniversary Meeting of the Sons of Clergy-
Men " on November 7th, 1678 (five months after the
granting of the Charter). By the way, we would gladly
exchange Pearson's sermon of 1675 and Gunning's of
1676 for this of Sprat's, but we can at least see what
light it throws on the history of the Festival.

> " These friendly and charitable meetings, Men,
> Fathers, and Brethren," he begins, " you have
> now, by the blessing of GOD, *for several years,*
> *renewed* with no just offence to any, tho with the
> grief, and envy perhaps of some, who are not of
> our Household of Faith. . . . Of these our Annual
> Solemnities there being two principal intentions

[to prove the propriety of clerical marriage and to encourage charity]. For your former worthy beginnings of this kind having lately received incouragement by a Royal Establishment ; I cannot but believe that this advantage has inspir'd all your hearts with the most chearful resolutions, to perfect . . . what you yourselves had before so generously attempted." " You are now," he says towards the end of his first hour, " you are now, with happy and auspicious beginnings, forming a Model of Charity. . . . The opportunity . . . is peculiar and extraordinary. Not only of this one day, or of other such days, which I trust will always succeed this once a year ; but the sure and solid foundation of a perpetual Corporation."

Such phrases are both definite and inconclusive. They establish the fact, which we know already, that the Charter only dignified a work which was already well in hand, but they give us no definite *data* as to the beginnings of the Festival, and are quite consistent with Freeman's record that the sermons were resumed in 1674.

At that date St. Paul's Cathedral was still a ruin, Wren having just abandoned his first design, and the Stewards turned to one of the first City churches which Wren rebuilt after the fire. In 1674 and 1675 John Dolben and John Pearson preached to the Sons of the Clergy at St. Michael, Cornhill, and from 1676 to 1696 the Festival made its home at St. Mary le Bow, Cheapside, whose rebuilding was not wholly accomplished till 1680. It was only in 1697 that they were admitted to Wren's great cathedral, which year by year they have visited ever since. We are therefore dealing with what is by far the oldest anniversary service of its kind in the English Church, and it may not be lost labour if we recall the system upon which it was organised.

THE STEWARDS

It is fair that the first place should be given to those who constituted the management of this ancient ceremony, and whose names are on record from 1674 onwards to this year of grace. We start with a list of sixteen, which continued to be the regular number till 1695, when they fell to twelve, and so continued till the opening years of the nineteenth century, when the willingness of the Royal Dukes to serve the office in turn tended to increase the number, which now cannot be too large for the good of the Charity. But in the early days the Stewards managed the anniversary in person. Their number therefore must not be too large to cause confusion, nor too small to compass the work. If they fixed on sixteen or on twelve, it was with this in view ; and the need of making up their *quorum* provoked one of the very few references to the Stewards in the early books of the Corporation. It is in 1715 and is to this effect :—

A representation being made to the Court by the present Stewards that there were four Stewards

wanting for the ffeast for this year and the great
difficulty to procure persons to serve, the Rev^d
Mr Houblon [1] and the Rev. Mr Lewis [2] were pleased
generously to offer themselves to bear the Charge
and Expense of two persons to represent them as
Stewards.

To the latter part of this minute we must return later ;
for the present it is useful, as showing their system
of having a certain number to do definite work.

If it be asked what sort of men undertook this office,
the answer is, first, that at the outset the men who
worked for the Festival were the men who were busy
in the Corporation. Of the Assistants appointed by
King Charles' Charter in 1678 over a score had served
as Stewards during the preceding years, 1674–7. But,
secondly, for at least forty years the Stewards were
composed entirely of laymen. Sprat's sermon in 1678
hinted that there was method in this arrangement,
according to the notion, not yet quite exploded, that
the clergy are " mere children " in business and
organisation. " If any shall think," he said, " that
in the practical prudence of managing such gifts, the
Laity may have some advantage over the Clergy ;
whose experience is and ought to be less of this World

[1] This is Rev. Jacob Houblon, Corpus Christi Coll., Camb. B.A.
1687 ; rector of Bobbingworth, Essex, 1692–1740. Venn, *Al.
Cantab.* ii. 412 f. His father, also Rev. Jacob Houblon, was admitted Perne Fellow of Peterhouse, July 24th, 1654, and was rector
of Moreton, Essex, 1662–98. Cf. T. A. Walker, *Admissions to
Peterhouse,* p. 106 f.

[2] Rev. George Lewis ; perhaps vicar of Westerham, Kent, 1706–
48.

than the others : That in your Corporation is most
wisely supplied. As there are Churchmen enough in
this Pious Foundation, most able to advise the good
Works ; so there are Laymen enough most able to
direct their Uses."   Anyhow, the first clergy to appear
among the Stewards were the two mentioned in the
minute quoted above, Jacob Houblon and George
Lewis. Freeman's " Compleat List " is most careful
to note one apparent exception.   In 1704 the list was
headed by " Thomas Sprat Esqre," and there is a
manuscript note that " he entered soon after into Holy
Orders and preached the next Sermon."   If anyone is
rude enough to remark that the lay Steward of 1704
was by 1705 " Arch Deacon of Rochester," of which
diocese his father was Bishop, it is not easy to deny
that young Sprat's circumstances were favourable to
fairly rapid promotion.[1]   But the clergy, having begun
to serve as Stewards, did not draw back.   Houblon
and Lewis were followed in 1716 by John Dolben, Sub-
Dean of the Chapel Royal—the Dolbens were always
ready for any work for the Sons of the Clergy—and
Archdeacon Cumberland[2] ; and after that there were

[1] Thomas Sprat, junior, was admitted K.S. at Westminster,
1692, and elected to Christ Church, 1697 ; was called to the Bar,
Middle Temple, 1700. Ordained deacon and priest, 1704. Prebendary and Archdeacon of Rochester, 1704 ; vicar of Boxley,
1705 ; rector of Stone, 1707 ; Prebendary of Winchester, 1712 ;
Prebendary of Westminster, 1713 ; and retained all these till his
death in 1720 at the age of forty-one. F.R.S. 1712.

[2] Richard Cumberland, Magdalene Coll., Camb. Archdeacon of
Northampton, 1707. Son of Richard Cumberland, Bishop of
Peterborough.

BISHOP SPRAT AND HIS SON.
From the engraving by I. Smith, 1712

188]

three or four parsons on each year's list, such as
Manningham, Sacheverell, Trapp, and Waterland.
Sherlock served in 1727, when he was " Lord Bishop
of *Bangor* Elect," but more as one of the most energetic
workers in the cause than as an incipient prelate.   The
first Dean to serve was Dr. Edward Cresset, of Hereford, in 1741, and in 1743 we come upon the first
Bishop Steward in the person of Dr. Herring, Archbishop of York, who was joined by Maddox, of St.
Asaph [1]; and from that time onward there has been
scarce a list without a Bishop upon it to this day.

The question still remains, who the laymen were.
Why could twelve or sixteen men be counted on to
come forward year after year to organise this great
service ?   A comparison of their names with those of
the Assistants would tend to show that about half the
Stewards were intimately engaged in the general work
of the Corporation.   Such men would be merchants
and tradesmen in the City, careful to enter themselves
as " M^r."   A not inconsiderable number were medical
men, doctors of law, and naval and military officers.
There is an occasional judge, and at least one budding
Lord Chancellor, Charles Talbot, who served in 1711.
But the satisfactory feature about these lists is the
recurrence of family names, Dolbens and Wrens and
Sedgwicks and Tenisons and Sherlocks and Atterburys

---

[1] The Festival that year was held on April 14th, and on June 3rd
Horace Walpole was writing to his friend Mann : " Madox of St,
Asaph has wriggled himself into the see of Worcester.   He makes
haste." (*Letters,* ed. 1846, i. 283.)

14

and Houblons and Stillingfleets. Humphrey Henchman, the Bishop of London's son, served in 1674, and
his son, Dr. Humphrey Henchman, Chancellor of the
diocese of London, served in 1717. Their internal
constitution is not obvious. In some years Freeman's
list indicates that they had three Treasurers and a
Vice-President ; in some there is nothing to indicate
any officialdom at all, and as to their place of meeting
I have found just one reference in the Corporation
records during the first half-century. In 1723, on Sir
Christopher Wren's death, the Hon. John Verney,
afterwards Master of the Rolls, was elected Vice-
President of the Corporation at a General Court held
in the Chapter House, St. Paul's. " Mᵣ Verney," the
record adds, " was attending with some of the Stewards
in the Chapterhouse," so " 3 of the Court were desired
to attend him and acquaint him therewith " ; whereupon Mr. Verney came from the room where the
Stewards were sitting into the large room of the Chapter
House, in which, no doubt, the Court would assemble,
and took the oath and the chair. It may be added
here that in 1744 the Stewards, having sent a petition
to the Archbishop, were allowed to meet in the Corporation House in Salisbury Court.

It was not to be expected that a body of this nature,
definitely pledged to definite work, would long remain
a mere appendage of the Corporation ; it would in
time desire an independent organisation. There is no
mention of it in the books of the Sons of the Clergy,
but there is surviving a printed copy of the constitution

which the Stewards set up for themselves in 1749, and which finally led to a separate charity altogether. It is worth giving as it stands :—

CONSTITUTIONS

OF THE

SOCIETY OF STEWARDS

OF THE

SONS OF THE CLERGY

𝔚𝔥𝔢𝔯𝔢𝔞𝔰 great Part of the Clergy of the Church of *England* are ſo ſcantily provided for, (altho' reſtrained from almoſt every *other* Profeſſion) that they are not able to *maintain* their Families, much leſs to *leave* them ſufficient to maintain themſelves in a Manner ſuited to their Character; *for* 𝕽𝖊𝖒𝖊𝖉𝖞 of which Misfortune (an Object of Triumph to the Enemies of the *Proteſtant* Religion) the Piety of our Anceſtors had Eſtabliſhed and endowed the Corporation *for Relief of the poor Widows, and Children of Clergymen,* 𝕬𝖓𝖉 𝖂𝖍𝖊𝖗𝖊𝖆𝖘 the Eſtates and Benefactions of this well-managed Charity fall greatly ſhort of the Number of its Objects; 𝕿𝖔 ſupply which Deficiency in ſome Measure, it has for many Years been the Deſire, and Endeavour of *the Stewards of the Feaſt of the Sons of the Clergy,* to promote an annual Collection towards the putting out ſome of theſe helpleſs Orphans to uſeful, and reputable Trades. 𝖂𝖊, therefore, being deſirous to encourage a conſtant *Succeſſion* of Stewards, in order to perpetuate and improve this very neceſſary and commendable Branch of Charity, and likewiſe to raiſe a Fund for *educating* ſuch of the ſaid Orphans as are not of a proper Age to be bound *Apprentices*, 𝔥𝔞𝔳𝔢 this eighth Day of *June* 1749, agreed to form ourſelves into a Society, and to ſubmit to the following Conſtitutions :—

The rules were twelve in number. The Society so formed was to consist of those who " shall have served, or declared themselves ready to serve, the Office of Steward " or " otherwise to promote " its " charitable intentions." Meetings were to be held monthly " at the *Queen's Arms* Tavern in St. *Paul's Church-Yard, London*," on the last Thursday in each month at 7 p.m. in winter and 8 p.m. in summer. Excepting annual subscribers of a guinea, each member was fined half-a-crown in case of absence from a meeting. At the February meeting they appointed by ballot their chairman, deputy-chairman, treasurer, and secretary. A new member must be proposed by two members at one monthly meeting and elected at the next. The forfeits " after a Deduction of the Charge of Printing, and other *extra* Expences of the Society " were to be applied to the " Maintenance, Education, or Relief of poor Clergymens Children." It is added in a note that " Letters and Benefactions to the SOCIETY are desired to be directed to Mr. GEORGE HAYTER in *Pancras Lane, London*."

This constitution synchronises with the appearance in the Stewards' lists of men not actively engaged in the work of the Corporation,[1] men of great place, too much occupied with other matters to serve the office personally. A few names will show what is meant :— The Earl of Dartmouth (1761), the Duke of Richmond (1762), the Earl of Northumberland (1764), the Duke of Marlborough (1766), the Marquis of Tavistock and the Earl of Bute (1767), the Earl of Radnor (1768), Lord Clive, who had then returned home in shattered health (1769), the Duke of Leeds (1770), the Duke of Grafton and Sir Watkin Williams Wynn (1771), the Duke of Devonshire (1772), Lord North, then First Lord of the Treasury (1774), Earl Bathurst, Lord Chancellor, and Sir John Skynner, Lord Chief Baron, (1778), Lord Thurlow, Lord Chancellor, a munificent friend of the Charity, (1779), the Earl of Salisbury (1783) and his relative the Earl of Exeter (1784), William Pitt, Prime Minister, (1785), Lord Fortescue and Mr. Gosling, the banker, (1786), Sir Richard Jebb, the King's Physician, (1787), Lord Fitzwilliam, Pepper

---

[1] It is clear that a certain amount of pressure was exerted in order to make people feel it a matter of conscience to be Stewards, if they could afford it. Edmund Pyle, D.D., had been asked by Dr. Kerrich to assist in getting a grant for a clergyman's child ; and this was his answer :—" Apr. 21, 1757 . . . I am a little shy of asking anybody to serve a clergyman's child, in the way you speak of, (when it can be done without me ;) because I have been threatened to be made a Steward, which I will not absolutely refuse, but will not perform, till many others, of much greater preferment than mine, have gone thro' that service. Then I am willing " (A. Hartshorne, *Memoirs of a Royal Chaplain*, p. 298). But, though threatened, he managed to evade it.

Arden, the Attorney-General, and the Warden of
Merton (1788), the Duke of Portland (1789) and his son
the Marquis of Titchfield (1790), Speaker Addington
(1791), the Duke of Bedford (1792), Lord Lough-
borough, Lord Chancellor, (1794), Earl Spencer, First
Lord of the Admiralty, (1795), Marquis Cornwallis
(1796), Earl Camden (1799), Sir Francis Baring, M.P.
(1800), Lord Harewood and Sir Robert Peel (1801),
" Right Hon. Robert Peel, Secretary of State for the
Home Department," (1822), the Duke of Rutland,
Lord Bridgewater, Lord Chesterfield, and " Viscount
Nelson, Duke of Brontè," (1804), the Dukes of Norfolk
and Somerset and William Manning, M.P., Cardinal
Manning's father, (1807), the Duke of Newcastle,
" Rev. and Right Hon. Earl Nelson (Duke of Brontè),"
and Viscount Castlereagh (1808), George Canning (1809),
Sir Vicary Gibbs, Knt., Attorney-General, (1811), the
Duke of Buccleuch and Lord Harrowby (1812), Lord
Rolle, of Coronation fame, (1813), the Duke of Devon-
shire, Viscount Palmerston, Lord Calthorpe, and
William Wilberforce (1815), Sir Thomas Dyke Acland,
M.P. (1816), John Archer Houblon, M.P., representative
of a friendly family, (1817), the Earl of St. Germans,
the Right Hon. Nicholas Vansittart, and Sir John
William Lubbock (1820), Lord Somers and Charles
Manners Sutton, the Speaker, (1821), and the Duke of
Wellington (1822). The list could easily be brought
to the present date with an equal number of famous
names, but these will suffice to show the change that
took place, largely through John Bacon's efforts, in the

character of the Stewards' lists during the latter half of the eighteenth century.

Anyone who will consider a list like this, containing the names of men of fame or station, will be able to watch the devolution of the Steward from an active into a merely benevolent friend of the Anniversary. It would be impossible to expect a Lord Chancellor or a Speaker, North or Nelson or Wellington, to do more than give their names and pay their quota, let alone the many members of the Royal House, beginning with the Duke of York in 1798, continuing down to His present Majesty, who served as Steward of the 250th Festival in 1904, and Her Majesty Queen Mary, a gracious helper: Of this we shall speak elsewhere. In the meantime the question is, how the work was done when the Stewards could not do it, and the answer is contained in the extract given above from the Corporation's minutes of 1715. There the two clergy nominated each a substitute, for whom they were at charges, and this no doubt continued to be done where personal service was impossible. Sixty years later, in 1775, we open John Bacon's minute-book, and the exception has become the rule. There are then twelve Stewards, each with his Deputy, and the Deputies are City clergy, such as Peter Whalley,[1] rector of St. Gabriel, Fenchurch Street and St. Margaret Pattens, and Upper Grammar Master of Christ's Hospital, where he had as his assistant the redoubtable James Boyer, of Charles Lamb's essay ; Whalley

[1] Cf. *Annals of Christ's Hospital*, p. 88.

acted as Deputy for a number of years, certainly from
1775 to 1787 and probably earlier. He had as one of
his fellow Deputies "the Revd Mr Disturnell," [1] who
as the head Grecian at Christ's Hospital in 1760 had
welcomed George III. to the City in the customary
Latin speech, which Peter Whalley composed, and
who lived all through the long reign of that King,
surviving him by fourteen years. The other Deputies
were laymen interested in the Charity, and a few, like
Edward Pomfret, the wine merchant, were also interested in the business to which the Anniversary might
lead. It may be added that the fee paid by each
Steward to cover his own and his Deputy's portion
of the expenses was in 1775 35 guineas ; in 1803
it rose to £40, in 1804 to £50, and in 1806 to 50
guineas, as the presence of the Royal Princes at
the anniversaries made the Stewards anxious to
be hospitable beyond their wont. For many years
past, the fee has been fixed at 30 guineas for the
first year and 20 guineas for subsequent years, but
it has now been decided to adopt a " flat rate " of
20 guineas.

The work of the Deputies has long since passed into
the hands of a permanent Festival Committee, over
which the Treasurer of the Festival presides. Apparently the yearly nomination of Deputies came to an
end in 1800, when it is stated that certain clergy
and laymen, eight in number, " were requested, as
a Committee, to assist the Secretary in making the

[1] *Ibid.,* p. 205.

necessary Arrangements for the Rehearsal and Feast Days." [1]

[1] Until recently the Festival Committee, as the modern equivalent of the " Deputies," used to have a rehearsal of the Festival dinner at Vintners' Hall by the kind permission of that ancient guild. We fixed our respective places at the Cathedral ; we settled the *menu* and the wine-list, holding a solemn interview with the caterer ; we made arrangements for the speeches at Merchant Taylors' Hall ; and we were as companionable as John Bacon himself. Then, quite suddenly, we realised that all this might be dispensed with. *Sic transit.*

CHAPTER XI

JOHN BACON AND HIS FRIENDS

THE mystery attaching to the way in which the Festival was organised up to 1775 is suddenly dispelled when we open the elaborate and often humorous minute-book kept by John Bacon [1] as Secretary of the Stewards. He appears to have accepted the office in 1769, when he was thirty-one years of age, and he resigned it in 1799, remaining Treasurer till his death in 1816. Apparently, therefore, he must have used some book previous to the one which survives, and which covers the years 1775 to 1815, when the old man, then not far short of eighty years of age, breaks off in the middle of his last Festival balance-sheet, having just entered £15 as the fee paid for an apprentice on the nomination of William Wilberforce. The minute-book itself is enough to indicate his keen and cheerful nature, as well as his devotion to the Festival, which he attended for forty consecutive years, then

---

[1] A correspondent, Mr. W. L. King, who wrote to me in 1914, and who was investigating the family history, told me that John Bacon's father was John Bacon of Lough Grange, Briscoe, Carlisle. The son was baptised at St. Cuthbert, Carlisle, June 29th, 1736. His mother was a Hetherington of Kirklington, and he inherited some property there. It has been stated, without proof, that he was secretary to Lord North during the American crisis. He was elected F.S.A. in 1774. He was twice married, and had three sons and a daughter by his first wife. At Friern Barnet he had portraits of Lord Keeper Bacon and Roger Bacon, as if to claim kinship, and a fine portrait of himself, which is lost and, it would seem, was never engraved.

missing one through breaking his leg, and returning to his place next year till 1815. In a sense, it was he who made it what it has since become, but what he did most was to promote a friendly companionship among those who took part in it. Hardly a festive gathering has its record in this book brought to a close without a statement that " the Secretary with a few friends stayed and spent the Evening joyously," or " enjoyed themselves till near 12 o'clock when they departed in peace according to the Word," or " spent the remainder of the day in a chearfull harmonious manner," or " with much glee and harmony," or " much festivity and glee." " We continued," he writes of an evening in 1780, " to keep up the Ball till near 11 o'clock when the Secretary was no longer able to support the Chair, so withdrew," and once in sheer merry sarcasm against himself he records that " Mr Bacon and his friends as usual did not stay the evening."

He is not as well known to fame as he ought to be, save at the office of Queen Anne's Bounty, where he is a household word. John Bacon passed most of his life in the First Fruits Office, first as junior clerk to the Deputy-Remembrancer, then as senior clerk (1778), and as Receiver from 1782. In 1786 he published under the title of *Liber Regis, vel Thesaurus Rerum Ecclesiasticarum*,[1] what was really an edition of Ecton's

---

[1] " The Registrar," says a minute of our Court of Assistants of 1795, " was desired to procure a Copy of Bacon's *Liber Regis* for the use of this Court." If he did so, it has disappeared.

Thesaurus, though he made no mention of his predecessor's labours. It is the standard work on the values of English benefices for First-Fruit purposes, but its interest to us lies in the evident sympathy for the poorer clergy which is displayed in Bacon's preface.

> Whoever (he says,) will compare the Greatness of the Duty in many Market Towns and other considerable Parishes with the Smallness of the Recompense for performing such Duty will, from the great Disproportion of the one to the other, be easily convinced of the Necessity of establishing some Method for the better Support of Persons officiating in such Cases. . . . What Fruit is to be expected from the Labours of a Pastor, who, we will suppose, is willing to do all the Good he can, is contented to drudge on with his little Allowance, in hopes of seeing some good Effect from his Labours among his Parishioners, but notwithstanding his best Endeavours falls into Contempt of the meanest of them, which his Poverty alone, without any Personal Demerit of his own to add to it, is sufficient to bring upon him ?

The sentiment might, no doubt, have been expressed in shorter sentences and fewer words, but the man who feels it has " the root of the matter " in him, as far as the work of the Corporation is concerned, and such a man was John Bacon. In his old age, having given the best years of his life, and many of them, to the

Festival, he became one of the Treasurers of the Corporation, then settled in its present abode. His first London home was in Hart Street, Bloomsbury, but about 1783 he went to live at Friern Barnet, and late in life he bought from the Dean and Chapter of St. Paul's their estate at that place, and died at the manor house there in 1816.

Let us, then, take a brief view of a year of John Bacon's work as Secretary to the Stewards of the Festival. As in the days of the 1749 Constitutions, they were still meeting at the " Queen's Arms " in St. Paul's Churchyard. Early in February he would call a meeting at this tavern of the twelve Stewards and their twelve Deputies. He wrote their names in a fine bold hand in his minute-book, with a cross against each of those present. A Steward, who in this case was always an Alderman and in later years the Lord Mayor, was appointed Treasurer, and John Bacon was chosen Secretary. Indeed, the Aldermen appear to have served in rotation, but in 1776 the particular Alderman due to serve refused, and the Lord Mayor agreed to take his place. The next business was to fix the date of the Rehearsal and the Feast, generally the second Tuesday and Thursday in May. There would also, as a rule, be a reference at this meeting to the printing of the last year's sermon ; *e.g.* in 1777 " at this meeting it was agreed to print off three hundred copies of Dr Porteus's Sermon with the addenda as drawn up by the Secretary, and it was ordered that care be taken to deliver the usual number to the

Bishops, Aldermen, Stewards and Deputy Stewards of last year, and that the Messenger have particular Directions respecting the same." After this they would have a preliminary talk about the preacher for the current year, who frequently offered his services, and, having agreed on a suitable date at the end of February for the Union Dinner, they adjourned till then.

The Union Dinner, at which the Stewards and their Deputies sat down together, was the sort of combination of the *utile* and the *dulce* which delighted John Bacon's heart. In describing the 1793 gathering, at which Cornewall,[1] Dean of Canterbury, presided during the first part of the evening, and " the Revd Mr Green,"[2] Prebendary of St. Paul's, for the rest of it—" a better never filled the chair," says Bacon—the Secretary's verdict is that it was " a day of *unanimity*, business, mirth and pleasure," and during his time the description would perhaps serve for most Union Dinners. For the present we return to 1777 and find a company of twenty-one at the " Queen's Arms "—Bishop Porteus, Sir James Eyre, Baron of the Exchequer, an Alderman, Dr. Waller,[3] Archdeacon of Essex, Dr.

[1] Folliott Henry Walker Cornewall. "Who is Dr. Cornewall, the new Dean of Canterbury, and what merit has raised him to that dignity ? " So Hurd wrote from Hartlebury to his friend Butler, Bishop of Oxford, little knowing that Cornewall was to succeed him in the see of Worcester. (Cf. E. H. Pearce, *Hartlebury Castle*, p. 312.)

[2] Probably Henry Greene, Prebendary of Oxgate, 1772–97. Son of Richard Greene, of Rolleston, Leics.

[3] James Waller, nephew of Richard Terrick, Bishop of London. Rector of St. And. Undershaft, 1764–70; rector of Finchley, 1767–

Richard Kaye, Sub-Almoner to the King, Dr. Majendie, Canon of Windsor, William Rix, Town Clerk of the City, a Lombard Street merchant, and the twelve Deputies. They made their arrangements to summon tradesmen to the next meeting and to have their accounts audited. " The day was spent with much Harmony and Glee ; and his Lordship of Chester [Dr. Porteus] quitted the Chair at 8 o'clock." It is probable that the £25 entered in the lower corner of the page signifies the consideration that passed to the Queen's Arms Tavern.

A fortnight later they met again, for the *utile* with considerably less of the *dulce*. The Stewards' fees were received by Orlton, the Corporation Messenger, who served his office from 1766 to 1810, " to be paid by Him into the hands of Mess[rs] Gosling Clive and Gosling, Bankers." Then " the Rev[d] M[r] Pearce." [1] a Deputy for many years, " was desired to settle with D[r] Boyce the Music that shall be performed and to request D[r] Howard to speak to the Directors of the Musicians Charitable Fund about the Band of Music " ; also " to wait upon the Dean of St. Paul's to request the use of the Cathedral for the Rehearsal and Anniversary Meetings, as also for the use of the Keys of the Stalls and *all* the Closetts." Further, " the Rev[d] M[r] Pearce

70 ; Prebendary of Hoxton, 1766–71 ; rector of St. Martin, Ludgate, 1770 ; vicar of Kensington, 1770 ; Prebendary of Mora, 1771 ; Archdeacon of Essex. He held the last four till his death. He resided at Waltham and was killed there by the fall of a chimney-stack, November 8th, 1795.

[1] Probably Rev. William Pearce, St. John's Coll., Camb. B.A. 1767 ; B.D. 1778. Master of The Temple, 1787.

was like wise desired to ask Dr Knares of his Majesty's
Chappel Royal, Mr Cook, and Mr Hudson, Almoner,[1]
for the Attendance of the Choristers of the Chappel
Royal, St. Pauls, and Westminster Abbey on the
Rehearsal and Feast Days." Then came the turn of
the Alderman Steward. He must wait on the Lord
Mayor to have the Court of Aldermen summoned, and
" inform his Lordship that Closetts would be appropriated for the Aldermens Ladies," and ask for the use
of the City Plate to adorn the Stewards' dinner-table.
The Secretary would next announce that he had
secured Merchant Taylors' Hall for the Feast, and this
would suggest an order to Mr. Pomfret for the wine,
" viz : a Hogshead of Port, ten Doz^n of Madeira and
eight Doz^n of White Wine." Next came the question
of the tickets, and instructions were given " to work
off 1000 Dinner Tickets in black, 6000 Rehearsal in
red and 4500 Choir Tickets in black for the Feast day,"
to be delivered a fortnight before the event. For
many years the Stewards and Deputies personally
superintended the distribution of the tickets. They
divided themselves into four bodies—" the City List,"
" the Middle List," " the Upper List," " the Westminster List," or, as we should say, " E.C.," " W.C.,"
" N.," and " S.W." But in 1796 they made a wise
change in this matter, resolving that " Tickets be
sent to each Friend of the Charity that can be selected
from a small publication called the *Visiting Book* . . .

[1] This is still the technical title of the Master of the Choir School
at St. Paul's Cathedral.

to be directed by the Messenger and sent by the Penny Post Free, and that the usual trouble given to the Stewards in the Delivery be done away." Having transacted this amount of business at a cost of only £2 8s. 7d. for refreshment, they could adjourn with an easy conscience till the Rehearsal and the Feast.

These claim separate treatment. We pass now to the Stewards' final meeting for the year, about a fortnight after the Feast. Here the Secretary would report the collections on the two great days and any benefactions received since; for instance, one year, 1777, brought four guineas from the Bishop of Salisbury,[1] five from the Lord Chief Baron, and £20 from the Earl of Hardwicke; the total being less than £1,100 by £2 6s. 6d., " John Bacon, Secry.," put himself down for that sum. All that remained to complete the year's work was that the Stewards should nominate forty-eight apprentices to receive each their share of the collection and that John Bacon should draw up his balance-sheet of the Festival expenses. This is worth looking at. On the " Dr " side stands £478 16s. subscribed by the Stewards. The " Contra " page shows that Edward Pomfret's bill for wine is £35, and the Cook's (William Angell) is £91 10s. The fee for the use of Merchant Taylors' Hall is ten guineas,

---

[1] Dr. John Hume, Prebendary of Westminster, 1742; Canon Residentiary of St. Paul's, 1748; Bishop of Bristol, 1756; Bishop of Oxford and Dean of St. Paul's, 1758; Bishop of Salisbury, 1766. Buried in the south aisle of Salisbury Cathedral, 1782.

15

and it may be noted that the minutes of the Feasts generally close with a statement that " the Hall was cleared before 12 o'clock, by which the Stewards were entitled to a return of five Guineas out of the 15 which they had deposited for the use of it." " Carpenters' work at Hall " cost a further £10, " Matting the Hall " £1 5s., and " the Whifflers and Waiters for the two days " £24 12s. These " Whifflers " were, of course, the fife-players, who led the processions from the tavern to the Cathedral and from the Cathedral to the Hall, and who at the Hall laid aside their instruments of music in order to wait at table. In 1792 it was decided to make a change in this respect, leaving the Butler to find the waiters, and allowing the Whifflers three shillings for each day's " whiffling." The reason for this appears in a note " that the Conduct of the servants be particularly attended to." The tavern-keeper's bill (£82 4s. 8d.) closes this part of their expenditure, and we turn to the cost of the service and the music. We start with £50 paid to the " Musicians' Fund " for the band, and two guineas " to Robert Hudson for the Attendance of the Choristers of St. Paul's." Gould, the verger, received eight guineas every year, and though in 1798, on Gould's death, when Hyde became verger, it was " agreed that in future the Vergers be only paid half a guinea each," subsequent accounts show that the payment of eight guineas continued as before. Dr. Cummings had in his possession a manuscript by Richard Gould, who seems also to have been Clerk of the Works, and I am indebted to his kindness for the following extract, which shows how the eight guineas were distributed :—

May 14th, 1766.

The Annual Fees from the Stewards of the Sons of the Clergy—To the Virgers and others belonging to St. Pauls at the Rehearsall and Feast Day

To the 4 Virgirs for the use of the church £6	6	0
To the Subsacrist for the use of the alter 0	10	6
To the use of the Scarlet Cloth the senior of the 3 Virgers . . . 0	10	6
To the Organ blower 1	1	0

8 8 0

Then come six guineas to Ann Burnell " for the use of the Forms," on which subject it occurred to the Stewards of 1781 that the Secretary might get this charge " mitigated " or " request them as a Donation for the use of the Charity ; and for this reason, because the sums of money already paid for the use of them are considerably more than the purchase money," with the result that Ann Burnell " mitigated " a guinea. " Matting the Church " cost £9 10s. and " Carpenter's Work " £20, while there is a small account " for Green Bays at the Bench at Church Door." Certain " sundries " connected with the music are not without interest. Dr. Nares, who brings the Children of the Chapel Royal, has £2 5s. 8d. for " Coach Hire, Breakfasts, &c." J. S. Smith's charge for " writing, correcting &c. the Musical parts " comes to £19 6s. 6d. There is an annual fee of a guinea to " the Revd Mr Champness for doing Duty at the Abbey," perhaps because the Minor Canons gave their services in the Festival choir. " Mast^r Russel for his various Exhibitions p. Order of the Stewards " and presumably for their delectation also receives a guinea, while the " Expences at the Rehearsal of New Anthem [the advertisement implies that this was Handel's " O come, let us sing unto the Lord "] at Crown and Anchor," £2 15s. Advertising cost £19 10s., and there was an annual " Gratuity to the Archbishops Servants " of two guineas. As early as 1729 it was the custom to have the bells of Bow Church and St. Michael, Cornhill (the two churches associated with the earlier history of the Festival), rung during the procession, and there was an annual charge of four guineas for this privilege.

THE REHEARSAL

The process by which a mere charity sermon in November in the seventeenth century was evolved into a great musical function, and one of the events of the London season in the eighteenth century, is not easy to follow for lack of minute-books. Probably it began in William III.'s reign, but Bacon's own information about the past is lacking in dates and definiteness. To make the matter clear I give his note in full :—

Dr. Godolphin, Dean of St. Paul's, had refused letting Music be introduced into the Church when

Queen Anne went in State to that Cathedral, to
a public Thanksgiving for some of the Duke of
Marlborough's Victories ; the Year after that Refusal, Dr. Tenison, Archbishop of Canterbury, the
Lord Keeper Wright, the then Lord Mayor of
London (all Clergymen's Sons) and John Forster
Esq., and others, Stewards, being desirous of
having Music, in order to increase the Collection,
applied to the Dean, who said he could not consent,
as he had refused the Queen the Year before.
Upon which the Archbishop, the Lord Keeper,
and the Lord Mayor were appointed a Committee
to wait upon the Queen for her Consent, if the
Dean's could be obtained, who graciously answered
She should be very glad if it could be, as she
thought it would be a great Means of drawing
Company, and increasing the Fund, to which she
earnestly wished success ; and perhaps the Dean
might be prevailed upon to be more obliging to
promote a Charity for his own Cloth than he had
been to her. Accordingly the Dean did give
Leave, and it is said, that either Dr. Purcel, or
Dr. Blow, conducted the Music, and that the Rev.
Mr Atterbury, Lecturer of St. Bride's, preached
the Sermon.

Fortunately for the Sons of the Clergy they were
dealing with two good friends. Queen Anne gave
them £500 and Godolphin £1,000, and what we have
to do is to arrive at a date when their friendship took
effect in permitting the Festival to become a feast of
music. Now Godolphin became Dean of St. Paul's

in 1707, and Mr. Richard Brocas, afterwards Lord Mayor, served as Steward in 1708, while Francis Atterbury, no longer [1] " Lecturer at St. Bride's," but Dean of Carlisle, preached the Festival sermon for the second time in 1709. Queen Anne attended a thanksgiving service for Oudenarde at St. Paul's in August, 1708, which was, no doubt, the occasion of Godolphin's refusal of her request. So we can hardly be wrong in attributing the change which Bacon implies to the year 1709. But Bacon's *on dit* about the conductor must be wrong, for Purcell died in 1695, and Dr. John Blow, who, by the way, was a Steward of the 1698 Festival, died in 1708. It is true that Daniel Purcell was in London in 1709, but he stood scarcely high enough in his profession to wield the *bâton* in the Cathedral.

Probably what this year 1709 saw, and what Queen Anne had wanted, was the introduction, not of music in the cathedral sense, but of orchestral accompaniments. But Bacon evidently had access to some previous minute-book, which told him that in 1727 and 1728 " Mr Green," by whom he means Maurice Greene, was paid £57 2s. 6d., each year, " for Music at St. Pauls," which consisted of Purcell's *Te Deum* and *Jubilate* and " a new Anthem composed by Mr Green."

---

[1] This needs correction. Atterbury continued to be Minister of Bridewell Precinct till June 15th, 1713. As such he retained his Fellowship of Sion College, was elected to the Court in 1709, and the same year preached the Latin sermon *Ad Clerum*. E. H. Pearce, *Sion College and Library*, p. 65 ; H. C. Beeching, *Francis Atterbury*, pp. 162-4.

It was, no doubt, Greene who introduced the custom of giving the Royal Society of Musicians, which he helped to found, £50 each year to provide the orchestra. We pass to 1771, and find an attempt to transplant the Rehearsal to the West End. A certain " Revd Mr Tilson [1] of Richmond, Surrey," says Bacon, " gave the sum of £200 to try the experiment of a Rehearsal of the Music in a Church or Chapel at the West End of the Town." The Stewards naturally chose St. George's, Hanover Square, where they collected £160 ; but next year " it was unanimously agreed to lay aside all Thoughts of any other Rehearsal than the usual one that has been held in St. Paul's Cathedral." Nothing seems more likely than that from the beginning of their musical efforts they should have such a rehearsal just before the actual anniversary, and that folk should be admitted to hear the various items practised, if they cared to contribute to the Charity. John Bacon could be trusted to turn the day to the account of good fellowship between the Stewards and their musical colleagues. This said, we may look at a specimen Rehearsal as described in his own words :—

9 May, 1775.

The Stewards met at the Queens Arms to breakfast at 9 oclock and afterwards ballotted for their

[1] George Tilson, son of Thomas Tilson, of Dublin. Eton and Trinity Coll., Camb. Admitted to Lincoln's Inn, 1732 ; ordained, 1739–40 ; Chaplain at Hampton Court. He resided at Richmond. Died 1778. Venn, *Al. Cantab.* iv. 243. He served as a Steward in 1772.

Stations and went in procession to the Church.
The performance of the Music was truly noble and
much to the satisfaction of the Audience in General.
A collection to the amount of £210 . 16 . 3 was
made ; afterwards the Stewards adjourned from
the Church to the Queens Arms to dinner ; where
they entertained Dᴿ Howard and the Gentlemen
of the three Choirs and much Glee and unanimity
appeared—At 7 o'clock the Stewards drank Tea,
and then a few select friends sat down jocundly
and at 11 o'clock departed.

It is obvious, especially when we fill in the picture
with details from other years, that this represents a
fairly long day's work.   The Feast Day meant just as
much, so that John Bacon's attendance at the First
Fruits Office and the Deputies' devotion to their
several occupations must have been somewhat nominal
during the Anniversary week.   We see them assembling
for their breakfast at the " Queen's Arms " at 9 a.m.,
and giving it a heed begotten of the thought that their
next meal would not be reached before 4 p.m.   At
10 a.m. they went in procession with their Whifflers to
the Cathedral and " opened the Church Doors."   The
collection began at once, and continued till twelve
o'clock, when " the Church was amazingly full "
with " a numerous and respectable company," or " a
company genteel to a degree," or " not without some
of the first Ladies in the Kingdom," and all these had
contributed according to a method set forth in an
advertisement in the *Public Advertiser* of May 7, 1790.

It may be found between an announcement of Mrs. Mountain's " benefit " at Covent Garden Theatre, and one of Dr. Johnson's *English Poets*, " published this day." " It is to be hoped," the Stewards there say, " that no Person will be desirous of being admitted, without first contributing to this Charity. The greatest Care will be taken, that those who contribute liberally shall be seated commodiously—a Circumstance that cannot fail to be agreeable." By 1832 they had become still more precise. " The Committee respectfully state "—so runs the advertisement—" that contributions of gold will admit each person (by a separate door, at the West end of the Cathedral, nearest Doctors' Commons) to the Galleries and Closets ; and express their hopes that, for admission into the Choir, no person will contribute less than half-a-crown. To the Individual, this latter small donation can be no object, whilst the aggregate is of the utmost importance to the interests of the Charity." Even when these broad hints had appeared in a public print, the Stewards realised that still much depended on their personal effort. When they had succeeded they would allow Bacon to say in his minutes that " from the favourableness of the Day and the Assiduity of the Stewards the amount was £201." When the result was less they accepted it philosophically, as thus : " The Collection, considering the Review by his Majesty of the Horse Guards on Blackheath and other public attractions is a tolerable good one." Whatever the apparent result of their " assiduity," there was generally a not inconsiderable deduction to be allowed later on, as, for instance, in 1781, when the balance sheet enters £4 15s. 0d. " by loss on Sale of Light and Base Money taken at the Collections."

The alteration of the date of the Festival, first from December to February in 1727 ; then to April in 1740, " at the instance of the Archbishop of Canterbury,[1] upon an Idea that it would be of much Advantage to the Charity " ; then to May in 1753, had its drawbacks as well as its advantages. Society was, of course, in town, and it was the time to catch visitors of distinction from abroad. In 1781 " the two Chiefs from the East Indies were introduced and sat in the Bishop of London's throne. They expressed much Reverence and Awe at the Performance and seem'd beyond measure pleased." It was a time when the Court would naturally hold its great functions, and in 1789 the Festival became a sort of aftermath of Thanksgiving Day ; for

> The Dean and Chapter being so kind as to give Directions that the Scaffolding and Erections for the reception of the Peeresses, the Members of the Houses of Lords and Commons &c. on the Day of general Thanksgiving shall remain entire . . . and for the gratification of all Persons in every part of the Choir the Orchestra was erected on each side of the Organ with a projected Gallery in the Front, which did not only add uniformity to the Building but harmony to the sound by the

[1] Dr. John Potter.

regular reverberation, which could but give universal pleasure from such a performance placed in so happy a situation under the direction of Dr. Hayes.

But such a season brought also a constantly increasing number of counter attractions. In 1790 when " the company was not so numerous as has been known, but very select," it is noted that the public was " much attracted " to a review on " Black Heath," " together with Mr Hastings Tryal and the proximity of the Grand Musical Meeting at Westminster Abbey, which will commence on the 26th inst., with various other Allurements for the Publick's Amusements." It is only fair to add that on at least one occasion the rival attraction at Westminster was really a rival in the same cause. Reference is made in the Court Book of 1792 to some " Musical Performances in Westminster Abbey in 1791," and it was reported that George III. had ordered that £500 of the money thence resulting should go " to the benefit of the families of necessitous Clergymen deceased, under the direction of the Archbishop of Canterbury." [1] His Grace, as President of the Corporation, assigned £250 to its funds.

So the Stewards, having at any rate done their best, rounded off the Rehearsal day with " Glee and Harmony." They retired to the Queen's Arms Tavern and entertained the various musicians who had taken part in the service, and Bacon's records show that the

[1] Dr. John Moore.

Rehearsal dinner was looked upon as part of the dignity of the Anniversary, and that the duty of making it a success lay upon him with quite a weight of responsibility. " After Dinner several excellent pieces of Musick were vocally performed by the Minor Canons, . . . and in particular the Catch of ' Bonny Christ Church Bells,' the words in Greek by Dr. Morell, as likewise ' Jack, thou art a Toper.' " Morell,[1] an Etonian and a King's man, will be remembered as Handel's librettist and the writer of " See the Conquering Hero comes," and as the compiler of a *Thesaurus* of Greek poetry. They sang his Greek catch in 1777 and 1779, and he died at the age of 81 in 1784. In 1782 their music pieces were " many of them accompanyed by Mr Dupée [Bacon means, no doubt, Dupuis of the Chapel Royal] on the Harpsichord," and there was " never a more convivial or jovial eve," except for " a small degree of Disturbance which took its rise from the imprudence of one of the Gentlemen of the Choir." In 1796, after " Mr Forster was requested to entertain the Company with his two Flutes, which he did to the wonderful satisfaction of all," the company was inspired with a wish to have some special music of its own. Men wrote anthems for the Cathedral service. Why not glees for the Rehearsal dinner ? Here is the result :—

At this meeting the healths of Dr Arnold and Dr Dupuis being noticed and given, as two of the

[1] Thomas Morell, D.D., F.R.S., F.S.A., rector of Buckland, Herts., 1737–84.

first Professional Men in their Line, with the kind
accompaniment of *three* times *three* Cheers, They
with the utmost kindness and civility to the Institution agreed for the attention shown to them
to compose against the next year a Glee to be sung
at the Meeting of the Stewards at their Rehearsal,
and thereby to establish *for ever* the conviviality
of the annual meeting of this Society. The Rev^d
Mr Tew and the Rev Dr Browning agreed at the
same time to furnish Dr Arnold and Dr Dupuis
with words suitable to the occasion.

Tew,[1] like Morell, was an Etonian, and by 1799 he had
produced his suitable words and Arnold had composed
the music. The ode was arranged for chorus, air,
duet, chorus, air, duet, and chorus. The words have
a general reference to the Stewards' work. If the poem
begins—

> " Mourn, ye afflicted Children, mourn ;
> And, as ye bend o'er Sorrow's urn,
> Let Life's illusive dream
> Be made the mournful theme :
> To softest notes of woe attune the lay,"

at least it ends with " Hallelujah—Amen " ; as for
the music, John Bacon's criticism is that it was composed by Dr. Arnold " in a stile that will perpetuate
his Memory, as to the Elegance and Harmony in the

---

[1] Rev. Edward Tew, Fellow of Eton, was a Steward in 1796.
He graduated in 1758 from King's Coll., Camb., and may have
been a son of Rev. Edmund Tew, B.A., Jesus Coll., 1719, rector of
Boldon, Durham, who was educated at Christ's Hospital, to which
he bequeathed a large benefaction for the benefit of sons of clergymen. E. H. Pearce, *Annals of Christ's Hospital*, p. 85.

Composition, which keep'd pace with the Words and which were appropriate and well-adapted for the occasion." Having listened to such music, some of the Stewards would retire comparatively early in the evening ; it was 8 p.m., for instance, on the Rehearsal day of 1783, when " Lord Salisbury quitted the chair." Sometimes the chairman stayed later, and yet rose too soon for the Stewards ; the Marquis of Carmarthen left in 1781 at 10 o'clock " to the great mortification of those that remained, who could only drown their regret in a Bumper to the health of their Convivial President." Then " the Secretary and a few select Friends stayed the evening."

CHAPTER XII

THE BANQUETS

HOWEVER much the Stewards might enjoy their work and their refreshment on Rehearsal Day, there was still the great day of the Feast to be gone through on the Thursday, and it may be said at once that from the beginning the day seems to have been a long one. Manton's undated sermon, which at any rate preceded the Restoration, has been already referred to. It closes with two practical paragraphs—the first as to the feast, the second as to the collection.

" Let me press you," he said in the former, " to sobriety and temperance. At a feast men grow loose, and abate of their severity and awe. Certainly there needs caution. When Job's sons were feasting, the father falleth a-sacrificing. Let it be a sober meeting, as becometh ministers' sons. You have begun well ; let not your crown fall to the dust. Do but consider what a dishonour it will be, not to yourselves only, but to this holy calling, yea, to the Lord Himself, when from a feast of ministers' sons some shall go away with staggering feet, inflamed countenances, and a faltering tongue. Oh ! let it not be. You do well to begin with a sermon to season your hearts ; and you will do as well to end and conclude with a psalm, that it may look like one of the sober and holy love-feasts the old Christians used "

We have no records at Corporation House to show how far such an injunction was needed by the Sons of the Clergy under Puritan auspices, nor the place of the Feast. We can only start with a specimen of John Bacon's *memorabilia* of what happened in his day.

14 May, 1778.

The Stewards and their Deputies met at the Queens Arms Tavern to breakfast at 9 o'clock, ballotted for their several stations at the Church and the Hall, and at 10 went in procession in the usual manner to the Church—The Collection begun soon after ten and the service of the Church soon after 11—The Sermon was preached by the Revᵈ John Warren [1] D.D. Chaplain in Ordinary to His Majesty and Prebendary of Ely from St. James Ch : 1 Ver : 27 " Pure Religion and undefiled before GOD and the Father, is this, to visit the Fatherless and Widows in their affliction " and met with general approbation, insomuch that the Stewards returned the Preacher thanks before they left the Hall and requested him to print—He readily acquiesced in their request and it was ordered to be printed accordingly—The Service concluded about 3 o'clock, and the sum of the Collection at the Church for the day was then ascertained, which proved to be £301 ,, 9 ,, 6—a very noble and liberal contribution ! in the above

[1] Son of Richard Warren, D.D., Archdeacon of Suffolk. Sizar of Caius Coll., Camb., 1747. Members' Prize, 1758. Prebendary of Ely, 1768–79. Bishop of St. David's, 1779–83, and of Bangor, 1783–1800.

sum was included a Bank note of £50. the kind
Donation of an unknown Benefactor—an Instance
of real Charity—The Stewards and Clergy then
proceeded in procession, the Lord Mayor, the
Archbishop of Canterbury, the Bishops, Aldermen
&c to the Hall, and after dining themselves, set
the Dinner before a numerous Company at ½ after
4 o'clock. There were present at this Anniversary in the Hall the Lord Mayor, His Grace the
Lord Archbishop of Canterbury, The Archbishop
of York, the Bishops of London, Ely, Bath and
Wells, Worcester, Peterborough, St. Davids,
Rochester, Lichf[d] and Cov[y] and Bangor, [various
Aldermen and the Sheriffs], Count O'Rourke, the
Chamberlain of the City, Many of the Deans,
Archdeacons, Residentiaries, Canons, and Preben-
daries, and an unprecedented number of the Clergy
and Laity. The Collection at the Hall amounted
to £506. The Hall was cleared before 12 o'clock.

The total of that Festival was £1,059 6s., and was
perhaps an answer to recent comments in the news-
papers. The Stewards had found that their good was
evil spoken of. The *Public Advertiser* had opened its
columns to a correspondence about the administration
of the charity, and " An Old Steward " replied on their
behalf. Why, he asked, does not the objector consult
our Secretary ? " You would there, I fancy, have
discovered that, instead of a Malapplication of the
sums collected, there was Liberality and a Series of
disinterested Charity throughout the whole. You
16

would have found a handsome Donation to that very valuable Institution, the Musicians Fund, . . . and the Remains and Fragments of the Dinner at which you are so indignant, carefully distributed to the Relief of upwards of one Hundred poor Indigent Creatures." " Your Correspondent," writes another champion in the same issue, May 7, 1777, " may think, if he pleases, that we assemble only to eat and drink ; but happily for many a poor Creature our Accounts speak a very different language." The matter is only worth mentioning because there are still those who complain of the dining even across the dinner-table, and the fault-finding of a century and a half ago will probably find its echo in the grumbling of as many years hence. The banquet was an adjunct, but merely an adjunct, to the music and the sermon, which can best be dealt with in a separate chapter.

MERCHANT TAYLORS' HALL

There is no record at Corporation House of the date when the valuable alliance between the Corporation and this ancient Guild was first cemented. But some information kindly supplied to me by Mr. Edward Nash, the late Clerk of the Company, sets all doubt at rest. He found that the first sum received by the Merchant Taylors from the Sons of the Clergy for the use of the Hall was £2 in 1677, and that a similar fee was paid in 1680 and 1682. The charge had risen to £3 in 1684 and 1685, and this was paid continuously

MERCHANT TAYLORS' HALL.

from 1687 to 1692. From then to the close of the century the fee was £7 yearly, and after that increased further, till we come to the fifteen guineas, which will be mentioned directly. From 1704 to 1709 the Hall was leased to the East India Company, but the relations existing between "John Company" and our Corporation would warrant the idea that the Festival might still be held in the Hall during their tenure. It will have been noticed that the above dates are not quite continuous. The years 1678, 1679, 1681, 1683, and 1686 have no entry of any fee paid by our Corporation, but the omission is hardly serious enough to throw doubt on the continuity of the connection between the Corporation and the great Guild, whose interest is shown by an order of its Court, dated 1795, that in future only the Sons of the Clergy should be granted the use of its Hall. When John Bacon began his minute-book in 1775, it was thus an ancient and accepted custom. We have seen him booking the Hall as a matter of course, and depositing his fifteen guineas in the hope of recovering five, if the company separated in time to get the Hall cleared by midnight. Inasmuch as they sat down about 5 p.m. this was not an extravagant hope. Service would be over at St. Paul's about half-past three. The Lord Mayor, the Archbishops and Bishops, and the great folk of the congregation would then go in procession, led, of course, by the whifflers through the City. "Bow and St. Michael's Bells rang merrily." The company seems to have consisted in Bacon's time of between one hundred and three hundred, or about its present numbers. The Stewards would be there of course, and Bacon has left a note in his list of Stewards that in 1769, which seems to have been the year when he became Secretary, " The Lord Mayor, the Archbishops and Bishops, the Nobility and Aldermen, dined together at this Anniversary for the first time at the High Table in Merchant Taylors Hall." But it was not an uncommon thing for the Stewards to dine first by themselves, in order that they might attend on the company during their repast and, no doubt, increase the collection thereby.

Whatever it might make up in quantity, the *menu* was certainly not the elaborate creation of modern times. You could not come in late and still find that there were several courses not yet served. Unpunctuality was thus a great inconvenience to the *ménage*, and in 1729 it was " ordered that every Steward that does not come within one Hour after the Time appointed in the Summons shall forfeit 2s. 6d. and the Treasurer and Secretary 5s." Bacon's record that the dinner of 1798 was " good (only one course) " must be read in interpretation of his statement about 1789 that " the Tables were covered and with great profusion. Turbot was fine and in g^t plenty. . . . Every person was perfectly satisfied." In 1728 " the Cook (Mr Miller) was ordered to provide a Dinner at £160 as per Bill delivered in." But in 1798, though the company had not decreased, the " one course " dinner cost them £89.

Nor was their wine-bill to any extent extravagant or progressive. In 1728 they " used one Hogshead and an Half of French Wine at £42." In 1741 there is a note : " French Wine rejected by an Order of the Stewards this year," but presumably they had a substitute. In 1788 Mr. Pomfret's bill for " a Hogshead of Port, 10 Doz^n of Madeira and 8 Doz^n of White Wine " was £37 ; but it is possible that there is some tragedy latent in Bacon's record of the year following, in which he tells us that " the Wine was served by Mr Lewis of the New London Tavern, Cheapside, and *no complaint*," especially as the italics are his.

In the earlier years of the gathering at Merchant Taylors' Hall there was music as part of the entertainment. Maurice Greene, in 1728—the organist of St. Paul's has indeed become a dignitary since then— " provided the Music in the Hall at the usual Price of Six Guineas and an Half. The Number of Musicians was Eleven." But in 1752, says Bacon, the music at the Hall was discontinued, " as being thought not only useless, but disagreeable." This, however, did not bind future generations. Bacon himself was a firm believer in the harmonising effects of music. If, as the *Globe* of May 13, 1803, stated, " His Grace the Archbishop of Canterbury [1] joined with the greatest good humour in the general festivity," who shall say how far the music had lured him to contentment ? For " a number of songs were sung, with much taste, by the singers of St. Paul's. *God save the King, Rule*

[1] Dr. John Moore ; he was then seventy-three.

Britannia, the Stormy Winds do Blow and the *Mid Watch* were the most worthy of notice." The former sentence would be true of a festival of to-day, but there would be a less nautical ring about the music selected.

Nothing in connection with the dinner seems to have given such trouble as the conduct of the servants. The important guests brought their own, the Stewards provided waiters and whifflers, and apparently anyone could come in to wait who chose to assume the part. It became so serious that in 1792 the Lord Mayor was asked " to order the Marshalmen to attend at the Hall door to prevent any Servants excepting those of the Stewards, Noblemen, Bishops, Lord Mayor, Sheriffs and the Aldermen entering the Hall, and that no Coachman without exception be permitted to enter." And there is a by no means archaic ring about a complaint in 1807 that " the Stewards were very much surprized and displeased by an application from the Servants of the Lord Mayor and others to have a supply of Wine found them previously to the dinner ; in resisting this unprecedented and unwarrantable demand they felt that they were only acting in conformity to the duty they owed to themselves and their successors."

But one incident in the history of the function at Merchant Taylors' Hall is worth longer notice. In 1793 and 1794 the Hall was under repair, and, no doubt at the Archbishop's instigation, the Stationers' Company offered a kind hospitality to the Festival.

John Bacon's story of the 1793 dinner has its own inherent merits :—

The Stewards having dined in an adjacent room " waited upon the Company in the Hall, but by a letter which the Sec : had received from Lord Thurlow saying that he would dine but could not be with them till 6 o'clock, on which account it was till then postponed to the great murmuring of most. By the Request of Dʳ Hayes the whole of the Vocal Performers were introduced to Dinner. . . . The Sec : and a few Friends stayed the Evᵍ and finished a Day happily. A singular circumstance happened. It was discovered that the Lord Mayor by the neglect of his proper Officers had left the Mace and Sword behind them. They were immediately placed before Mʳ Bacon after Supper. Having such Ensignia before him he felt all the authority of a Lord Mayor and acted accordingly. The Power was but short. A message was sent to the real Lord Mayor who ordered a proper officer to take it home."

The company, we may add, need not have murmured at Lord Thurlow, who, with all his eccentricities, was a munificent benefactor to the Charity. During his long occupation of the Lord Chancellorship under Lord North he generally gave a donation of £50, either bringing it himself or sending it by his bishop brother, besides serving as Steward in 1779 ; and in 1795 after his retirement his gift was increased to £100, when he had every excuse for reducing it.

For some not very obvious reasons the dinner at Merchant Taylors' Hall was omitted in 1832 and 1833. There were hints given to the public in inspired paragraphs in the *Standard* and *Old England* that it was " determined upon in consequence of the expence which it entailed on those Noblemen and Gentlemen, who from time to time accepted the office of Stewards . . . and defrayed all the expences both of the Dinner and the Festival." Naturally some of the friends were very angry, and a " Constant Reader," discussing the difficulties in the *Standard* [June 18th, 1833] said that " there is such a thing as secretly asking those you formally solicit to refuse," and mentioned a report " that some, high enough in the Church to know better . . . wished to get rid of the trouble &c of the whole thing," so that " the service at the Cathedral will very soon follow the dinner." But the dinner came back to its place in the programme of 1834, and the only change resulting from this *lacuna* in the tradition was that from henceforth the Festival Stewards, instead of themselves distributing the sums raised, handed them over to the Corporation, as is done to-day.

THE LAMBETH DINNER

The City banquet generally closed with an invitation from the Archbishop of Canterbury to the Lord Mayor and Sheriffs, the Stewards, and the Preacher to dine with him at Lambeth the following week. I have no

data for deciding when this custom arose. It was a
recognised ceremony in 1775. What is remarkable is
that an event which is now fixed some ten or twelve
months in advance could then be arranged on a week's
notice. Thus in 1779 " the Archbishop [1] mentioned
Thursday for the Stewards to dine with Him but
did not absolutely fix it because of the engagements
of the Lord Chanc' and Ld George Germaine " (two
of the Stewards). So again on May 23rd, 1793, " the
Secretary waited upon the Archbishop of Canterbury [2]
this Morning, who desired him to invite the Stewards
&c to dine with His Grace on Friday (!) the 31st Ins^t :
Letters accordingly were wrote and given to the Messenger this day." In the days when the family of
King George III. were taking an active and regular
interest in the Festival the Archbishop's entertainment
became a great function. In 1807, when Archbishop
Manners Sutton entertained George, Prince of Wales,
and the Duke of Kent, their Royal Highnesses

> arrived at Lambeth about half-past five o'clock, by
> which time the Nobility, Clergy and others invited
> by his Grace the Archbishop were assembled. The
> Archbishop followed by his Chaplains . . . and
> attended by the Preacher, the Treasurer and Secre-
> tary, went to the top of the great Stair Case,
> adjoining the Grand Hall, to receive their Royal
> Highnesses. The Prince of Wales addressing the
> Archbishop expressed the pleasure he felt at the

[1] Dr. Frederick Cornwallis.
[2] Dr. John Moore.

Idea that his Name and assured Patronage had
been productive of such beneficial effects, and
graciously promised his favour and protection to
the Sons of the Clergy.

Their Royal Highnesses entering the Gallery
Drawing Room the Archbishop presented the
Stewards and Officers of the Charity to the Prince
who was pleased to receive them with His accustomed graciousness and Courtesy.

Dinner was then announced, the arrangements,
attendance, and splendour of which was worthy
of the Royal Guests and of the princely and mag-
nificent spirit of the most Reverend President.

The customary Toasts being given after dinner
the Treasurer rose to make his report of the sums
already received for the service of the year and
those which might reasonably be expected in
addition thereto. The Report was received with
the most flattering approbation of His Royal
Highness, the Archbishop, and the Stewards.

After the Archbishop had thanked the preacher of that
year and nominated the preacher of the next year,

His Royal Highness the Prince of Wales declared
his intention of nominating his Royal Brother the
Duke of York, to represent him as Steward the
following year. . . . His Royal Highness retired
a little past nine and the rest of the guests followed
soon after, all expressing the utmost satisfaction
at their hospitable reception and the arrangements
of the Day.

Such was the round of a Steward's duties in the latter half of the eighteenth century, when John Bacon managed the Festival with the strenuous ease of a Receiver of First Fruits. It may seem that to attend committees with refreshments, the Union Dinner, the Rehearsal and subsequent dinner, the Anniversary and Merchant Taylors' Hall, and the function at Lambeth, was a life in somewhat glaring contrast with the poverty it was intended to relieve. The defence, if defence it is, lies in this, that the collection was going on more or less all the time, and certainly no other motive inspired John Bacon. He was never more pleased than when he could write down in 1789 that at the Rehearsal dinner " the following Toast was given by a benevolent Steward, ' May Avarice lose its Purse and Benevolence find it.' " It has already been stated that after thirty years' service as secretary and treasurer he decided in 1799 to resign the former office, retaining the latter. " J. Bacon's speech on the Occasion," he says, was " taken down in Shorthand by a Deputy Steward." For J. Bacon's sake it is worth its space, and was as follows :—

I feel on the present Occasion, as I have ever felt since I have been honor'd by the Stewards with their Nomination as Secretary of this Institution an ardent wish to do my duty and a singular degree of Happiness at the Idea of having it in my power to alleviate the Distresses of the indigent and particularly those of our Brethren of the established Church. I presume not to say with what success my weak endeavours may have been attended, that circumstance being sufficiently known to many of the respectable company now present. But I have now to regret that it will be no longer in my power to proceed.—Various causes have arisen, such as my non-residence in Town, my magisterial situation in the country [Barnet], the urgency and weight of business under the Executorships of Wills of my deceased Friends, and other matters of equal Moment,—all of which contribute to deny any longer my fulfilling the duties of this station as they ought to be filled. —I therefore beg leave to inform you that I have obtained leave of his Grace of Canterbury and of other valuable Friends of this Institution, after I have performed the Duties of my office this year, to resign and after thirty years services to shut my Book, and I hope of this Resignation you will have the goodness to bear testimony, and I beg leave to assure you at the same time that it is the most sincere wish of my heart that my Successor may be more successful, and that he may feel at the termination of his office the same degree of gratification and satisfaction which I at this moment experience. I beg leave to drink prosperity to the Charity, and Health and Happiness to the Stewards and Deputy Stewards of the day.

After all he did not " shut his book " for a time. It contains no more of his genial minutes, and his suc-

cessors were without humour as recorders of events ;
but for fifteen years more he kept the accounts and
attended the Festivals. He was a fine old English
gentleman, and the Sons of the Clergy should have
him in remembrance.

CHAPTER XIII

THE MUSIC AND THE SERMON

THE Rehearsal and the Anniversary found their common ground in the rendering of a considerable musical programme. Even before Maurice Greene's time at St. Paul's (1718–55) the Handelian influence was already asserting itself. Probably the first-love of the Anniversary was Purcell's *Te Deum* and *Jubilate*, " for voices and instruments, perform'd before the Sons of the Clergy." This had been composed in 1694, and was performed on St. Cecilia's Day at St. Bride, Fleet Street, where Francis Atterbury was then lecturer. Sir W. H. Cummings told me that it was probably given at our Festival in 1697, and this is credible on other grounds, as that year was the date of the return of the Anniversary to St. Paul's Cathedral. He was also kind enough to lend me his copy of the work, the frontispiece of which is here reproduced. It bears upon it the signature of Robert Hudson, who has already been referred to as the Almoner of St. Paul's, and who was also the Song School Master of Christ's Hospital. Purcell's music remained in the programme till 1713, when Handel's Peace of Utrecht *Te Deum* took its place, and the two were given in alternate years down to 1743, when both were elbowed aside by Handel's Dettingen *Te Deum*

234

TE DEUM
ET
JUBILATE,
FOR
VOICES
AND
INSTRUMENTS

Perform'd before the

SONS of the CLERGY
at the

Cathedral-Church of St. *PAUL*.

COMPOS'D

By the late Mr. HENRY PURCEL

Note. Where these are Sold may be had great variety of Church-Musick.

London. Printed for and Sold by John Walsh Musick Printer and Instrument maker to his Majesty at the Harp and Hoboy in Catherine Street in the Strand.

and *Jubilate*.[1] Nevertheless the Purcell influence was not extinct. Boyce succeeded Maurice Greene in 1755, and in that year arranged some additional orchestral accompaniments to Purcell's work for the express object of having them used at the Anniversary. It is in connexion with this that we get some idea of the orchestra of the early Festivals. Purcell wrote for a string quartette and two trumpets. Boyce's re-arrangement added two hautboys, two bassoons, and drums, and made the setting a third longer than it was originally, not to speak of his barbarity in Han-delising Purcell. By 1775 we are on the sure ground of Bacon's yearly minutes, and know that from then to 1825, when C. J. Blomfield was on the list of Stewards as Bishop of Chester, the music was almost without variation as follows :—

1. The overture of *Esther*.
2. The Old Hundredth Psalm, as the opening hymn.
3. "Mr Handel's grand Dettingen *Te Deum* and *Jubilate*."
4. The Hallelujah chorus, after the Third Collect.
5. Dr. Boyce's anthem, "Lord, Thou hast been our refuge," specially composed for the Festival, "to be sung immediately before the Sermon."

[1] I am afraid that this general statement must be qualified. My old friend, Dr. A. H. Mann, organist of King's Coll., Camb., sent me in 1920 a newspaper record as follows :—"On Thursday [Dec. 14, 1721] the Rev. Dr. Waterland preach'd before the Sons of the Clergy at St. Paul's, where Te Deum and an Anthem composed by Dr. Green were performed with solemnity." This may mean that both Te Deum and Anthem were Dr. Greene's work ; it certainly means that the Anthem was.

6. " Mr Handel's Grand Coronation Anthem, to be sung after the Sermon."

It is obvious that the result of cleaving so steadfastly [1] to this programme was a desire for at least occasional deviations. They found they could make their change, where we should least expect it, in connection with the Old Hundredth. Thus in 1778 this Psalm, " with Instrumental parts by the late Dr Hayes (*i.e.* William Hayes, who had died in 1777), was performed for the first time and had a very pleasing effect." In 1797, and for many years after, they had the Psalm " as harmonised by Mr Greatorex." Again, they could if they liked vary the anthem. Boyce, by whose death in 1779 they realised that " the Charity had sustained a very great loss," wrote them a special anthem for the Festival of 1755, when he became conductor. This was his " Lord, Thou hast

---

[1] This steadfast cleaving to a programme applies also to the incidental parts of the service such as Psalms and Lessons. The selection vexed Scott Holland's righteous soul. "Would you write" —so he urged his sister from Rome in April 1890—" to Bowman, Sons of Clergy Secretary, begging him from me to see whether the Psalms and First Lesson of the Festival may be reconsidered. Tempers and minds are changed, and it now seems to us a terrible irony to sing ' Happy is the man who has his quiver full of them '— on an occasion like this. Such a psalm raises all the problem of the families of the clergy. . . . And then, could we not read something less exalted in key than ' The wilderness and the solitary place ' ? We are thinking of giving some necessary and scanty aid to pinched children, and we cannot attribute to our gifts the highest fulfilment of Messianic joy." Stephen Paget, *Henry Scott Holland* (Murray), p. 146. Very characteristic. One would delight to be in Chapter when the appropriateness of Ps. 127 was being discussed between the eugenic Dean and the bachelor Canon.

17

been our refuge," with a verse " for the Children only " from the words, " We are orphans and fatherless : our mothers are as widows. The joy of our heart is turned into mourning." To this anthem they clung with great tenacity, but Boyce was not Handel, and they need not be called Goths if they were willing to substitute something else. So they record on their minutes with hope and satisfaction that " Mr Linley expressed his Inclination to accommodate this Charity with the best efforts of his Musical Abilities on any future occasion by setting such words by way of Anthem to musick as may be provided with the approbation of the Stewards." This must be Thomas Linley the elder, for young Thomas Linley had been drowned off the coast of Lincolnshire in 1778. Old Linley was at this time director of the music at Drury Lane, and some members of the Festival orchestra were under him in that capacity. But the promise was apparently not fulfilled. On Boyce's death the conductorship of the Festival passed for one year to Dr. Samuel Howard, who was followed in 1780 by Philip Hayes. The latter was soon ready with a special anthem, which was given in 1782, when, as Bacon says, " some of the first musical characters in the Kingdom " were present, " All of whom expressed their satisfaction at the performance, and gave a general fiat to the honest endeavours for the benefit of the Charity of Dr Phil. Hayes, whose Anthem, notwithstanding the ill-nature of a few, will remain a lasting Memorial of his Musical Abilities." This is

somewhat faint praise, of which I cannot measure the
justice, as the kind efforts of Mr. John S. Bumpus,
the well-known authority on the Church music of the
period, have failed to identify the particular composition. Anyhow, for the next ten years, in spite
of Mrs. Boyce's bill of three guineas " for the use of
Dr Boyce's Anthem," they returned to the old love.
In 1794 they agreed to try the Hayes anthem again,
when it " gave great satisfaction " ; so also in 1796,
when " the D^r appeared very ill," but " the Music went
off well."

In 1797, on the death of Hayes, the Stewards chose
as their conductor Samuel Arnold, of Westminster
Abbey, who had frequently acted as organist under
Hayes. In 1802 it is noted that " Dr. Arnold the
conductor of the Band was ill and could not attend " ;
and in 1803 they secured in his stead Sir William
Parsons, Master of the King's band. The *Oracle* of
May 13, 1803, speaking of his appointment, said that
" it was certainly a bold and an arduous task, after
such predecessors as Boyce, Hayes and Arnold, men
who were esteemed in private and admired in public,"
and that Sir William " seemed to know and feel the
honour of this professional distinction " ; while the
Globe of the same date noted that " the Chorusses were
delivered in a most impressive and awful style." Yet
there were signs that the music was losing its effect
as an attraction to the benevolent, for the collection
at the Rehearsal was as low as £70, and there was an
obvious feeling that the music should be varied. In

1807, when George, Prince of Wales, served as Steward for the second time, the question came up during the business portion of the Union Dinner at the Thatched House Tavern. "A Letter was read by the Secretary addressed to him by Charles Ashley, Esq., recommending the substitution of Purcell's *Te Deum* and *Jubilate* for that of Handel"; so "it was agreed that the decision should be left to the Prince, who on his arrival was graciously pleased to signify his Royal pleasure that the Music for the present year should be without variation the same as on preceding anniversaries." So for many years they clave to Handel and Boyce, though Crotch succeeded Parsons as conductor in 1814, and Greatorex followed Crotch in 1817. Owing to a fire which destroyed many of the Festival records, there is some difficulty in giving the exact dates at which some subsequent conductors took up the work. But Greatorex was still conducting in 1825, and no doubt continued till his death in 1831. In the following year the conductor was Sir George Smart, with Attwood at the organ. In 1839, after Attwood's death, the music was in the hands of "Mr. Goss," who was destined to render the greatest service to the Festival till his retirement in 1872. In his time there were several conductors, such as Dr. Elvey from 1851 to 1866, Henry Buckland (who also held the *bâton* at the Charity Children's services) in 1867, and Winn, the vocalist, in 1868. But these were merely there as time-beaters; the power was with Goss. What he did the following extracts from *The*

Times will show. They may no doubt be attributed
to its musical critic, James William Davison. The
first refers to the Festival of 1851.

> The interest that might attach to such a cere-
> mony, in which music is made to play so solemn
> and sublime a part, may be imagined. But, un-
> fortunately, our cathedral music, while the art is
> making rapid strides in profaner quarters, has
> remained for a long time, and is likely to remain
> still longer, *in statu quo*. The choirs are meagre
> and ill paid, and by consequence the members
> cannot devote any important portion of their time
> to their official duties. When we say that the
> choir of St. Paul's consists of *six persons*, and
> that these six persons are very inefficiently re-
> munerated, some idea may be entertained of the
> state of things we are compelled to arraign as a
> discredit to our cathedrals, which have the means,
> and ought to be compelled to assume a more
> respectable position. If music be indispensable in
> our church service (which we devoutly maintain),
> it should be represented effectively, and not in
> such a manner as to degrade the service by an
> exhibition of incompetence which would be in-
> sufferable in a minor place of public entertain-
> ment. . . . It is no use in 1851, when all England
> understands and loves and flocks to hear such
> grand and immortal compositions as *Israel in
> Egypt* and *Elijah*, as thoroughly and as eagerly as
> it appreciates and runs after *Don Giovanni* and
> *Masaniello* at the Opera,—it is no use . . . pro-

nouncing that to be splendid and impressive which
is really incompetent and ridiculous. We must,
therefore, in spite of the regret it causes us, un-
equivocally condemn the music and the performance of the music which celebrated the Festival
of the Sons of the Clergy yesterday afternoon.
The choirs . . . cannot be brought to learn anything out of the common track; and thus Dr.
Hayes is allowed to praise God in our cathedrals,
while Mendelssohn is condemned to silence, al-
though the one was a nonentity and the other a
lofty genius. . . . For the meeting of the choirs
yesterday, there was, we understand, *one* rehearsal
only. How, then, could an efficient execution be
expected? Under such circumstances . . . Mr.
Goss showed wisdom in adhering to the tattered
conventionalities of Attwood and Dr. Hayes. Dr.
Elvey beat time strenuously from the organ loft,
but to very little purpose. He followed Mr. Goss,
but the respective choirs went each its own way.

It is thus that the idols of one generation become the
footballs of another, where great composers are in
question. But the passage is worth looking at as a
means of reckoning up what both the Cathedral and
the Festival owe to Sir John Goss, to Sir John Stainer,[1]

[1] A kindly notice of the first edition in the *Guardian* gave the
information that, after having had the help of an orchestral band
for 150 years, the committee dispensed with this aid in 1843 at the
instigation of Bishop Blomfield, and for the next thirty years were
content with the accompaniment of the organ. At the Festival of
1873, a year after Stainer's appointment, the orchestra was restored. Stainer composed for this occasion his Evening Service
in A, and Mendelssohn's *Hymn of Praise* was the anthem.

and to Sir George Martin, who for many years, out
of sheer love towards a good cause, was able to put
the music beyond such criticism.[1] The complaint
about the conservatism of the selection has long ceased
to be justified. Nothing remains of the regular eigh-
teenth-century programme but the Old Hundredth
and (in alternate years) the Hallelujah Chorus.

Indeed, the *Times* critic soon had an opportunity
of acknowledging that things were improving. At
the Bicentenary Festival, which the Prince Consort
attended in 1854, the choral service, says Davison,
" had an effect of grandeur and sublimity, of which
no conception can be formed by those who did not
hear it." Attwood's *Deus misereatur*, no longer a
" tattered conventionality," now seemed to the critic
of Printing House Square " one of the finest specimens
of our English ecclesiastical harmony," while Goss's
anthem, " Praise the Lord, O my soul," specially
composed for the occasion, struck him as being " grand,
broad, and massive " in its harmony, " but free from
any servile adherence to models." It was in 1859
that Mendelssohn came first into the programme with
what the *Morning Post* of May 19 called " Bartholdy's
Anthem on Psalm xliii.," but the *Times* critic was
apparently not present. He reserved himself for the
production, in 1862, of Goss's " Wilderness " anthem,

---

[1] It is hard to realise that since Sir George's death we have had,
and have too early lost, the help of Dr. Charles Macpherson. His
successor, Dr. Stanley Marchant, received his first post as organist
of Christ Church, Newgate Street. I record his name with pride
and affection.

" a work," he says, " no less admirable for its purity
than for its scholarly correctness and intrinsic musical
charm." The same authority was on the watch at
the Festival of 1865, which King Edward VII. attended
as Prince of Wales, and at which Goss's special setting
of the then Dean's " Brother, thou art gone before
us," seemed to the critic to be " one of the most
melodious and expressive movements in the whole
range of modern music for the Church."

The instrumentalists and vocalists do not figure
prominently in the records. But Bacon notes " M^r
Richards playing the first violin " in 1780, " Mr Shaw,"
afterwards Leader at Drury Lane, in 1790, and " M^r
Serjeant " (Trumpeter) and Mr. Archer (second violin,
Drury Lane) in 1793. And Bacon, as the very soul
of good humour, was sometimes not a little disturbed
at the incompatibilities of temper among the musicians.
Philip Hayes, who " enjoyed the reputation of pos-
sessing the largest person and the most unsociable
temper in England," [1] had in 1783 what the Secretary
describes as " a trifling altercation " with Mr. Toaper
" respecting the performance of the latter, which
however at that time could not be adjusted." Much
difficulty, Bacon adds, " arises in the management of
the different performers both vocal and instrumental,
and it is much to be lamented that such should be the
case where Charity exists, and by which a charitable
institution may be affected." Again, in 1793, when
Arnold was asked to preside at the organ, great offence

[1] *Dict. Nat. Biog.*, s.v.

was given to John Jones, the St. Paul's organist
(1755–96). He was ill, and "was hurt at his not
being consulted or asked for permission ; on which
account the D [Arnold] has since rec^d an insolent
letter from Mr Jones's deputy, who he meant should
have done the Duty." But Bacon can find consola-
tion even here. " Very fortunate "—so he sums the
matter up—" this did not happen till the next Morn^g
or such a Discord would have unharmonized the Day,
which was as pleasant as the Sun was bright." Certainly King George III. set the musicians a better
example ; for in 1787 Bacon had to write to the
Archbishop (Moore) in a serious dilemma and to the
following effect :—

The Royal Reviews of the Oxford Blues and
the Brigade of Horse are fixed for the 8th and
10th of May, the Days which have been publicly
announced for the Rehearsal and Anniversary of
the Charity of the Sons of the Clergy at St. Paul's
Cathedral. . . . The brief State of the Fact is
that the Charity being deprived of the best Wind
Instruments in consequence of these Reviews must
suffer exceedingly in the Execution of the Music
and it is generally believed that such a defalcation
may greatly injure the Collections ; and the
Stewards are so circumstanced by the whole of
their Tickets being printed off, and their absolute
Agreement with the Members of the Musicians
Fund for the band, that it is impossible for them
to alter their days.

This letter was sent on April 19th, and the Archbishop's reply was both concise and satisfactory :—

> The Sons of the Clergy,
>   The Archbishop mentioned the substance of the Inclosed to His Majesty this Morning, Who condescended to say that the Review on the 8th should not take the Wind Instruments from the Stewards of the Charity ; and that He might possibly find some way of preventing the inconvenience which they are afraid of on the Tenth.
>
> J. C.
>
> LAMBETH.

It is added that in consequence " His Majesty was graciously pleased to alter the Day of Review to Friday the 11th instead of Thursday the 10th of May " —a striking tribute to the hold which the Festival had gained over public attention and concern.

It has been already mentioned that the orchestra was furnished by the Royal Society of Musicians, which Maurice Greene helped to found. In 1739 the Governors of this Society " resolved *nem. con.* that they would supply an able Band of Music at the Rehearsal and Anniversary of the Sons of the Clergy for the sum of £50 and, upon payment of that Sum annually to their Charitable Fund, that they would never increase the Demand upon any future Occasion." This arrangement lasted till within living memory. Sir W. H. Cummings, late Principal of the Guildhall School of Music, told me that, having sung at Festivals as a choir boy, he remembered the band of the Royal Society of Musicians taking part. He also most kindly placed at my disposal some information in regard to the early connection between this Society and the Sons of the Clergy. His rare copy of " The Laws and Resolutions of several General Meetings for the future Regulation and Management of the Fund for the Support of Decayed Musicians and their Families " (1761) shows that in 1751 the following rule was made :—

That all Lists of Performers to be appointed out of the Members of this Society, for performing at the annual Feasts of the Sons of the Clergy, (so long as the present Agreement subsists between that Corporation and this Society, in relation to musical Performances at those Feasts) be made and appointed by the Governors of this Charity as heretofore ; and it is most strongly recommended to all such Members . . . that they do attend such Performances and the Rehearsal thereof regularly, that the above-mentioned Agreement . . . may be continued, to the mutual Advantage of both Charities, and which will prevent any Proposals being made hereafter, that may be disagreeable to any member or members of this Society.

At another general meeting in 1753,

upon a Motion made by Dr. Greene from the Chair That all Persons appointed . . . to perform

at St. Paul's . . . that shall refuse or neglect giving
their Attendance after due Notice given them in
Writing, without giving satisfactory reasons . . .
shall be excluded the Society, . . . it was *resolved
in the Affirmative.*

In 1754 they decided " that no Allowance whatsoever
shall be made to any Member of this Society out of
the Fund for his performance at St. Pauls." After
the Society was incorporated in 1790, every member
had to declare on his election that he would " attend,
when summoned, in person, or with permission . . .
by Deputy, at St. Paul's . . . to assist in such manner
as the Governors or Committee shall appoint." Also
a rule was made that the Governors of the Musicians'
Society,

in March annually, make a list of the Performers
for St. Paul's ; the said list to be made from the
junior Members . . . excepting the Leader, and
such principal Performers whose assistance may
be requisite on that occasion, and that notice be
immediately sent to such Members.

As soon as the day fixed for our Festival was known,
the date was communicated to each musician on the
list, with this admonition :—

And it is hoped every Member will think it incumbent on him to exert himself on this occasion.
But in case you should be applied to, by mistake,
to perform in a way you think likely to injure

you in your profession, it is expected that you immediately acquaint the Governors, that they may consider the propriety of admitting a Deputy.

Such a partnership between the charitable societies of the two professions is of historical interest, and it is a pity that it should be altogether forgotten.

THE PREACHERS

The Anniversary was distinguished from the Rehearsal by the fact that a sermon was added to the long programme of music. There are scarcely any signs that the proceedings were shortened to make room for the sermon, save that in 1779 it was arranged for " Handel's Chorus to be omitted and the *Jubilate* chanted." It is true that on a rough calculation the discourses of the Festival preachers at that period were only twice the length of what is thought necessary to-day, whereas, in the days before elaborate music was introduced, a preacher such as Henry Sacheverell, in 1713, would be five times as long as the preacher of to-day. In either case, whether the sermon was the thing in itself or only an addendum to the music, one cannot but wonder at the patience and the leisure of the generations of old.

The invitation to the preacher came in early times from the Stewards, but a natural tendency arose to consult the Archbishop as President of the Corporation, and with him to-day, if not by the letter of the

constitution, yet by a natural tendency, the choice of
the preacher rests. John Bacon introduces us in 1775
to a state of things in which a preacher appointed
himself. " Rev^d Mr. Burnaby [1] being present was so
kind as to offer his services to preach the Anniversary
Sermon." In 1776 " the Rev^d Dr. Porteus " [then
rector of Lambeth] had offered to preach, and the
Secretary was asked " to signify to Him the great
Respect and satisfaction which the Stewards have
expressed on the Occasion." They did not consider
it absolutely necessary to fix upon a preacher until
the Union Dinner day, and in 1778 they are found
desiring " that the opinion of the Bishop of Oxford
should be first ascertained on that Head." This was
John Butler, a popular preacher of the time, who was
chaplain to George III., and was afterwards promoted
to Hereford.

It will be remembered that the earlier preachers
were mostly bishops ; it was so from 1674 to 1680.
Turner, Bishop of Ely, preached in 1684, and Edward
Fowler, Bishop of Gloucester, John Bunyan's former
adversary, in 1692. But from the time that the
Festival settled at St. Paul's it came to be the very
rare exception for a prelate to be the preacher. Isaac
Maddox, of St. Asaph, in 1742, is the only case between
1692 and 1854, when Archbishop Sumner preached
the Bicentenary sermon. Since then the rule has

---

[1] Andrew Burnaby, son and grandson of two of the same name,
rectors of Asfordby, Leics. K.S. at Westminster, 1748. Vicar
of Greenwich, 1769–1812. Archdeacon of Leicester, 1786–1812.
Author of *Travels through North America*. (D.N.B.)

been slightly relaxed. Magee and four other bishops of English or Welsh dioceses have advocated the claims of the Corporation in and since 1874. It is evident from one of John Bacon's notes that the task of preaching on these occasions was held to belong to the " inferior clergy," and that the Stewards of 1790 and later did not quite acquiesce in the notion. Bacon then had " a Letter from the Bp. of Chester [de Quincey's friend, William Cleaver, an incorrigible non-resident,] declining the office of Preacher notwithstanding his *promise* of last year. The Secretary reported that he had a very respectable person who had promised, if one could not be procured from the Bench of Bishops by the interference of His Grace of Canterbury, whom the Secretary promised to apply to for that purpose." But the Archbishop " declined applying to any of the Bishops." However, nothing daunted, they tried again in 1792. Beadon, Bishop of Gloucester, one of the Stewards of the previous year, " was solicited, but refused, partly from its *not being known that a Bishop ever accepted that office*, but principally upon his being full of engagements. Dr. Pearce [Master of the Temple, who has already been referred to as one of the active workers in the Festival arrangements,] was likewise asked, but excused himself upon its being too hard to perform double duty, viz Steward and Preacher. The Revd Mr Barton [of St. Andrew, Holborn,] rejected for the same reason. The Secretary was requested *to take out of his Pocket a Preacher*, when he produced the name of Dr Rich^d

Nicholl, Chancellor of Wells, &c. &c." So in 1795 the Bishop of Bristol (Dr. Courtenay), being a Steward that year, was asked to nominate a preacher, but preferred to leave the choice to the Stewards. There is not much doubt that the present plan of a private conversation between the Archbishop and the Registrar is a more delicate mode of arriving at the same result. One can sometimes see John Bacon, as the selector, preening himself over the success of his selection. In 1789 he notes that "the Sermon was preached by W. Vincent, D.D. &c. &c. &c. and with a command of voice that every one distinctly heard every word of his most excellent Discourse." Vincent, who was at this time headmaster of Westminster, sub-almoner to the King, and incumbent of All Hallows, Thames Street, was, with all his pluralism, a generous friend to the Corporation, and no doubt deserved Bacon's praise. Having secured their preacher and seen him safely into the pulpit, the Stewards had nothing to do but decide whether they would ask him to print the sermon at their expense.[1] Sometimes they gave this invitation before the preacher left the church. Sometimes they hesitated. For instance, they acknowledged the sermon of 1792 to be a "very excellent

---

[1] And they were read. Pyle (A. Hartshorne, *Memoirs of a Royal Chaplain*, p. 226) reported to Dr. Kerrich on January 11th, 1755, among the "literary news" of the week from Bishop Hoadly's house at Chelsea :—" The Bishop of Norwich's Chaplain, Dʳ Butler, minister of Yarmouth, has published a mighty clever sermon preached before the Sons of the Clergy." The sermon was preached on May 9th, 1754, and the preacher, then "Chaplain to the Princess Dowager of Wales," afterwards became Bishop of Oxford and of Hereford.

discourse," but the preacher "was not requested to print till the Stewards had ascertained the opinion of his Grace of Cant^y their President on that Head, which could not be done with any propriety before their dining at Lambeth."

It is not surprising that an occasion of this sort should have called to its aid in two centuries and a half a very remarkable list of preachers. It includes, with many names whose significance is lost, many which stand for what is great in theology or thought —Pearson, Gunning, Beveridge, Tenison, Atterbury, White Kennett, T. Sherlock, Waterland, Mangey, Porteus, Vincent, Henry Phillpotts, Samuel Wilberforce, Melvill, Dale, Vaughan, Alford, Daniel Moore, W. F. Hook, Liddon, Magee, James Moorhouse and William Boyd Carpenter. Out of the sixty-eight preachers for the period 1860–1928, twenty-two were afterwards Bishops of English dioceses and seven became Deans of English cathedrals.

This long series of nearly two hundred and seventy-five sermons on one and the same subject, the great majority of which have been printed, affords a unique opportunity of watching the choice of texts. In a few cases these are not on record, but an examination shows that out of the first one hundred and fifty eighty took texts which no one else chose, while nineteen texts appear more than once. The palm for popularity goes to Galatians vi. 10 : "As we have therefore opportunity, let us do good unto all men, especially unto them who are of the household of faith," which

18

was the preachers' gambit on seven occasions ; 2 Kings
iv. 1, 2—Elisha and the prophet's widow—on six ;
St. James i. 27 [1]—the " pure religion " passage—on
five ; Jeremiah xlix. 11 and Psalm cxxii. 8, 9 on four ;
and 1 Corinthians ix. 13, 14 on three. No text chosen
verges on the extravagant, except perhaps Lamen-
tations iv. 5 : " They that were brought up in scarlet
embrace dunghills."

[1] This text is inscribed in Greek on Dr. Thomas Turner's monument in the church at Stowe.

CHAPTER XIV

THE CORPORATION AND THE STATE

A BODY of men like the Sons of the Clergy, established under Royal Charter to relieve the wants of those whom loyalty had brought low, was not likely to be altogether without its relations with the Heads of the State.

From political propaganda they must needs hold sternly aloof, and must see that their subordinates did the like. Nothing but shipwreck could follow any other course, and the following incident, which dates from 1748, shows their natural anxiety to avoid such a catastrophe :—

Mr Comyn [the Register] acquainted the Comittee that a Complaint had been made to him by several Members of the House of Commons of Thomas Baseley Agent of the Corporation for their Estate at Stow in North'tonshire for influencing the Tenants of the Corporation and threatning to turn them out of their Farms unless they voted as he directed at the next Election for the said County. And the Comittee taking the same into consideration and hearing read a Letter from the President relating thereto, are of opinion that it is highly improper for any Agent of this Corporation to make any use of such power to influence the Tenants at any Election as the same may turn to the prejudice of the Charity, and that the

Register write to him and acquaint him that it is the direction of the Comittee that he leaves the Tenants at their Liberty to vote at such Election in such manner as they shall think proper. And that the Register do also write to George Carpenter Tenant of the Manor House to signify this opinion of the Comittee to such Tenants as are Freeholders.

Whatever faults may be laid at the door of the clergy and their families, unfaithfulness to the Crown is scarcely one, and, if we had the old-time toast-lists surviving, we could perhaps trace " Church and King " further back in the history of our Corporation than in that of any other society in the kingdom. Indeed, there were times when their feelings became too exuberant to be content with the customary modes of expression. For at the Rehearsal dinner held at the London Coffee-House in May, 1808, after *Non nobis, Domine*, had been " sung in a most masterly style by the gentlemen of the Choir, accompanied in the Choral parts by all the parties present," they took up " God save the King," and gave it an additional verse, which could now be, not inappropriately, revived :—

" O May the Royal Line
In every virtue shine
Like George our King,
And when to Kindred Skies
His happy spirit flies
May other Georges rise
Like George our King."

But they could still be loyal and yet keep to humbler levels in expressing their feelings. Naturally their first efforts were in the direction of gratitude to the Merry Monarch, their Royal Founder, and they had only enjoyed their Charter five years when the Rye House Plot gave them an opportunity to present their first address to the Crown. The Court, in the presence of the Stewards, ordered it " to be faire engrossed and to passe the Seale," and it was arranged through Sir Leoline Jenkins, who had risen out of Doctors' Commons to the Secretaryship of State, that they should " know his Maties pleasure when he will be attended therewith." The address was as follows :—

Dread Soveraign

All other loyall Societys in the Kingdome having dutifully layd at your Majesties feet theire zealous Acclamations for the miraculous deliverance of your Majesty and your dearest Brother the Duke of Yorke from the late damnable conspiracy of Fanaticall and wicked men, enemies alike implacable to Monarchy and to the Church of England Wee the Sons of the Clergy might justly be condemned of extreme Ingratitude to GOD and the King if wee should neglect to expresse our unfeigned joy and congratulations upon this most happy occasion, since wee have not only the same obligations of Duty and Fidelity to your Majesty with all your other subjects in that wee plentifully enjoy the blessings of Heaven and Earth under your most mercifull and benigne reigne But wee are a Corporation entirely your Majesties, framed and erected by your Royall goodnesse into a body of men, in whome Loyalty

and obedience to the Crowne is naturall and in-
bred, derived to us from our Fathers, confirmed
by our Education, encouraged by your Majesty's
patronage and protection, and immoveably fixd in
us by our holy Religion. Wee have therefore
unanimously made use of this first Returne of our
solemne annuall feast of Charity to declare our
vows of inviolable affection and zeale for the
safety and honour of your Maties sacred person
(whome GOD Allmighty long preserve) and to
publish to all the world our utter detestation of
all Rebellious principles and practices under whatsoever pretence of Liberty property or Religion
they would recommend themselves : And wee take
the boldnesse humbly to assure your Ma^{ty} that
Wee are firmly resolved to save and defend (if
need be) with our Lives and Fortunes the just
prerogatives of your Imperial Crowne and Dignity,
the right of Lineall Succession in the Royall
Family and the happiest government upon Earth
as under your Majesty it is by Law established in
Church and State.

Our particular Relation to and zeale for the best
of Reformed Churches make us joyne in Devout
Prayers that GOD would be pleased to turne the
Hearts of all your misguided subjects to theire
bounden Duty and Allegiance and incline them
to judge of the Truth of the protestant Religion
not by the Schismaticall or factious Tenents of
any evill sect or party that usurps its name but
by that steddy Loyalty and Primitive Christian
Subjection to Kings which has been always owned

JOHN DOLBEN, BISHOP OF ROCHESTER, THE FIRST PRESIDENT.
From the engraving by R. Tompson.

and practised by the Church of Christ and remarkably by this of England.

The address was graciously received, and printed in the *Gazette* ; nor is there any reason to discount its sentiments. The men who founded the Corporation were ardent Royalists to a man. John Dolben, the first President, while still a Student of Christ Church, Oxford, had been wounded at Marston Moor, and returned to the University a major. Peter Gunning's Royalist sermons filled Little St. Mary's by Peterhouse. Tobias Rustat had been attached to Charles II., when Prince of Wales, and had gone to and fro between him and his unfortunate father. Sprat, indeed, was not made of such stern stuff, but no one spoke more loudly for Divine Right, and it is possible to pity his trembling hand as he read James II.'s Declaration in Westminster Abbey. Humphrey Henchman was the son of the Bishop who had assisted Charles II. to escape after the battle of Worcester, while Pearson had been chaplain to the last remnant of the Royalist forces in the West under Goring at Exeter in 1645.

With the accession of James II. there came to them, perhaps, some searchings of heart. For if they were Royalists, they were no Romanists. During the Commonwealth Dolben had maintained, penal laws or no penal laws, the regular and ritual celebration of the Holy Communion at Oxford, as Peter Gunning did at Exeter House in the Strand. Such men had not rescued their rites from Geneva to sacrifice them to Rome, and it is possible to gather from the address presented to James II. that they were glad of his assurances, and meant to hold him to them. Here at least is what they permitted themselves to say to him on March 17, 1685, taking Sir Christopher Wren to the palace with them :—

As Wee cannot but have a just sense of the publick losse and of ours particularly in the decease of the late King your Majesty's dearest Brother and our most Gracious Founder of ever blessed Memory, so it is to our unspeakeable comfort and joy to behold your Sacred Majesty peaceably settled on the Throne of your Royall Progeniture. To this most Auspicious beginning for which Wee are ever bound to blesse GOD Wee are deeply sensible how much your Majesty hath added by your most Gracious Declaraçon at your first comeing to Councell and particularly by your declaring that you will make it your Endeavour to preserve this Government both in Church and State as it is now by Law established which also adds a further obligation of gratitude to that which Wee had before by our Haereditary Principle of Unconditionall and unchangeing Loyalty.

And as Our Fathers have also taught Us Wee make it our dayly Prayer to GOD that he would grant your Majesty in health and wealth long to live, strengthen you that you may vanquish and overcome all your Enemies and finally after this Life you may attaine Everlasting joy and felicity.

So they left him with their apt quotation from the national liturgy in the vulgar tongue. But when he lost the confidence of the country and his own in himself, it did not follow that a Corporation of Toryism all compact could throw itself at the feet of " Dutch William," and there was no address drawn up when he and his Queen came to the throne. Not, perhaps, that none of the Sons of the Clergy would have been willing to bow to the new-comers. But their President's name must appear on any address that was likely to be accepted, and Francis Turner, Bishop of Ely, had thrown in his lot with the Nonjurors. How was it possible, moreover, for the Sons of the Clergy to take part in the congratulations addressed to William, when Sancroft, the Primate, was not consenting to the counsel and deed of those who would ? It may be that the Corporation was saved from paroxysm by Tenison. He had joined the Court in 1688 as rector of St. Martin in the Fields. He would bring in his tendency to Whig Latitudinarianism, but in the Court Room it would show itself in a desire that for an object of this charitable nature all parties might work together. So in 1689 we find as Vice-President Sir William Gregory, who when baron of the Exchequer had been suspended in 1685 for giving a decision against the " dispensing power " of the Crown. In 1690 William Lloyd, one of the Seven Bishops, became President, replacing Turner, and Edward Fowler, a notorious Whig, joined the Court. The transformation was outwardly complete in November, 1697, when

Tenison was elected President. Exactly a month later
an address was presented to William III. " Such of
the Court of Assistants as please to goe are desired to
attend the president . . . to-morrow att five of the
Clock in the afternoone att Kensington, when his
Grace is to waite upon the King with it." It is
obviously inspired by a wish to make up for lost
opportunities :—

Wee your Majesties most dutifull subjects the
Corporation of the Sons of the Clergy doo humbly
beg leave to take this first opportunity of our
Annuall meeting for offering in your Royall
presence

ffirst our Sacrifice of praise to almighty GOD
for restoring your Majestie safe to your people in
all the glories of an honourable peace,

Next to your Royall self our most unfeigned
thanks for that unparallelld Magnanimity and in-
defatigable zeal employed on our behalfe to which
the Reformed Religion your owne Kingdomes and
the whole western world do owe the Restauration
of their present quiet and the prospect of their
future security.

The more imediate Relation wee of this Body
bear to that establish'd Church of which God
hath made you soe eminently the protector and
deliverer, as it gave us Dread S^r a constant and
most sensible concerne for all your hazards in
War, so does it fill our hearts with a proportion-
able Joy for all your Maties Honours and Successes

as the most valuable blessings which can divolve upon our selves.

Our gratefull thanks whereof wee shall ever labour to express by a distinguishing zeal for your Maties services and by our daily fervent prayers to the King of Kings that your Maties may long continue to reap the ffruit of all your Toils and Dangers by living the happy peacefull glorious Ruler of an affectionate United prosperous people by seeing vice and Irreligion effectually suppressed and truth justice and piety flourish under your most auspicious Government and by attaining att length a Crowne of Everlasting Joy and ffelicity.

As William's reign drew to a close the Jacobite cause began to raise its head again, and the Corporation saw a fresh chance of asserting its assent to the Act of Settlement by presenting another address, this time at Hampton Court, through the Archbishop, " accompanied by the Right Honble Sr Nathan Wright, K^t, Lord Keeper of the Great Seal of England," and several others. The Lord Keeper's presence and his keen interest in the Charity is itself an instance of the mutual toleration of the Sons of the Clergy, for he had been junior counsel for the Crown against the Seven Bishops. In this second Address they submitted

that the present indignation which wee now feel upon the Accompt of the French Kings late attempt against y^r Imperial Crowne and the Succession in the Protestant line by setting up the pretended prince of Wales, doth only make the Loyalty and gratitude of the Nation to increase and to exert themselves the more vigorously in very numerous and most affectionate Addresses.

Wherefore amongst the crowds who wait to express their just resentments against the French King and their greatest obligations to your most Excellent Majesty We the Sons of the Clergy who are a Society that cant expect to subsist under none but a protestant prince humbly desire to give y^r Majesty fresh assurances of our haereditary Loyalty to the Crowne and of our deliberate and long resolved adherence both to the sacred person and to the noble cause you are ingaged in of piously maintaining the protestant Religion and generally opposing the French King in all his unjust ambitions and enslaving designs.

Within six months they were waiting on Queen Anne " at her Court at St. James," and claiming " that our Corporation is an evidence (notwithstanding the Objections of our Adversaries of the Church of Room) that a married clergy may be prosperous and usefull to the nation and government unto which they belong," and thanking the Queen for her " timely care to discourage all manner of prophanesse and Immorality." As a body the clergy soon had other things for which to thank her, in the shape of the First Fruits grant of 1704. No doubt she did not think worse of the Corporation because in 1710, the year of his trial and sentence, Henry Sacheverell was elected an Assistant and, being suspended from preaching, became a most regular attendant at Courts and Committees. But the Sons of the Clergy must not take sides. Benjamin Hoadly was made a Governor in 1704, the year of his appointment to St. Peter-le-Poer, though he took no active part in the management. Sacheverell's Sancho Panza, the Rev. Joseph Trapp, the High Church and Tory tract-writer, and afterwards Vicar of Christ Church, may be set against Charles Trimnell, Archdeacon of Norfolk, who joined the Court in 1707, and, as an advocate of the rights of the Crown against Convocation, became Bishop of Norwich and died Bishop of Winchester—a very good man, " whom even the Tories valued, though he preached terrible Whig sermons." [1] When Trimnell defeated Atterbury in 1721 in the contest for the presidency of the Corporation, his son Hugh became his father's representative in the routine work of the Charity.

But seven years before that the Sons of the Clergy were again anxious to stand before kings. In June, 1714, the Committee of Ways and Means had before them " a Draught of a Peticon to her Ma'tie for granting a Charter to enable the Corporation to purchase £3000 p. Ann. more," and the Register was told to " ingrosse it and attend the Attorney Generall therewith for his approbation and offer him 2 Guineas for his ffee for perusing the same." The petition was approved by the next Court, and it was resolved " that

---

[1] Abbey and Overton, *English Church in the Eighteenth Century*, p. 61, note (ed. 1902).

the Treārers attend the Ld Bishopp of Rochester with
the Peticon and desire the favour of him to gett the
same presented to her Majestie." Francis Atterbury's
action during these last days of Queen Anne's life has
been the subject of much investigation, and has inspired
one famous passage in historical fiction. Whether
he was preparing to proclaim James III. at Charing
Cross or not, it may be taken for certain that his
time during those weeks was too fully occupied even
for the affairs of the Sons of the Clergy, whose colleague
he had been so long. So a month later it was reported
to them that the Bishop " excused himself from being
concerned in the matter." In any case, the Queen
was ill, and it must wait. Then, in September, came
the question of approaching her successor. The Committee of Ways and Means " at the Chapter House
belonging to St. Paul's," met " to prepare an Addresse
. . . to congratulate his Maties Accession to the
Throne," and requested Dr. Sacheverell, Dr. Trapp,
and Dr. Higden, with several others, to " withdrawe
into another Roome and draw up the Addresse." But
when the matter came before the Court of Assistants,
it was apparently thought well to put the question
whether such an address should be presented, and it
was " carried in the affirmative (*nemine contradicente*)."
Then they went to Tenison in order to have it presented, but not without some doubts whether " His
Grace's Health or business " would " permitt him to
present it himselfe." Notice was given to the Assistants to be present at the function. But October came,

and the new King had not received the bow of the
Sons of the Clergy. Tenison had told one of the
Treasurers " that the King was tired with the Crowds
of People attending upon these occasions and that it
was his (Tenison's) opinion the more privately it was
done the better, and that his Grace recommended them
to the Bishopp of Norwich . . . who had undertaken
to do it." However, if the King was too tired to
receive their address in public, he gave them the
extension of purchasing power, which they had hoped
to obtain from Queen Anne, and their new Charter
was granted in December, 1714. Only one other
Corporation event in George I.'s reign is worth notice
—the contest for the Presidentship in 1721. It lay
between Trimnell, who was for the King, and Atterbury, who was for the Pretender. Considering that
in 1720 Atterbury had been sent to the Tower on a
charge of endeavouring to bring the Stuarts back, we
are forced to the conclusion that there was some
political significance in his being put forward for
election at all, and his retirement from the Court of
Assistants in the following year, 1722, no doubt tended
to the peace of its proceedings.

We need not follow their addresses further. The
gracious answer of George II. to their greeting in
1722 was followed early in 1723 by the Treasurer's
announcement that he " had received the £500 his
Majesties Benefaction which was attended with the
Charge of the usuall ffees," and no doubt Trimnell
deserved the thanks which the Court tendered to him

" for the share he has had in procuring " the gift. Henceforward the interest passes to the connexion of the House of Brunswick with the annual Festival, and to the untiring ambition of John Bacon for the success of his undertakings.

Even before his day the interest had begun to show itself. In 1738 the Festival collection included £50 from Frederick, Prince of Wales, who, by the way, did not like Handel, and " an Address was framed by the Stewards to his Royal Highness and spoken by Thomas Potter, Esq., the youngest son to the Archbishop of Canterbury." In 1747 " Prince George [afterwards George III., then nine years of age] and Prince Edward were at the Rehearsal . . . and their Royal Highnesses contributed £100 on the Day following," which called forth another address to the Prince of Wales. This visit was due to Dr. Francis Ayscough, whose family name appears frequently among those of the Corporation's early beneficiaries, and who was tutor to the young Princes. A newspaper account says " they were in a coach of State, drawn by six horses, richly dressed with orange-coloured ribands, and escorted by a party of the Horse Grenadier and Life Guards." Frederick, Prince of Wales, replying next day to an address of thanks presented by the Stewards, said : " I am glad to have had an opportunity to convince the Clergy of the high regard I have for them ; and it shall be the study of my life to imprint the same sentiments on my children." Thirteen years afterwards, when their youthful visitor, Prince George, came to the throne, the Corporation in its address reminded him " of the Honor it once received by the Presence of your most illustrious Person " ; and, that nothing might be wanting to express their gratitude, it had been ordered that an advertisement should appear in the papers giving the Governors notice of the day of presentation. " N.B. that the Coaches will go from the Corporation Office in the Temple Precisely at 12 o'clock."

But Bacon was determined to have Royal patronage on a permanent basis, if dutiful supplication could secure it. In 1794 he submitted a plan to Sir John Skynner, formerly Chief Baron and then Vice-President of the Corporation, and the gist of it was this :— " Could his Majesty and the Royal Family be allured to the Anniversarys, the Prosperity of the Institution would be at once established." And Bacon was not the man to miss chances. For in 1797 the Princess Royal's marriage to the " Prince of Wirtemberg " clashed with the Stewards' date and necessitated a postponement of the Festival. So Bacon got himself instructed to send a message to the Archbishop from the Rehearsal dinner expressing " the Honor which they have this day had in proposing and drinking the Health of their Serene Highnesses [he is a little amiss here] the Prince and Princess of Wirtemberg, with an earnest hope that they might be indulged with their Presence at St. Paul's at their Anniversary on Wednesday, where proper and suitable accommodation would be furnished for them and for their suite, and

19

the Stewards the rather indulge their Imaginations to a degree of Compliance, upon a supposed Idea that the Charity may have suffered from the prolongation of the time owing to the Royal Nuptials." The amiable plan did not succeed, but as " the Church began to fill unusually fast on account of a Belief " that the young couple would be present, and was " very crowded with people of the first distinction," the Secretary no doubt consoled himself.

He was getting nearer his desire when in 1798 he secured the Duke of York as Steward. If " the pressure of Public Business " kept His Royal Highness from attending the Anniversary, he at any rate accepted Archbishop Manners Sutton's invitation to Lambeth, and it was perhaps at his instigation that George, Prince of Wales, became a Steward in 1799. With that achieved, Bacon could retire from the secretariat, and his account of the day's proceedings was his swan-song as a writer of minutes. It is long, but characteristic.

This Anniversary (it says) was never so eminently distinguished as on this day in consequence of His Royal Highness the Prince of Wales not only having condescended to accept the Office of Steward of the Music Meetings in the Cathedral of St. Paul but honouring it by His Royal presence —The previous notification which had been given by the Secretary to the Stewards of this favourable circumstance proved highly advantageous to the Charity—The Honourable the Artillery Company

and the Loyal London Association were prepared
to receive His Royal Highness with the Military
Honours due to the Heir Apparent when visiting
the City of London on a public and solemn occasion—About ½ past 11 o'clock the Prince arrived
in his Coach at Temple Barr accompanied by
General Leigh and Thomas Tyrwhit Esq, His
Royal Highness's Secretary, parties of the City
Associations being arranged on each side of the
Street. On his Royal Highness coming near
St. Dunstan's Church he was received by the City
Marshals and the Artillery Company with the
accustomed ceremony of Drums beating and
colours flying and by them escorted to St. Paul's,
where His Royal Highness was also welcomed by
the Loyal London Association.—On the Prince's
allighting from his Carriage at the Gates the
Association Band struck up, and continued playing
till He came to the Porch where the Archbishop
of Canterbury and several of the Bishops with
the Dean and Chapter and his Brethren Stewards
were waiting to receive Him.   Immediately on His
Royal Highness's entering the Church, and whilst
he was conducted by the Archbishop Bishops and
Stewards to the door of the Choir, a masterly
Voluntary was played on the Organ.

The Prince was ushered to the Bishop of London's
throne, the Lord Mayor taking his stall on the opposite
side. Dr. Arnold conducted, and the music was performed " with appropriate taste and spirit." Greatorex'
harmonisation of the Hundredth Psalm " failed not

to excite in the attentive congregation a glow of Devotion." The rest of the usual programme " produced all the effect these inestimable compositions are calculated to inspire." Indeed, Bacon himself becomes as one inspired, when he tries to describe it all.

The whole of the Service was conducted in a very grand and impressive stile. It was not over till half past three. His Royal Highness was dressed in the uniform of the Tenth Light Dragoons of which He is Colonel—Upon the whole it was a most pleasing spectacle to every true and Loyal Briton—whether we consider the dignifyed affability and endearing manners of the accomplished *Prince* or the great and solid grandeur attending this exhibition by his wealthy and liberal Fellow-Subjects united in one divine object, by which our *Constitution* as well as our Morals are upheld ; namely in cherishing and supporting the orphans of those good Men whose Lives have been devoted to the propagation of British Virtue and British patriotism—The Prince retired about half past 7 o'clock eagerly solicitous to pay His respects to His *Royal Parents* at Covent Garden Theatre.

It may be added that an entry, " The Prince of Wales his whole expence £46. 15," acknowledges that the Prince qualified for his Stewardship by something more than his actual attendance on the occasion, and that the sum raised by the anniversary was £1,150.

Thenceforward for half a century, with the single exception of the year 1804, when Nelson served the office, the Sons of the Clergy were never without a Royal Steward, and at a meeting at Willis's Rooms on January 17, 1807, with the Duke of Sussex in the chair, this princely habit was ordained as an ordinance for ever. The minute-books sometimes refer to " that precious pledge given on a memorable occasion by six of the Royal Family in person, that so long as a Prince of the House of Brunswick was alive, our Charity should never want a royal Name at the head of its list of Stewards." The following figures will show that they were as good as their word : George, Prince of Wales, was Steward on two occasions, the Duke of York on four, William IV. as Duke of Clarence on five, the Duke of Kent on three, the Duke of Cumberland (once as King of Hanover) and the Duke of Sussex on seven each, the Duke of Cambridge on ten, and the Duke of Gloucester on five. In more modern days the Prince Consort was three times Steward, the last time being at the Bi-centenary in 1854. King Edward VII. served in 1865 ; the late Dukes of Saxe-Coburg and Albany and the Duke of Connaught have each given their names twice,[1] while the late Duke of Cambridge, true to his father's example and his own loyalty to all long-established institutions, was a Steward five times, and lived through 1903 to see the continued prosperity of an institution to which his father first gave his name in 1803. The

[1] H.R.H. Prince Arthur of Connaught served in 1914.

Duke had been a member of the Court of Assistants since 1842.[1]

In consenting to take a Steward's part in the 250th Festival, King George, who was also a Steward in 1895, had a wealth of precedent behind him, and has since then encouraged his children to follow in his steps.[2] He does not forget the Prince Consort's eloquent wish, expressed at the Bicentenary in 1854, that the Corporation might " continue for further hundreds of years as a bond of union between clergy and laity, and on each recurring centenary . . . find the nation ever advancing in prosperity, civilization, and piety " ; nor his Royal Father's plea in 1865, that " this society has been formed to mitigate the anxiety of many a hard-working clergyman, and to soothe the aching heart of many a widow and orphan in their hour of affliction."

[1] H.R.H.'s record was remarkable. 1834, May 10th, aged 15 : " Yesterday I went with the Queen to St. Paul's for the Festival of the Sons of the Clergy. Though the ceremony lasted very long—5 hours—yet it was a very fine and imposing service." 1890, May 8, aged 71 : " At 3 went to St Paul's Cathedral as Royal Steward for the year [a significant phrase] for the Sons of the Clergy Corporation—a very fine choral service, with addition of a large Choir and Orchestra. Dined with the Corporation at Merchant Taylors' Hall in the evening." Edgar Sheppard, *George, Duke of Cambridge*, i. 15 ; ii. 215.

[2] H.R.H. the Prince of Wales was a Steward in 1921 ; H.R.H. The Princess Mary, Viscountess Lascelles, in 1923 ; H.R.H. the Duke of York, in 1920 ; and H.R.H. the Duke of Gloucester in 1927. In 1828 H.R.H. the Duke of Gloucester was a Steward for the fourth time.

CHAPTER XV

SINCE 1904

IT is fitting that a few words should be added by way of giving an account of our stewardship for the time which has elapsed since the 250th Festival. To be alive at all in the last five and twenty years has been a testing and a moving experience alike for societies and for individuals, and it is naturally the oldest societies which have been most led to wonder whether, in the new and strange conditions wrought by the War and its consequences, they should find themselves among the things that are shaken and ready to vanish away.

In actual fact the 250th Festival did much to explain the Corporation and its work to a large public and to set us forward on the way to wider activities ; indeed, in many respects we stand on a broader and deeper basis alike of security and of usefulness than we did in 1904.

Let us talk of persons first. We remain for the time being the willing and grateful subordinates of the President of 1904. Dr. Davidson will cease to be Archbishop of Canterbury within a few weeks of the publication of this edition. But it is certain that the Court of Assistants will not willingly allow him to cease to be one of themselves. His Grace was elected to the Court in November, 1886, being then Dean of Windsor. He remained a member as Bishop of

Rochester and of Winchester, and in 1903 the Court followed the precedents, which go steadily back to the election of Archbishop Wake, by asking him to accept the President's office. He has quite frequently presided over their deliberations. He has made a long and unbroken series of speeches—full alike of history, as to the past, and of suggestiveness as to present needs and future developments—at Merchant Taylors' Hall ; until, the other day, that ancient and exclusive guild welcomed him to its honorary freedom as being almost one of themselves. With gracious and large hospitality the Archbishop and Mrs. Davidson have maintained the old-time custom of inviting the Stewards to dine at Lambeth Palace. No change of policy or of persons has ever been projected by the Court without seeking his wise and understanding counsel, and without accepting his view, when there was any difference, as surer and sounder than their own.

The 275th Festival will go forward under a new Archbishop of Canterbury, to whose guidance the Corporation can trust itself in full assurance ; for already Dr. Lang has been several times a Steward of the Festival and was himself the preacher at the Festival of 1900.

But there has also been a change of persons at 2 Bloomsbury Place. Fifty years ago the Court chose Mr. Paget Bowman as their Registrar, and " Sir Paget," as he became in due course, proved to be the very embodiment of the Corporation in the eyes of its particular public. He was assiduous in caring for and personally visiting its estates. He was like Mr. Mandeville B. Phillips of the Poor Clergy Relief Corporation in his accurate knowledge of the personal circumstances of the poorer clergy and their dependents. He stood for all that kind understanding and that ready sympathy and that close trustworthiness which have always marked the relations of " the Sons of the Clergy " towards those who seek their aid. He admirably prepared the business to be discussed by Courts and committees. He was a tactful and genial chairman of the independent committee of the Festival.

Sir Paget passed away in January 1917, when we could not yet see the end of the War, and when the men who were of an age to succeed him were still occupied in the service of the country. The Court was fortunate to be able to leave the affairs of the Charity, temporarily, in the hands of his son, Mr. Guy P. Bowman, who for some time had acted as his father's helper and deputy.

So it was not till the first memorial of the Armistice —on November 11, 1919—that at the Annual Court we were able once more to have a Registrar, when the choice fell most happily upon Mr. Aldred C. Rowden. He graduated from New College, Oxford, and came to us with a warm recommendation from Dr. Spooner, the late Warden. After several years in the publishing firm of Mr. Edward Arnold, he " joined up " in the first year of the War, served in Egypt and Palestine,

(captain and adjutant, 1915, and later major), was
severely wounded at Gaza, was " lent " during con-
valescence to the Ministry of Pensions, where he was
afterwards an inspector, and was for a time on the
personal staff of Sir Frederick Sykes at the Air Ministry.
He has amply fulfilled for us the promise implied in
such a record, and it is enough to say that the mantle
of Sir Paget has fallen upon him. The President
himself has borne true witness to Mr. Rowden's " quiet
effectiveness from the first day until now."

As it has been with persons, so is it also with the
various branches of the Corporation's life. Let us
take the Festival first because that is its historical
order. It would have been easy to prophesy that
after the War the glamour would pass away from a
great orchestral service, such as the cathedral saw in
plenty during those stirring years. But, nevertheless,
the Festival holds its own. Eminent musicians still
feel a pride in writing special compositions for it.
Eminent preachers feel honoured by an invitation to
emphasise the need for our work and the thoroughness
of our methods. Even in a St. Paul's which seems
but a fraction of its usual self the congregation is still
large, and will expand—let us hope, along with the
collection—whenever, two or three years hence, the
great space under the dome is once more the Festival's
auditorium.

The Stewards, who are the very backbone of
the whole organism of our annual commemoration,
continue to serve in welcome numbers, and since

1920 we have admitted ladies to the office, with
the result that there are ladies who have served
every year since the opportunity was first given
to them.

It is, in fact, the stedfastness of the Stewards which
is the glory of each Festival. In the list for 1927,
which happens to lie before me, there are 112 names.
Of these, only thirteen appear for the first time, of
whom two were Sheriffs and six were Masters of City
Guilds—the changing representatives of offices which
are a constant source of help. Thus, there were really
five recruits, and death makes as many gaps as that.
For 1929 in particular the Registrar hopes for a large
accession of strength to the ranks. He aims at a
total of 275 Stewards.

Meanwhile, the Corporation has been steadily con-
solidating its affairs and its finances. In the course
of the notes added to this edition it has been revealed
that we are no longer the landed proprietors that we
were in 1904. Very wisely, advantage was taken of
the " boom " in agricultural property, which was one
of the *sequelæ* of the War. Stowe-Nine-Churches and
Adstone ; Saltagh Grange ; Willingham—all these
were converted into Government securities ; and we
should have parted with Frank's Farm at Farningham,
if the chance had come. Few of us have skill to manage
an estate, even when it is immediately under our eyes,
and some of these properties lay at a far distance from
town. So it is of no use to pretend that there is not
a feeling of greater comfort and security, when we

receive our Stock-dividends on the appointed days, even though the percentage may be slightly less on the whole.

Our only anxiety now, as before, is that people should not assume that the Corporation has endowments for all its need, whereas in fact we are crippled in our beneficent work, unless each year brings its additional volume of voluntary contributions.

And one other happening of these last twenty-five years is serving to emphasise the lead which the Corporation could give, if it were adequately supported. The " Enabling " legislation and the financial activities of the Church Assembly have led both to inquiries and to projects which must bring us still further to the fore. The Commission of Enquiry into the Property and Revenues of the Church, which was appointed by the Archbishops in 1921 in pursuance of a resolution of the Church Assembly, was naturally anxious to have our Registrar's evidence. He put before them a careful statement of the Corporation's aims, and was examined about it on November 29th, 1922.[1]

But the long discussions on the Clergy Pensions Measure, 1925, inevitably brought up the question " What is the Church of England doing for the widows of the clergy ? " It became clear that pensions for widows could not be incorporated in the Measure without a great addition to the rate of premium. But it was arranged that the whole question should

[1] *Report* (ed. A. T. Lawrence), pp. 159–163.

be referred to a committee, of which Lord Selborne is chairman, and which has this reference :—

> to examine into the provision now made for the Widows and Orphans of Clergy of the Church of England, and the mode in which it may be strengthened, increased, or developed, and to report thereon.

The interim report [1] of that committee is dated October 21st, 1925. We appear in it as one of " the [five] great general societies," and the committee stated its hope to arrange interviews with the officials of each society.

So our review of long years of activity in a splendid cause closes at a moment of some interest. In the preface to the first edition it was suggested that in our Corporation " the Church has her central charitable organisation, to which the hundred minor societies of the same sort should be in some way affiliated." I wonder if that suggestion is to be supplanted by another—that for the purpose of pensioning widows and helping children, as well as of pensioning clergy, the " central charitable organisation " should be set up by the Church Assembly.

In any case, we hold on our way, knowing that we, and the other " great central societies," are constantly in receipt of contributions which might otherwise be lost to the cause, and steadily accumulating that

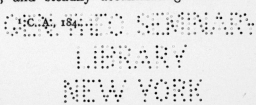

knowledge of our poorer folk and their needs, without which all central organisations must fail. We hold on our way, the older of us thankful for the long years during which we have been permitted to have our little part in so sacred a task, and the younger trusting by the goodness of God to be spared to celebrate the tercentenary of the Festival of the Sons of the Clergy.

APPENDIX

DR. THOMAS TURNER

REFERENCE has been made more than once in the course of our story (cf. pp. 79–81, 118–121) to the great benefaction, variously stated at £18,000 and £20,000, which Thomas Turner, President of Corpus Christi College, Oxford, left to the Sons of the Clergy on his death in 1714. Like Francis Turner, Bishop of Ely, and William Turner, Archdeacon of Northumberland, he was the son of Thomas Turner, Dean of Canterbury, his mother being Margaret, daughter of Sir Francis Windebank, Charles I.'s Secretary of State, who fled the country in 1640 owing to accusations brought against him of partiality to the Jesuits. Dr. Turner, as his monument in the old church at Stowe states, left £4,000 to friends and relations; £6,000 to Corpus Christi College, Oxford, and £20,000 in trust for his executors to buy land and hand it over " Societati quæ sublevandis per universam Angliam clericorum viduis liberisque fide non minore quam diligentia invigilat." Our records show that the executors in selecting the Manor of Stowe as the best purchase acted on a resolution of our Court of Assistants that the choice was in their view a wise one. It was the executors who placed the cenotaph in Stowe Church and the Court who printed engravings of it as an advertisement for their Charity. " Corpus ejus," says the Stowe inscription, " collegium Christi corpori dicatum die ultimo reddendum servat."

This cenotaph is described in Bridges' history of the county (p. 92) as being " made of a very curious variegated marble " and " arched over at the top." The arch is supported by " two neat pillars of the composite order." By the eastern pillar stands " a virgin on a celestial globe charged with a miter," holding a font on which is inscribed in Greek a portion of St. James i. 27. On the opposite side, also on a globe, stands Dr. Turner himself. Below are two shields, one bearing the inscription, *Clerus Anglicanus heres meus esto*, the other, *Filii Clericorum Ecclesiæque Anglicanæ*.

It is added by Baker (*History of Northamptonshire*, p. 443) that the person from whom the executors acquired the estate was Mr. Edward Harley, of Lincoln's Inn, who in 1699 had bought it of Lord Wharton for £14,000. Edward Harley, son of Sir Edward Harley, Governor of Dunkirk, a keen Parliamentarian, held the rich office of Auditor of the Imprest from 1702, and was greatly interested in the London charity schools, whose trustee he was, and whose yearly festival at St. Paul's was the companion function to our festival. As to the advowson of Stowe-Nine-Churches, the sale of which by auction has been described on page 119 f. of this volume, I am indebted for some further information to the late rector, the Rev. Henry Hughes Crawley. It appears that John Lloyd, whom we have seen making the highest bid, presented, in 1720, his son William Lloyd, who held the benefice till 1754, and was succeeded by his nephew, John Lloyd, who survived till 1789. He also was followed by his nephew, Charles Crawley, who died in 1849 and was succeeded by his grandson, the Rev. Henry Crawley, who died in 1895. Mr. Henry Hughes Crawley, the late incumbent, was his predecessor's nephew, and was inducted in 1896.[1] Thus during the period of 175 years which begins with the year 1720 and closes with the late incumbent's death there were but four rectors, and the average length of their occupation of the benefice is over forty-three years. This

---

[1] He died in 1921. The present patron is Lord Wraxall, of Clyst St. George, and the present incumbent is the Rev. Morgan Stanley Davies, sometime curate of Wraxall.

may be taken to imply that the Sons of the Clergy were the landlords of a fairly salubrious property. But further, the five rectors, including the last incumbent, have been members of one and the same family. The cynic may say that there is thus all the more reason to congratulate the highest bidder in 1717 on his bargain. But to-day the Church of England is inclined to rejoice when it sees a family steadily supplying men to serve God in its clerical ranks to the fifth generation, each in turn being content with the sphere which satisfied and engrossed his forbears.

PRESIDENTS

1678 John Dolben, Bishop of Rochester.
1683 Peter Gunning, Bishop of Ely.
1684 Francis Turner, Bishop of Ely.
1690 William Lloyd, Bishop of St. Asaph.
1697 Thomas Tenison, Archbishop of Canterbury.
1716 William Lloyd (second time), Bishop of Worcester.
1717 Philip Bisse, Bishop of Hereford.
1721 Charles Trimnell, Bishop of Winchester.
1723 William Wake, Archbishop of Canterbury.
1737 John Potter, Archbishop of Canterbury.
1747 Thomas Herring, Archbishop of Canterbury.
1757 Matthew Hutton, Archbishop of Canterbury.
1758 Thomas Secker, Archbishop of Canterbury.
1768 Hon. Frederick Cornwallis, Archbishop of Canterbury.
1783 John Moore, Archbishop of Canterbury.
1805 Charles Manners Sutton, Archbishop of Canterbury.
1828 William Howley, Archbishop of Canterbury.
1848 John Bird Sumner, Archbishop of Canterbury.
1862 Charles Thomas Longley, Archbishop of Canterbury.
1868 Archibald Campbell Tait, Archbishop of Canterbury.
1883 Edward White Benson, Archbishop of Canterbury.
1896 Frederick Temple, Archbishop of Canterbury.
1903 Randall Thomas Davidson, Archbishop of Canterbury.

VICE-PRESIDENTS

1678 Sir Christopher Wren.
1683 Sir William Wren.
1689 Sir William Gregory, Justice of the King's Bench.
1696 Sir Thomas Meres, M.P.
1705 Sir Nathan Wright, Lord Keeper of the Great Seal.
1706 Sir Thomas Meres, M.P.

1707   Sir Gilbert Dolben, Knt. (Bart. 1709).
1722   Sir Christopher Wren.
1723   The Hon. John Verney, Master of the Rolls.
1741   Sir John Willes, Lord Chief Justice.
1762   Sir Sidney Stafford Smythe, Baron of the Exchequer.
1778   Sir John Skynner, Lord Chief Baron.
1806   Lord Ellenborough, Lord Chief Justice.
1818   Sir Richard Richards, Lord Chief Baron.
1823   Sir Charles Abbott, Lord Chief Justice.
1827   Lord Tenterden, Lord Chief Justice.
1829   Sir N. C. Tindal, Lord Chief Justice.
1846   Lord Denman, Lord Chief Justice.
1854   Lord Cranworth, Lord Chancellor.
1868   Lord Chelmsford, Lord Chancellor.
1878   Lord Hatherley, Lord Chancellor.
1880   The Earl of Powis.
1891   Lord Herschell, Lord Chancellor.
1899   Earl Egerton of Tatton.
1909   Lord Alverstone, Lord Chief Justice.
1916   Lord Parmoor.

REGISTERS OR REGISTRARS

1678   Henry Symonds.
1679   Thomas Tyllott.
1711   William Pocklington.
1731   Valens Comyn.
1741   Stephen Comyn.
1759   Thomas Wall.
1788   John Topham (the first to be called Registrar).
1803   Henry Stebbing.
1808   John Matthew Grimwood.
1833   Oliver Hargreave.
1848   Charles J. Baker.
1878   Sir W. Paget Bowman, Bart.
1919   Aldred C. Rowden.

FESTIVAL PREACHERS

THE following is a list of the Festival Preachers, with the offices to which they ultimately attained :—

AT ST. PAUL'S CATHEDRAL

1655 George Hall, D.D., Minister of St. Botolph, Aldersgate, and previously Archdeacon of Cornwall.

(?) Thomas Manton, B.A., Rector of St. Paul, Covent Garden.

AT ST. MICHAEL'S, CORNHILL

1674 John Dolben, D.D., Bishop of Rochester and Dean of Westminster ; Archbishop of York.

1675 John Pearson, D.D., Bishop of Chester.

AT BOW CHURCH, CHEAPSIDE

1676 Peter Gunning, D.D., Bishop of Ely.

1677 John Fell, D.D., Bishop of Oxford and Dean of Christ Church.

1678 Thomas Sprat, D.D., afterwards Bishop of Rochester and Dean of Westminster.

1679 William Lloyd, D.D., Dean of Bangor.

1680   ,,   ,,   Bishop of St. Asaph.

1681 Thomas Tenison, D.D., Vicar of St. Martin-in-the-Fields and afterwards Archbishop of Canterbury.

1682 Arthur Bury, D.D., Rector of Exeter College, Oxford.

1683 William Beveridge, D.D., Rector of St. Peter, Cornhill, and afterwards Bishop of St. Asaph.

1684 Francis Turner, D.D., Bishop of Ely.

1685 Edward Pelling, D.D., Rector of St. Martin, Ludgate, and Prebendary of Westminster.

1686   Henry Dove, D.D., Vicar of St. Bride, Fleet Street,
     and Archdeacon of Richmond.

1687 ⎱
1688 ⎰ Adam Littleton, D.D., Rector of Chelsea and Pre-
1689 ⎰   bendary of Westminster.

1690   Thomas Lynford, D.D., Rector of St. Edmund the
     King, Lombard Street.

1691   Thomas Tenison, D.D., Bishop of Lincoln, elect.

1692   Edward Fowler, D.D., Bishop of Gloucester.

1693   Edward Lake, D.D., Rector of St. Mary-at-Hill and
     Archdeacon of Exeter.

1694   Thomas Manningham, D.D., Rector of St. Andrew,
     Holborn, and afterwards Bishop of Chichester.

1695   Thomas Whincup, D.D., Rector of St. Mary Ab-
     church.

1696   Zaccheus Isham, D.D., Rector of St. Botolph,
     Bishopsgate.

AT ST. PAUL'S CATHEDRAL

1697   George Stanhope, D.D., Chaplain in Ordinary to His
     Majesty, and afterwards Dean of Canterbury.

1698   Francis Atterbury, M.A., Lecturer of St. Bride,
     Fleet Street ; afterwards Bishop of Rochester.

1699   William Assheton, D.D., Rector of Beckenham.

1700   Richard West, M.A., Fellow of Magdalen College,
     Oxford.

1701   Thomas Lamplugh, D.D. ; afterwards Prebendary
     of York.

1702   White Kennett, D.D., Rector of St. Botolph, Ald-
     gate ; afterwards Bishop of Peterborough.

1703   Nathaniel Resbury, D.D., Rector of St. Paul,
     Shadwell.

1704   Lilly Butler, D.D., Minister of St. Mary, Alderman-
     bury.

1705   Thomas Sprat, M.A., Archdeacon of Rochester.

1706 Roger Altham, D.D., Rector of St. Botolph, Bishopsgate.

1707 Charles Trimnell, D.D., Rector of St. James, Westminster ; afterwards Bishop of Winchester.

1708 Philip Bisse, D.D., F.R.S., Fellow of New College, Oxford ; afterwards Bishop of Hereford.

1709 Francis Atterbury, D.D., Dean of Carlisle and Preacher at the Rolls ; afterwards Bishop of Rochester.

1710 Thomas Sherlock, M.A., Master of the Temple ; afterwards Bishop of London.

1711 Nathaniel Marshall, B.C.L., Rector of Finchley.

1712 George Bell, M.A., Chaplain to the Lord Privy Seal.

1713 Henry Sacheverell, D.D., Rector of St. Andrew, Holborn.

1714 Edmund Chishull, B.D., Vicar of Walthamstow.

1715 William Savage, B.D., Rector of St. Andrew by the Wardrobe.

1716 Thomas Bisse, D.D., Preacher at the Rolls.

1717 William Lupton, B.D., Preacher of Lincoln's Inn and Prebendary of Durham.

1718 John Rogers, D.D., Rector of Wrington, Somersetshire.

1719 Joseph Smith, D.D., Rector of St. Dionis Backchurch.

1720 Joseph Trapp, M.A., Rector of Dauntsey, Wilts.

1721 Daniel Waterland, D.D., Master of Magdalene College, Cambridge, and Rector of St. Augustine and St. Faith.

1722 Pawlett St. John, D.D., Rector of Yelden, Bedfordshire.

1723 William Delaune, D.D., President of St. John's College, Oxford, and Canon of Winchester.

1724 Samuel Edgley, M.A., Vicar of Wandsworth, Surrey.

1725 Joseph Roper, B.D., Rector of St. Nicholas Cole Abbey.

1726 Sir John Dolben, Bart., D.D., Rector of Burton Latimer and Vicar of Finedon.

1727 Michael Hutchinson, D.D., Minister of Hammersmith.

1728 Robert Kilburn, D.C.L., Prebendary of St. Paul's.

1729 Ralph Brideoake, B.C.L., Archdeacon of Winchester.

1730 Thomas Spateman, M.A., Prebendary of St. Paul's and Rector of St. Bartholomew the Great.

1731 Robert Warren, D.D., Rector of St. Mary, Stratford-le-Bow.

1732 Henry Stebbing, D.D., Preacher of Gray's Inn.

1733 Thomas Mangey, D.D., Prebendary of Durham and Rector of St. Mildred, Bread Street.

1734–5 George Lavington, D.C.L., Canon Residentiary of St. Paul's; afterwards Bishop of Exeter.

1735–6 Philip Barton, D.C.L., Canon of Christ Church, Oxford.

1737 William Berriman, D.D., Rector of St. Andrew Undershaft and Fellow of Eton.

1738 Edmund Martin, D.C.L., Dean of Worcester.

1739 Edward Banyer, D.D., Afternoon Preacher at Gray's Inn.

1740 Edmund Bateman, D.D., Archdeacon of Lewes.

1741 Edward Yardley, B.D., Archdeacon of Cardigan.

1742 Isaac Maddox, D.D., Bishop of St. Asaph and afterwards of Worcester.

1743 Edward Cobden, D.D., Archdeacon of London.

1744 Andrew Trebeck, D.D., Rector of St. George, Hanover Square.

1745 Henry Hervey Ashton, M.A., Rector of Shotley, Suffolk.

1746 Samuel Nicholls, D.C.L., afterwards Master of the Temple.

1747 Francis Ayscough, D.D., Clerk of the Closet to Frederick, Prince of Wales; afterwards Dean of Bristol.

1748 Thomas Hayter, D.D., Archdeacon of York; afterwards Bishop of London.

1749 Sir G. Williams, Bart., M.A., Vicar of Islington.

1750 Henry Stebbing, M.A., Fellow of Catherine Hall, Cambridge, and Preacher at Gray's Inn.

1751 Arnold King, B.C.L., Rector of St. Michael, Cornhill.

1752 James Townley, M.A., Rector of St. Benet, Gracechurch Street; afterwards Head Master of Christ's Hospital.

1753 Thomas Ashton, D.D., Fellow of Eton and Rector of St. Botolph, Bishopsgate.

1754 John Butler, D.C.L., Chaplain to the Princess Dowager of Wales; afterwards Bishop of Hereford.

1755 Samuel Salter, D.D., Master of the Charterhouse.

1756 Thomas Church, D.D., Vicar of Battersea and Prebendary of St. Paul's.

1757 Glocester Ridley, B.C.L., Minister of Poplar and Prebendary of Salisbury.

1758 James Ibbetson, D.D., Archdeacon of St. Albans.

1759 Stotherd Abdy, M.A., Rector of Theydon Garnon, Essex.

1760 William Dodwell, D.D., Archdeacon of Berks.

1761 John Burton, D.D., Fellow of Eton and Vicar of Mapledurham, Oxon.

1762 George Horne, B.D., Fellow of Magdalen College, Oxford; afterwards Bishop of Norwich.

1763 Thomas Franklin, Vicar of Ware and Minister of Queen Street Chapel.

1764 Richard Hind, D.D., Rector of Sheering, Essex.

1765 James Halifax, D.D., Vicar of Ewell, Surrey.

1766 Cutts Barton, D.D., Dean of Bristol.

1767 Richard Eyre, D.D., F.R.S., Rector of Bright Waltham, Berks.

1768 Robert Pool Finch, D.D.; afterwards Rector of St. Michael, Cornhill, and Prebendary of Westminster.

1769 Thomas Percy, D.D., Vicar of Easton Maudit ; afterwards Bishop of Dromore.

1770 Peter Whalley, B.C.L., Rector of St. Gabriel, Fenchurch Street, and Head Master of Christ's Hospital.

1771 William Parker, D.D., Rector of St. James, Westminster, and Chaplain to George II. and George III.

1772 Thomas Morell, D.D., Fellow of Eton and Rector of Buckland, Herts.

1773 Samuel Glasse, D.D., Chaplain in Ordinary and Rector of Hanwell.

1774 Josiah Tucker, D.D., Dean of Gloucester.

1775 Andrew Burnaby, M.A., Vicar of Greenwich and afterwards Archdeacon of Leicester.

1776 Beilby Porteus, D.D., Rector of Lambeth ; afterwards Bishop of London.

1777 Hon. James Cornwallis, D.D., Dean of Salisbury ; afterwards Bishop of Lichfield and Coventry and fourth Earl of Cornwallis.

1778 John Warren, D.D., Prebendary of Ely ; afterwards Bishop of Bangor.

1779 Robert Richardson, D.D., Rector of St. Anne's, Westminster, and Prebendary of Lincoln.

1780 John Law, D.D., Archdeacon of Carlisle ; afterwards Bishop of Elphin.

1781 Robert Markham, D.D., Rector of St. Mary, Whitechapel.

1782 William Jones, M.A., F.R.S., of Nayland, Rector of Paston, Northamptonshire.

1783 Richard Kay, LL.D., Archdeacon of Nottingham.

1784 Samuel Carr, D.D., Rector of Finchley.

1785 Thomas Jackson, D.D., Prebendary of Westminster ; afterwards Canon of St. Paul's.

1786 Samuel Horsley, D.C.L., F.R.S., Archdeacon of St. Albans ; afterwards Bishop of St. Asaph.

1787   Anthony Hamilton, D.D., Archdeacon of Colchester.

1788   Phipps Western, B.D., Canon Residentiary of Wells.

1789   William Vincent, D.D., Head Master, and afterwards Dean, of Westminster.

1790   Durand Rhudde, D.D., Rector of Brantham and Wenham, Suffolk.

1791   Joseph Holden Pott, M.A., Archdeacon of St. Albans and afterwards of London.

1792   Richard Nicoll, D.D., Chancellor of Wells.

1793   Griffith Griffith, M.A., Rector of St. Mary-le-Bow.

1794   William Langford, D.D., Canon of Windsor.

1795   Charles P. Layard, D.D., Prebendary of Worcester.

1796   Thomas Rennell, D.D., Rector of St. Magnus, London Bridge ; afterwards Dean of Winchester.

1797   George Gretton, D.D., Vicar of Dartmouth.

1798   Gerrard Andrewes, M.A. ; afterwards Rector of St. James, Westminster, and Dean of Canterbury.

1799   Charles Moss, D.D., Canon of St. Paul's ; afterwards Bishop of Oxford.

1800   H. W. Majendie, D.D., Canon of St. Paul's ; afterwards Bishop of Bangor.

1801   William Lisle Bowles, M.A., Rector of Dumbleton, Gloucestershire ; afterwards Canon of Salisbury.

1802   George Henry Law, M.A., Prebendary of Carlisle ; afterwards Bishop of Bath and Wells.

1803   George H. Glasse, M.A., Rector of Hanwell, Middlesex.

1804   Robert Hodgson, M.A., Rector of St. George, Hanover Square.

1805   Charles Barker, B.D., Canon Residentiary of Wells.

1806   Robert Price, D.C.L., Prebendary of Durham.

1807   William Coxe, M.A., F.R.S., Archdeacon of Wilts and Rector of Bemerton.

1808   Francis Randolph, D.D., Prebendary of Bristol.

1809   Sir Henry Rivers, Bart., M.A.

1810   J. S. Clarke, LL.B., F.R.S., Vicar of Preston, Sussex ; afterwards Canon of Windsor.

1811   William Douglas, M.A., Prebendary of Westminster.

1812   Charles Burney, D.D., Rector of St. Paul, Deptford ; afterwards Prebendary of Lincoln.

1813   Hon. Henry Ryder, D.D., Dean of Wells ; afterwards Bishop of Coventry and Lichfield.

1814   Henry Phillpotts, M.A., Prebendary of Durham ; afterwards Bishop of Exeter.

1815   George Mathew, M.A., Vicar of Greenwich.

1816   John Cole, D.D., Rector of Exeter College, Oxford.

1817   Laurence Gardner, D.D., Minister of Curzon Chapel.

1818   D. W. Garrow, D.D., Rector of East Barnet, Herts.

1819   Charles Goddard, M.A., Archdeacon of Lincoln.

1820   Robert Stevens, M.A., Rector of St. James, Garlick Hythe.

1821   Thomas Rennell, B.D., Vicar of Kensington.

1822   Charles J. Blomfield, D.D., Archdeacon of Colchester ; afterwards Bishop of London.

1823   George D'Oyly, D.D., Rector of Lambeth and Sundridge, Kent.

1824   John B. Jenkinson, D.D., Dean of Worcester ; afterwards Bishop of St. David's.

1825   James Henry Monk, D.D., Dean of Peterborough ; afterwards Bishop of Gloucester and Bristol.

1826   Christopher Benson, M.A., Canon of Worcester and Rector of St. Giles-in-the-Fields.

1827   John Hume Spry, D.D., Rector of St. Marylebone.

1828   P. N. Shuttleworth, D.D., Warden of New College, Oxford ; afterwards Bishop of Chichester.

1829   Charles Webb Le Bas, M.A., Rector of St. Paul, Shadwell, and Prebendary of Lincoln.

1830   Edmund Goodenough, D.D., Canon of Westminster ; afterwards Dean of Wells.

1831   George Chandler, D.C.L., Dean of Chichester.

1832 William Dealtry, D.D., Prebendary and Chancellor of Winchester ; afterwards Archdeacon of Surrey.

1833 George Davys, D.D., Dean of Chester ; afterwards Bishop of Peterborough.

1834 John Merewether, D.D., Dean of Hereford.

1835 George Pellew, D.D., Dean of Norwich.

1836 Hugh N. Pearson, D.D., Dean of Salisbury.

1837 Thomas Calvert, D.D., Warden of Manchester Collegiate Church.

1838 John Lonsdale, B.D., Prebendary of St. Paul's ; afterwards Bishop of Lichfield.

1839 Lord John Thynne, D.D., Canon of Westminster.

1840 W. T. P. Brymer, M.A., Archdeacon of Bath.

1841 W. Hale Hale, M.A., Archdeacon of London and Master of the Charterhouse.

1842 Samuel Wilberforce, M.A., Archdeacon of Surrey ; afterwards Bishop of Winchester.

1843 George Butler, D.D., Dean of Peterborough.

1844 Henry Melvill, B.D., Principal of E. I. College, Haileybury ; afterwards Canon of St. Paul's.

1845 R. W. Jelf, D.D., Canon of Christ Church and Principal of King's College, London.

1846 J. Giffard Ward, M.A., Dean of Lincoln.

1847 Henry Howarth, B.D., Rector of St. George, Hanover Square.

1848 Thomas Dale, M.A., Vicar of St. Pancras ; afterwards Dean of Rochester.

1849 Edward M. Goulburn, M.A., Perpetual Curate of Holywell, Oxford ; afterwards Dean of Norwich.

1850 Charles Musgrave, D.D., Archdeacon of Craven.

1851 Charles John Vaughan, D.D., Head Master of Harrow School ; afterwards Master of the Temple and Dean of Llandaff.

1852 G. B. Blomfield, M.A., Rector of Stevenage, Herts.

1853 John Sinclair, M.A., Archdeacon of Middlesex.

1854 John Bird Sumner, D.D., Archbishop of Canterbury, President of the Corporation.

1855 Charles A. Thurlow, M.A., Rector of Malpas and Chancellor of Chester.

1856 James Amiraux Jeremie, D.D., Regius Professor of Divinity, Cambridge ; afterwards Dean of Lincoln.

1857 Henry Alford, B.D., Dean of Canterbury.

1858 Thomas Garnier, B.C.L., Rector of Trinity Church, Marylebone ; afterwards Dean of Lincoln.

1859 Daniel Moore, M.A., Incumbent of Camden Church, Camberwell ; afterwards Prebendary of St. Paul's.

1860 Archibald Boyd, M.A., Incumbent of Paddington ; afterwards Dean of Exeter.

1861 William Carus, M.A., Canon of Winchester.

1862 Anthony W. Thorold, M.A., Rector of St. Giles-in-the-Fields ; afterwards Bishop of Winchester.

1863 Hon. Augustus Duncombe, D.D., Dean of York.

1864 Walter Farquhar Hook, D.D., Dean of Chichester.

1865 Harvey Goodwin, D.D., Dean of Ely ; afterwards Bishop of Carlisle.

1866 William G. Humphry, B.D., Prebendary of St. Paul's and Vicar of St. Martin-in-the-Fields.

1867 J. R. Woodford, M.A., Vicar of Kempsford, Gloucestershire ; afterwards Bishop of Ely.

1868 John Saul Howson, D.D., Dean of Chester.

1869 Thomas James Rowsell, M.A., Rector of St. Margaret, Lothbury.

1870 Henry Parry Liddon, D.D., D.C.L., Canon of St. Paul's.

1871 J. C. Miller, D.D., Vicar of Greenwich and Canon of Worcester.

1872 James Moorhouse, M.A., Vicar of Paddington ; afterwards Bishop of Manchester.

1873 Francis J. Holland, M.A., Minister of Quebec Chapel ; afterwards Canon of Canterbury.

1874 William Connor Magee, D.D., D.C.L., Bishop of Peterborough and afterwards Archbishop of York.

1875 Frederic W. Farrar, D.D., Master of Marlborough College ; afterwards Dean of Canterbury.

1876 William Boyd Carpenter, M.A., Vicar of St. James, Lower Holloway ; afterwards Bishop of Ripon and Canon of Westminster.

1877 Ernest R. Wilberforce, M.A., Vicar of Seaforth, Liverpool ; afterwards Bishop of Chichester.

1878 James Fleming, B.D., Canon of York and Vicar of St. Michael, Chester Square.

1879 Hon. Edward Carr Glyn, M.A., Vicar of Kensington ; afterwards Bishop of Peterborough.

1880 Charles Marson, M.A., Vicar of Clevedon, Somerset.

1881 Henry Montagu Butler, D.D., Head Master of Harrow School ; afterwards Master of Trinity.

1882 Edward White Benson, D.D., Bishop of Truro ; afterwards Archbishop of Canterbury.

1883 S. Reynolds Hole, M.A., Prebendary of Lincoln and Vicar of Caunton, Notts ; afterwards Dean of Rochester.

1884 Arthur J. Mason, M.A., Vicar of Allhallows, Barking ; afterwards Master of Pembroke College, Cambridge, and Canon of Canterbury.

1885 Randall T. Davidson, M.A., Dean of Windsor ; now Archbishop of Canterbury and President of the Corporation.

1886 John Gott, D.D., Dean of Worcester ; afterwards Bishop of Truro.

1887 J. E. C. Welldon, M.A., Head Master of Harrow School ; afterwards Bishop of Calcutta ; now Dean of Durham.

1888 John G. Richardson, M.A., Vicar of St. Mary, Nottingham ; afterwards Archdeacon of Nottingham.

1889   Charles J. Ridgeway, M.A., Vicar of Christ Church, Lancaster Gate ; afterwards Bishop of Chichester.

1890   Edward S. Talbot, D.D., Vicar of Leeds ; afterwards Bishop of Winchester.

1891   William C. E. Newbolt, M.A., Canon of St. Paul's.

1892   Alfred George Edwards, D.D., Bishop of St. Asaph ; now Archbishop of Wales.

1893   Arthur T. Lloyd, D.D., Vicar of Newcastle-on-Tyne ; afterwards Bishop of Newcastle.

1894   Francis B. Sowter, M.A., Archdeacon of Dorset.

1895   Alfred Ainger, M.A., Master of the Temple and Canon of Bristol.

1896   Bernard R. Wilson, M.A., Rector of Kettering ; afterwards Vicar of Portsea.

1897   Robert William Forrest, D.D., Dean of Worcester.

1898   Arthur F. Winnington-Ingram, D.D., Bishop of Stepney ; now Bishop of London.

1899   Henry E. J. Bevan, M.A., Rector of Holy Trinity, Sloane Street ; now Archdeacon of Middlesex and Rector of St. Luke, Chelsea.

1900   Cosmo Gordon Lang, M.A., Vicar of Portsea ; Archbishop-designate of Canterbury.

1901   Philip F. Eliot, D.D., Dean of Windsor.

1902   John Wogan Festing, D.D., Bishop of St. Albans.

1903   Edgar C. S. Gibson, D.D., Vicar of Leeds and Prebendary of Wells; afterwards Bishop of Gloucester.

1904   William Boyd Carpenter, D.D., Bishop of Ripon.

1905   Cecil Henry Boutflower, D.D., Bishop Suffragan of Dorking (now Southampton).

1906   John Henry Bernard, D.D., Dean of St. Patrick's, Dublin ; afterwards Archbishop of Dublin and Provost of Trinity College.

1907   William Hartley Carnegie, M.A., Rector of St. Philip, Birmingham ; now Canon of Westminster and Rector of St. Margaret.

1908 Hon. Edward Lyttelton, B.D., Headmaster of Eton.

1909 Ernest Harold Pearce, M.A., Vicar of Christ Church, Newgate Street ; now Bishop of Worcester.

1910 Henry Reginald Gamble, M.A., Rector of Holy Trinity, Sloane Street ; now Dean of Exeter.

1911 Henry Russell Wakefield, Dean of Norwich ; afterwards Bishop of Birmingham.

1912 William Ralph Inge, D.D., Dean of St. Paul's.

1913 Lionel G. B. J. Ford, M.A., Head Master of Harrow ; now Dean of York.

1914 Herbert Gresford Jones, M.A., Archdeacon and Vicar of Sheffield ; now Bishop Suffragan of Warrington.

1915 Harold E. Bilbrough, M.A., Rector of Liverpool ; now Bishop of Newcastle.

1916 Sydney A. Alexander, M.A., Canon of St. Paul's.

1917 H. St. J. Woollcombe, M.A., Vicar of Armley, Leeds ; now Bishop Suffragan of Whitby.

1918 F. Homes Dudden, D.D., Rector of Holy Trinity, Sloane Street ; now Master of Pembroke College, Oxford, and Canon of Gloucester.

1919 E. W. Barnes, SC.D., Master of the Temple and Canon of Westminster ; now Bishop of Birmingham.

1920 Bernard O. F. Heywood, M.A., Vicar of Leeds ; afterwards Bishop of Southwell.

1921 L. J. White-Thomson, M.A., Archdeacon of Canterbury ; now Bishop of Ely.

1922 Arthur C. Headlam, D.D., Regius Professor of Divinity and Canon of Christ Church, Oxford ; now Bishop of Gloucester.

1923 Cyril A. Alington, D.D., Head Master of Eton.

1924 Vernon F. Storr, M.A., Canon of Westminster.

1925 T. Guy Rogers, B.D., Rector of Birmingham and Honorary Canon.

1927 F. C. N. Hicks, D.D., Vicar of Brighton ; now
   Bishop of Gibraltar.

1928 Bertram F. Simpson, B.D., Vicar of St. Peter,
   Cranley Gardens.

1929 William Ralph Inge, D.D., Dean of St. Paul's.

THE COURT OF ASSISTANTS, 1927–8

President.
The Lord Archbishop of Canterbury, G.C.V.O
Vice-President.
The Right Hon. Lord Parmoor, K.C.V.O.
Treasurers.
The Lord Bishop of Worcester, C.B.E.
Sir Frederick M. Fry, K.C.V.O.
Sir J. E. Kynaston Studd, O.B.E., Alderman.

The Earl of Ancaster.
Norman C. Armitage, Esq.
James H. Batty, Esq.
Ormond A. Blyth, Esq.
The Very Rev. the Dean of Christ Church, D.D.
The Viscount Clifden.
George W. Currie, Esq.
Harry J. Dare, Esq.
Howson F. Devitt, Esq.
The Lord Ebbisham, G.B.E., Alderman.
The Very Rev. the Dean of Exeter, D.D.
The Rev. Thomas W. Gibson, M.A.
Sir Ernest Musgrave Harvey, K.B.E.
Henry L. Hopkinson, Esq.
The Hon. Evelyn Hubbard.
Robert L. Hunter, Esq.
The Lord Hylton.
Harry Lloyd, Esq.
The Lord Bishop of London, K.C.V.O.
The Right Hon. Lord Marshall, K.C.V.O., LL.D., Alderman.
Sir Miles W. Mattinson, K.C.
The Rev. Cecil Graham Moon, M.A.

Richard R. Ottley, Esq.
Walter J. Payne, Esq.
Francis W. Percival, Esq., F.S.A.
The Rev. Prebendary L. J. Percival, C.V.O., M.A.
The Rev. Prebendary G. H. Perry, M.A.
Sir William Plender, Bart., G.B.E., F.C.A.
Arthur G. Roby, Esq., K.C.
The Earl of Shaftesbury, G.C.V.O., K.P., C.B.E.
The Rev. H. R. Cooper Smith, D.D.
Sir Henry A. Steward.
The Hon. Sir Edward P. Thesiger, K.C.B.
Alfred C. Thompson, Esq.
William J. Thompson, Esq., Junr.
The Rt. Rev. Bishop H. Russell Wakefield, D.D.
Colonel Sir Charles C. Wakefield, Bart., C.B.E., Alderman.
The Rt. Rev. Bishop Watkin H. Williams, D.D.
The Rev. George C. Wilton, M.A.
The Rev. T. Basil Woodd, M.A., LL.B.
Hugh Wyatt, Esq.

THE COMMITTEE OF THE FESTIVAL, 1928

President.
The Lord Archbishop of Canterbury, G.C.V.O.
Vice-President.
The Right Hon. Lord Parmoor, K.C.V.O.

N. C. Armitage, Esq.
Rev. W. P. Besley, M.V.O., M.A.
The Ven. Henry E. J. Bevan, M.A., Archdeacon of Middlesex.
Guy E. P. Bowman, Esq.
Rev. Maurice F. Foxell, M.A.
G. C. Gibson, Esq.
Rev. T. W. Gibson, M.A.
Rev. E. T. R. Johnston, M.A.
Gerard B. Laurence, Esq.
Stanley Marchant, Esq., Mus.D.
A. E. W. Marshall, Esq.

Arthur C. Morgan, Esq.
Rev. Preb. G. H. Perry, M.A.
S. Forde Ridley, Esq., J.P.
Aldred C. Rowden, Esq., Secretary.
Rev. H. R. Cooper Smith, D.D.
Rev. Hugh Alexander Tapsfield, M.A.
Rev. R. Thornber, M.A.
Rev. George C. Wilton, M.A.
The Lord Bishop of Worcester, C.B.E., Treasurer.
Hugh Wyatt, Esq.

Registrar.
Aldred C. Rowden, Esq.,
Corporation House,
2 Bloomsbury Place, W.C.1.

INDEX

Accountant, the, 59–61, 71
Accounts Committee, 37
Addison, Joseph, 33
Addresses, Royal, 19, 255–264
Adstone, property acquired at, 120 f.
—, John Bacon's visitation of, 121–123
—, advowson in hands of Corporation, 123
Albert, Prince Consort, attends Bicentenary Festival, 243
—, Steward, 274
Alliance Assurance Company, 107 f.
Almoner of St. Paul's Cathedral School, 204
Almshouses, bequest for erecting, 99
—, for widows, 148–152
—, dispute among the tenants, 150 f.
Altham, Roger, 35
Anderton's Coffee House, meetings held at, 68, 79
Andrewes, Bishop, 165
Anne, Queen, address to, 19, 264–266
—, visit to St. Paul's, 209–210
—, her gift, 209
—, First Fruits grant, 264
—, petition to, for further purchasing powers, 265 f.
Apprentices, fees paid, 16, 131, 163–169, 176, 198
—, bequest for binding, 86, 93, 172
—, clothes provided, 164
—, Stewards responsible for, 191 f., 205
Arms, grant of, 64–66
Arnald, Richard, Tutor of Emmanuel, 175
Arnold, Dr. S., 216 f., 239, 245, 271
Assheton, William, 100 f., 149
Assistants, Court of, 4–5, 32–37, 302
—, —, oath, 5
—, —, names of the first, 8
—, sworn before Lord Chancellor, 7
—, meeting places, 13–14, 46, 66–75
—, Governors elected as, 29–30
—, City clergy elected, 35
—, retire by rotation, 36

Assistants, register of attendances kept, 36
—, Collect before business, 37
—, first meeting, 6–7, 45, 52
—, not always sons of clergy, 62 f.
—, Book on Wills circulated by, 100 f.
—, to investigate claims for pensions, 133
—, pensions given to poor relations of, 145
Atterbury, Francis, Bp. of Rochester, 20, 35, 55 n., 139 n., 209, 234, 253, 266
—, Lewis, 35
Attwood, Thomas, 240–243
Audit, 38
Ayscough, Dr. Francis, 268

Bacon, John, 167, 198–233
—, visitation of Stowe, etc., 121–124
—, Secretary to the Stewards, 166–167, 198, 220, 223, 229, 236, 251
—, sympathy with poor clergy, 200
—, Treasurer of the Corporation, 201
—, house at Friern Barnet, 198 n., 201
—, resigns office of Secretary, 231–233
—, efforts to secure Royal patronage, 269 f.
Bank of England, Corporation doubtful about, 27
Bank Stock, considered a bad investment, 105
Banquets, 219–233. See also Festival dinner, Lambeth dinner, Union dinner.
Basin for the collection, 17 n.
Bedell, Bishop, apprenticeship fees of his grandson paid by Corporation, 16
Bedford Row, Corporation Office in, 75
Bell, The, New Exchange, Strand, 34
Benefactors, 50, 60, 76–101

304

Petites, School for the, 142
Pictures in Corporation House, 74
Plumtree Street almshouse, 150–152
Pocklington, William, Register, 48, 50, 287
Porteus, Dr. B., Bp. of London, 201, 241, 250, 293
Potter, Dr. John, Abp. of Canterbury, 115, 214, 286
Preachers, list of, 253, 288–301
—, Bishops seldom chosen, 250 f.
—, mode of selecting, 251 f.
President, sworn before Lord Chancellor, 7
—, election of, 12–21
—, contested election, 20 f., 267
—, the Abp. of Canterbury, regularly since Wake, 21
—, summoned to all meetings, 19, 53
Presidents, list of, 286
Princess Royal, her marriage, 269 f.
Procession at Festival, 212, 221, 223
Property, purchases of, 107–124
Property and Revenues of the Church, Commission on, 280
Purcell, Daniel, 210
Purcell, Henry, 209, 234–236, 240
Pyle, Dr. Edmund, 173 n., 193 n., 252 n.

Queen Anne's Bounty, 199
Queen Street, Cheapside, 34
Queen Victoria Clergy Fund, 157
Queen's Arms Tavern, St. Paul's Church Yard, 192, 201 f., 211 f., 215
Queen's Head Tavern, Paternoster Row, 69

Raymond, Thomas, 31
Register, or Registrar, 7, 45–52
—, widows paid by, 42, 50–52
—, origin of title, 45 f.
—, salary first given, 46–48
—, guarantee required, 48
—, title altered to Registrar, 48 f.
—, preference given to clergymen's sons at election, 52
—, to be a lawyer, 52, 55
—, resides in Corporation house, 71
—, burials of pensioners arranged by, 136
—, list of, 287
Registrar. See Register
Rehearsal, date of, 201
—, music, 208 f.

Rehearsal, request for loan of City plate, 204
—, dinner, 204, 212
—, glee composed for the, 217
—, 6,000 tickets, 204
—, expenses of, 205–207
—, attempt to transplant to the West End, 211
—, collection, 239
—, no sermon, 249
Rents, collected by Accountant, 60
—, collected by the Messenger, 109
Reynolds, Edward, Archdeacon of Norfolk, 163
Reynolds, Edward, Bp. of Norwich, 163
Reynolds, Sir Joshua, Assistant, 33, 66
Reynolds, Mary, her bequest, 163
Reynolds, Richard, Bp. of Lincoln, 60
Roderick, Rev. Dr. Charles, Governor, 81
Roderick, Rev. Dr. Richard, Governor, 81, 87
Rogers, Henry, Treasurer, 34, 70
Rogers, Dr. John, 80
Rowden, Aldred C., Registrar, viii, 277 f., 303
Russell, Sir William, proposed purchase of his estate in Essex, 106
Rustat, Tobias, 10, 33 f.
—, gives statue of James II to Whitehall, 33
—, his scholarships, 171
—, attached to Charles II, 259
Rye House Plot, 257

Sacheverell, Henry, 27, 37, 147
—, Collect for Assistants, preparing, 37
—, Assistant, 264 f.
St. George, Hanover Square, Rehearsal held at, 211
St. George, Sir Henry, arms granted by, 64 f.
St. John's College, Cambridge, exhibition at, 176
St. Martin-in-the-Fields, 9 n., 15 n., 17 n., 18, 164
St. Mary-le-Bow, 9, 13, 17, 185 f., 208, 223, 288 f.
St. Michael, Cornhill, 12, 185, 208, 223, 288
St. Paul's Cathedral, Festival held at, 2, 82, 178, 183, 186, 203, 207, 234 ff., 289 ff.